The Kama Sutra
The Perfumed Garden

Vatsyayana

The Kama Sutra

Cheikh Nefzaoui

The Perfumed Garden

Translated by Sir Richard Burton
and F.F. Arbuthnot

Diadem Books
New York

© by Hasso Ebeling International Publishing München GmbH
Published 1984 by Diadem Books
Typesetting: Fotosatz Weihrauch, Würzburg, West Germany
ISBN 1-85007-095-4

Preface

In the literature of all countries there will be found a certain number of works treating especially of love. Everywhere the subject is dealt with differently, and from various points of view. In the present publication it is proposed to give a complete translation of what is considered the standard work on love in Sanscrit literature, and which is called "The Vatsyayana Kama Sutra", or Aphorisms on Love, by Vatsyayana.

While the introduction will deal with the evidence concerning the date of the writing, and the commentaries written upon it, the chapters following the introduction will give a translation of the work itself. It is, however, advisable to furnish here a brief analysis of works of the same nature, prepared by authors who lived and wrote years after Vatsya had passed away, but who still considered him as the great authority, and alway quoted him as the chief guide to Hindoo erotic literature.

Besides the treatise of Vatsyayana the following works on the same subject are procurable in India: —

1. The Ratirahasya, or secrets of love.
2. The Panchasakya, or the five arrows.
3. The Smara Pradipa, or the light of love.
4. The Ratimanjari, or the garland of love.

5. The Rasmanjari, or the sprout of love.

6. The Anunga Runga, or the stage of love; also called Kamaledhiplava, or a boat in the ocean of love.

The author of the "Secrets of Love" (No. 1) was a poet named Kukkoka. He composed his work to please one Venudutta, who was perhaps a king. When writing his own name at the end of each chapter he calls himself "Siddha patiya pandita", i.e., an ingenious man among learned men. The work was translated into Hindi years ago, and in this the author's name was written as Koka. And as the same name crept into all the translations into other languages in India, the book became generally known, and the subject was popularly called Koka Shastra, or doctrines of Koka, which is identical with the Kama Shastra, or doctrines of love, and the words Koka Shastra and Kama Shastra are used indiscriminately.

The work contains nearly eight hundred verses, and is divided into ten chapters, which are called Pachivedas. Some of the things treated of in this work are not to be found in the Vatsyayana, such as the four classes of women, viz., the Padmini, Chitrini, Shankini and Hastini, as also the enumeration of the days and hours on which the women of the different classes become subject to love. The author adds that he wrote these things from the opinions of Gonikaputra and Nadikeshwara, both of whom are mentioned by Vatsyayana, but their works are not now extant. It is difficult to give any approximate idea as to the year in which the work was composed. It is only to be presumed that it was written after that of Vatsyayana, and previous to the other works on this subject that are still extant. Vatsyayana gives the names of ten authors on the subject, all of whose works he had consulted, but none of which are extant, and does not mention this one. This would tend to show that Kukkoka wrote after Vatsya, otherwise Vatsya would assuredly have mentioned him as an author in this branch of literature along with the others.

The author of the "Five Arrows" (No. 2 in the list) was one Jyotirisha. He is called the chief ornament of poets, the treasure of the sixty-four arts, and the best teacher of the rules of music. He says that he composed the work after reflecting on the aphorisms of love as revealed by the gods, and studying the opinions of

Gonikaputra, Muladeva, Babhravya, Ramtideva, Nundikeshwara and Kshe-mandra. It is impossible to say whether he had perused all the works of these authors, or had only heard about them; anyhow, none of them appear to be in existence now. This work contains nearly six hundred verses, and is divided into five chapters, called Sayakas or Arrows.

The author of the "Light of Love" (No. 3) was the poet Gunakara, the son of Vechapati. The work contains four hundred verses, and gives only a short account of the doctrines of love, dealing more with other matters.

"The Garland of Love" (No. 4) is the work of the famous poet Jayadeva, who said about himself that he is a writer on all subjects. This treatise is, however, very short, containing only one hundred and twenty-five verses.

The author of the "Sprout of Love" (Nr. 5) was a poet called Bhanudatta. It appears from the last verse of the manuscript that he was a resident of the province of Tirhoot, and son of a Brahman named Ganeshwar, who was also a poet. The work, written in Sanscrit, gives the descriptions of different classes of men and women, their classes being made out from their age, description, con-duct, etc. It contains three chapters, and its date is not known, and cannot be ascertained.

"The Stage of Love" (No. 6) was composed by the poet Kullianmull, for the amusement of Ladkhan, the son of Ahmed Lodi, the same Ladkhan being in some places spoken of as Ladana Mull, and in others as Ladanaballa. He is supposed to have been a relation or connection of the house of Lodi, which reigned in Hindostan from A.D. 1450-1526. The work would, therefore, have been written in the fifteenth or sixteenth century. It contains ten chapters, and has been translated into English but only six copies were printed for private cir-culation. This is supposed to be the latest of the Sanscrit works on the subject, and the ideas in it were evidently taken from previous writings of the same nature.

The contents of these works are in themselves a literary curiosity. There are to be found both in Sanscrit poetry and in the Sanscrit drama a certain amount of poetical sentiment and romance, which have, in every country and in every language, thrown an immortal halo round the subject. But here it is treated in a plain, simple, matter of fact sort of way. Men and women are divided into classes and divisions in the same way that Buffon and other writers on natural history have classified and divided the animal world. As Venus was represented by the Greeks to stand forth as the type of the beauty of woman, so the Hindoos describe the Padmini or Lotus woman as the type of most perfect feminine excellence, as follows:

She in whom the following signs and symptoms appear is called a Padmini. Her face is pleasing as the full moon; her body, well clothed with flesh, is soft as the Shiras or mustard flower, her skin is fine, tender and fair as the yellow lotus, never dark coloured. Her eyes are bright and beautiful as the orbs of the fawn, well cut, and with reddish corners. Her bosom is hard, full and high, she has a good neck; her nose is straight and lovely, and three folds or wrinkles cross her middle – about the umbilical region. Her yoni resembles the opening lotus bud, and her love seed (Kam salila) is perfumed like the lily that has newly burst. She walks with swan-like gait, and her voice is low and musical as the note of the Kokila bird, she delights in white raiments, in fine jewels, and in rich dresses. She eats little, sleeps lightly, and being as respectful and religious as she is clever and courteous, she is ever anxious to worship the gods, and to enjoy the conversation of Brahmans. Such, then, is the Padmini or Lotus woman.

Detailed descriptions then follow of the Chitrini or Art woman; the Shankhini or Conch woman, and the Hastini or Elephant woman, their days of enjoyment, their various seats of passion, the manner in which they should be manipulated and treated in sexual intercourse, along with the characteristics of the men and women of the various countries in Hindostan. The details are so numerous, and the subjects so seriously dealt with, and at such length, that neither time nor space will permit of their being given here.

One work in the English language is somewhat similar to these works of the Hindoos. It is called "Kalogynomia: or the Laws of Female Beauty", being the elementary principles of that science, by T. Bell, M.D., with twenty-four plates, and printed in London in 1821. It treats of Beauty, of Love, of Sexual Intercourse, of the Laws regulating that Intercourse, of Monogamy and Polygamy, of

Prostitution, of Infidelity, ending with a catalogue raisonnée of the defects of female beauty.

Other works in English also enter into great details of private and domestic life. "The Elements of Social Science, or Physical, Sexual and Natural Religion", by a Doctor of Medicine, London, 1880, and "Every Woman's Book", by Dr. Waters, 1826. To persons interested in the above subjects these works will be found to contain such details as have been seldom before published, and which ought to be thoroughly understood by all philanthropists and benefactors of society.

After a perusal of the Hindoo work, and of the English books above mentioned, the reader will understand the subject, at all events from a materialistic, realistic and practical point of view. If all science is founded more or less on a stratum of facts, there can be no harm in making known to mankind generally certain matters intimately connected with their private, domestic, and social life.

Alas! complete ignorance of them has unfortunately wrecked many a man and many a woman, while a little knowledge of a subject generally ignored by the masses would have enabled numbers of people to have understood many things which they believed to be quite incomprehensible, or which were not thought worthy of their consideration.

Introduction

It may be interesting to some persons to learn how it came about that Vatsyayana was first brought to light and translated into the English language. It happened thus. While translating with the pundits the "Anunga runga, or the stage of love", reference was frequently found to be made to one Vatsya. The sage Vatsya was of this opinion, or of that opinion. The sage Vatsya said this, and so on. Naturally questions were asked who the sage was, and the pundits replied that Vatsya was the author of the standard work on love in Sanscrit literature, that no Sanscrit library was complete without his work, and that it was most difficult now to obtain in its entire state. The copy of the manuscript obtained in Bombay was defective, and so the pundits wrote to Benares, Calcutta and Jeypoor for copies of the manuscript from Sanscrit libraries in those places. Copies having been obtained, they were then compared with each other, and with the aid of a Commentary called "Jayamangla" a revised copy of the entire manuscript was prepared, and from this copy the English translation was made. The following is the certificate of the chief pundit: —

"The accompanying manuscript is corrected by me after comparing four different copies of the work. I had the assistance of a Commentary called 'Jayamangla' for correcting the portion in the first five parts, but found great difficulty in correcting the remaining portion, because, with the exception of one copy thereof which was tolerably correct, all the other copies I had were far too incorrect. However, I took that portion as correct in which the majority of the copies agreed with each other."

The "Aphorisms on Love", by Vatsayayana contain about one thousand two hundred and fifty slokas or verses, and are divided into parts, parts into chapters, and chapters into paragraphs. The whole consists of seven parts, thirty-six chapters, and sixty-four paragraphs. Hardly anything is known about the author. His real name is supposed to be Mallinaga or Mrillana, Vatsyayana being his family name. At the close of the work this is what he writes about himself: —

"After reading and considering the works of Babhravya and other ancient authors, and thinking over the meaning of the rules given by them, this treatise was composed, according to the precepts of the Holy Writ, for the benefit of the world, by Vatsyayana, while leading the life of a religious student at Benares, and wholly engaged in the contemplation of the Deity. This work is not to be used merely as an instrument for satisfying our desires. A person acquainted with the true principles of this science, who preserves his Dharma (virtue or religious merit), his Artha (worldly wealth) and his Kama (pleasure or sensual gratification), and who has regard to the customs of the people, is sure to obtain the mastery over his senses. In short, an intelligent and knowing person, attending to Dharma and Artha and also to Kama, without becoming the slave of his passions, will obtain success in everything that he may do."

It is impossible to fix the exact date either of the life of Vatsyayana or of his work. It is supposed that he must have lived between the first and sixth century of the Christian era, on the following grounds: — He mentions that Satkarni Satvahan, a king of Kuntal, killed Malayevati his wife with an instrument called kartari by striking her in the passion of love, and Vatsya quotes this case to warn people of the danger arising from some old customs of striking women when under the influence of this passion. Now this king of Kuntal is believed to have lived and reigned during the first century A.C., and consequently Vatsya must have lived after him. On the other hand, Virahamihira, in the eighteenth chapter of his "Brihatsanhita", treats of the science of love, and appears to have borrowed largely from Vatsyayana on the subject. Now Virahamihira is said to have lived during the sixth century A.D., and as Vatsya must have written his works previously, therefore not earlier than the first century A.C., and not later than the sixth century A.D., must be considered as the approximate date of his existence.

On the text of the "Aphorisms on Love", by Vatsyayana, only two commentaries have been found. One called "Jayamangla" or "Sutrabashya", and the other "Sutra vritti". The date of the "Jayamangla" is fixed between the tenth and thirteenth century A.D., because while treating of the sixty-four arts an example is taken form the "Kávyaprakásha", which was written about the tenth century A.D. Again, the copy of the commentary procured was evidently a transcript of a manuscript which once had a place in the library of a Chaulukyan king named Vishaladeva, a fact elicited from the following sentence at the end of it: –

"Here ends the part relating to the art of love in the commentary on the 'Vatsyayana Kama Sutra', a copy from the library of the king of kings, Vishaladeva, who was a powerful hero, as it were a second Arjuna, and head jewel of the Chaulukya family."

Now it is well known that this king ruled in Guzerat from 1244 to 1262 A.D., and founded a city called Visalnagur. The date, therefore, of the commentary is taken to be not earlier than the tenth and not later than the thirteenth century. The author of it is supposed to be one Yashodhara, the name given him by his preceptor being Indrapada. He seems to have written it during the time of affliction caused by his separation from a clever and shrewd woman, at least that is what he himself says at the end of each chapter. It is presumed that he called his work after the name of his absent mistress, or the word may have some connection with the meaning of her name.

This commentary was most useful in explaining the true meaning of Vatsyayana, for the commentator appears to have had a considerable knowledge of the times of the older author, and gives in some places very minute information. This cannot be said of the other commentary, called "Sutra vritti", which was written about A.D. 1789, by Narsing Shastri, a pupil of a Sarveshwar Shastri;

the latter was descendant of Bhaskur, and so also was our author, for at the conclusion of every part he calls himself Bhaskur Narsing Shastri. He was induced to write the work by order of the learned Raja Vrijalala, while he was residing in Benares, but as to the merits of this commentary it does not deserve much commendation. In many cases the writer does not appear to have understood the meaning of the original author, and has changed the text in many places to fit in with his own explanations.

A complete translation of the original work now follows. It has been prepared in complete accordance with the text of the manuscript, and is given, without further comments, as made from it.

Part I
The Vatsyayana Sutra

Introductory Preface

Salutation to Dharma, Artha and Kama

In the beginning, the Lord of Beings created men and women, and in the form of commandments in one hundred thousand chapters laid down rules for regulating their existence with regard to Dharma, Artha and Kama. Some of these commandments, namely those which treated of Dharma, were separately written by Swayambhu Manu; those that related to Artha were compiled by Brihaspati; and those that referred to Kama were expounded by Nandi, the follower of Mahadeva, in one thousand chapters.

Now these "Kama Sutra" (Aphorisms on Love), written by Nundi in one thousand chapters, were reproduced by Shvetaketu, the son of Uddvalaka, in an abbreviated form in five hundred chapters, and this work was again similarly reproduced in an abridged form, in one hundred and fifty chapters, by Babhravya, an inheritant of the Punchala (South of Delhi) country. These one hundred and fifty chapters were then put together under seven heads or parts named severally.

1st. Sadharana (general topics).

2nd. Samprayogika (embraces, etc.).

17

3rd. Kanya Samprayuktaka (union of males and females).

4th. Bharyadhikarika (on one's wife).

5th. Paradika (on the wives of other people).

6th. Vaisika (on courtesans).

7th. Aupamishadika (on the arts of seduction, tonic medicines, etc.).

The sixth part of this last work was separately expounded by Dattaka at the request of the public women of Pataliputra (Patna), and in the same way Charayana explained the first part of it. The remaining parts, viz., the second, third, fourth, fifth, and seventh were each separately expounded by –

Suvarnanabha (second part).

Ghotakamukha (third part).

Gonardiya (fourth part).

Gonikaputra (fifth part).

Kuchumara (seventh part), respectively.

Thus the work being written in parts by different authors was almost unobtainable, and as the parts which were expounded by Dattaka and the others treated only of the particular branches of the subject to which each part related, and moreover as the original work of Babhravya was difficult to be mastered on account of its length, Vatsyayana, therefore, composed his work in a small volume as an abstract of the whole of the works of the above-named authors.

II

On the acquisition of Dharma, Artha and Kama

Man, the period of whose life is one hundred years, should practice Dharma, Artha and Kama at different times and in such a manner that they may harmonize together and not clash in any way. He should acquire learning in his childhood, in his youth and middle age he should attend to Artha and Kama, and in his old age he should perform Dharma, and thus seek to gain Moksha, i.e., release from further transmigration. Or, on account of the uncertainty of life, he may practice them at times when they are enjoined to be practised. But one thing is to be noted, he should lead the life of a religious student until he finishes his education.

Dharma is obedience to the command of the Shastra or Holy Writ of the Hindoos to do certain things, such as the performance of sacrifices, which are not generally done, because they do not belong to this world, and produce no visible effect; and not to do other things, such as eating meat, which is often done because it belongs to this world, and has visible effects.

Dharma should be learnt from the Shruti (Holy Writ), and from those conversant with it.

19

Artha is the acquisition of arts, land, gold, cattle, wealth, equipages and friends. It is, further, the protection of what is acquired, and the increase of what is protected.

Artha should be learnt from the king's officers, and from merchants who may be versed in the ways of commerce.

Kama is the enjoyment of appropriate objects by the five senses of hearing, feeling, seeing, tasting and smelling, assisted by the mind together with the soul. The ingredient in this is a peculiar contact between the organ of sense and its object, and the consciousness of pleasure which arises from that contact is called Kama. Kama is to be learnt from the Kama Sutra (aphorisms on love) and from the practice of citizens.

When all the three, viz., Dharma, Artha and Kama come together, the former is better than the one which follows it, i.e., Dharma is better than Artha, and Artha is better than Kama. But Artha should always be first practised by the king, for the livelihood of men is to be obtained from it only. Again, Kama being the occupation of public women, they should prefer it to the other two, and these are exceptions to the general rule.

Objection 1

Some learned men say that as Dharma is connected with things not belonging to this world, it is appropriately treated of in a book; and so also is Artha, because it is practised only by the application of proper means, and a knowledge of those means can only be obtained by study and from books. But Kama being a thing which is practised even by the brute creation, and which is to be found everywhere, does not want any work on the subject.

Answer

This is not so. Sexual intercourse being a thing dependent on man and woman requires the application of proper means by them, and those means are to be learnt from the Kam Shastra. The non-application of proper means, which we see in the brute creation, is caused by their being unrestrained, and by the females among them only being fit for sexual intercourse at certain seasons and no more, and by their intercourse not being preceded by thought of any kind.

Objection 2

The Lokayatikas say: — Religious ordinances should not be observed, for they bear a future fruit, and at the same time it is also doubtful whether they will bear any fruit at all. What foolish person will give away that which is in his own hands into the hands of another? Moreover, it is better to have a pigeon to-day than a peacock to-morrow; and a copper coin which we have the certainly of obtaining, is better than a gold coin, the possession of which is doubtful.

Answer

It is not so. 1st. Holy Writ, which ordains the practice of Dharma, does not admit of a doubt.

2nd. Sacrifices such as those made for the destruction of enemies, or for the fall of rain, are seen to bear fruit.

3rd. The sun, moon, stars, planets and other heavenly bodies appear to work intentionally for the good of the world.

4th. The existence of this world is effected by the observance of the rules respecting the four classes of men and their four stages of life.

5th. We see that seed is thrown into the ground with the hope of future crops. Vatsyayana is therefore of the opinion that the ordinances of religion must be obeyed.

Objection 3

Those who believe that destiny is the prime mover of all things say: — We should not exert ourselves to acquire wealth, for sometimes it is not acquired although we strive to get it, while at other times it comes to us of itself without any exertion on our part. Everything is therefore in the power of destiny, who is the lord of gain and loss, of success and defeat, of pleasure and pain. Thus we see that Bali was raised to the throne of Indra by destiny, and was also put down by the same power, and it is destiny only that can re-instate him.

Answer

It is not right to say so. As the acquisition of every object pre-supposes at all events some exertion on the part of man, the application of proper means may be said to be the cause of gaining all our ends, and this application of proper means being thus necessary (even where a thing is destined to happen), it follows that a person who does nothing will enjoy no happiness.

Objection 4

Those who are inclined to think that Artha is the chief object to be obtained argue thus. Pleasures should not be sought for, because they are obstacles to the practice of Dharma and Artha, which are both superior to them, and are also disliked by meritorious persons. Pleasures also bring a man into distress, and into contact with low persons; they cause him to commit unrighteous deeds, and produce impurity in him; they make him regardless of the future, and encourage carelessness and levity. And lastly, they cause him to be disbelieved by all, received by none, and despised by everybody, including himself. It is notorious, moreover, that many men who have given themselves up to pleasure alone, have been ruined along with their families and relations. Thus, King Dandakya, of the Bhoja dynasty, carried off a Brahman's daughter with evil intent, and was eventually ruined and lost his kingdom. Indra, too, having violated the chastity of Ahalya, was made to suffer for it. In a like manner the mighty Kichaka, who tried to seduce Draupadi, and Ravana, who attempted to gain over Sita, were punished for their crimes. These and many others fell by reason of their pleasures.

Answer

This objection cannot be sustained, for pleasures, being as necessary for the existence and well being of the body as food, are consequently equally required. They are, moreover, the results of Dharma and Artha. Pleasures are, therefore, to be followed with moderation and caution. No one refrains from cooking food because there are beggars to ask for it, or from sowing seed because there are deer to destroy the corn when it is grown up.

Thus a man practising Dharma, Artha and Kama enjoys happiness both in this world and in the world to come. The good perform those actions in which there is no fear as to what is to result from them in the next world, and in which there is no danger to their welfare. Any action which conduces to the practice of Dharma, Artha and Kama together, or of any two, or even one of them, should be performed, but an action which conduces to the practice of one of them at the expense of the remaining two should not be performed.

III

On the arts and sciences to be studied

Man should study the Kama Sutra and the arts and sciences subordinate thereto, in addition to the study of the arts and sciences contained in Dharma and Artha. Even young maids should study this Kama Sutra along with its arts and sciences before marriage, and after it they could continue to do so with the consent of their husbands.

Here some learned men object, and say that females, not being allowed to study any science, should not study the Kama Sutra.

But Vatsyayana is of opinion that this objection does not hold good, for women already know the practice of Kama Sutra, and that practice is derived from the Kama Shastra, or the science of Kama itself. Moreover, it is not only in this but in many other cases that though the practice of a science is known to all, only a few pesons are acquainted with the rules and laws on which the science is based. Thus the Yadnikas or sacrificers, though ignorant of grammar, make use of appropriate words when addressing the different Deities, and do not know how these words are framed. Again, persons do the duties required of them on auspic-

25

ious days, which are fixed by astrology, though they are not acquainted with the science of astrology. In a like manner riders of horses and elephants train these animals without knowing the science of training animals, but from practice only. And similarly the people of the most distant provinces obey the laws of the kingdom from practice, and because there is a king over them, and without further reason. And from experience we find that some women, such as daughters of princes and their ministers, and public women, ware actually versed in the Kama Shastra.

A female, therefore, should learn the Kama Shastra, or at least part of it, by studying its practice frome some confidential friend. She should study alone in private the sixty-four practices that form a part of the Kama Shastra. Her teacher should be one of the following persons, viz., the daughter of a nurse brought up with her and already married, or a female friend who can be trusted in everything, or the sister of her mother (i.e., her aunt), or an old female servant, or a female beggar who may have formerly lived in the family, or her own sister, who can always be trusted.

The following are the arts to be studied, together with the Kama Sutra: –
1. Singing.
2. Playing on musical instruments.
3. Dancing.
4. Union of dancing, singing, and playing instrumental music.
5. Writing and drawing.
6. Tattooing.
7. Arraying and adorning an idol with rice and flowers.
8. Spreading and arranging beds or couches of flowers, or flowers upon the ground.
9. Colouring the teeth, garments, hair, nails and bodies, i.e., staining, dying, colouring and painting the same.
10. Fixing stained glass into a floor.
11. The art of making beds, and spreading out carpets and cushions for reclining.
12. Playing on musical glasses filled with water.
13. Storing and accumulating water in aqueducts, cisterns and reservoirs.

14. Picture making, trimming and decorating.

15. Stringing of rosaries, necklaces, garlands and wreaths.

16. Binding of turbans and chaplets, and making crests and top-knots of flowers.

17. Scenic representations. Stags playing.

18. Art of making ear ornaments.

19. Art of preparing perfumes and odours.

20. Proper disposition of jewels and decorations, and adornment in dress.

21. Magic or sorcery.

22. Quickness of hand or manual skill.

23. Culinary art, i.e., cooking and cookery.

24. Making lemonades, sherbets, acidulated drinks, and spirituous extracts with proper flavour and colour.

25. Tailor's work and sewing.

26. Making parrots, flowers, tufts, tassels, bunches, bosses, knobs, etc., out of yarn or thread.

27. Solution of riddles, enigmas, covert speeches, verbal puzzles and enigmatical questions.

28. A game, which consisted in repeating verses, and as one person finished, another person had to commence at once, repeating another verse, beginning with the same letter with which the last speaker's verse end. Whoever failed to repeat was considered to have lost, and to be subject to pay a forfeit or stake of some kind.

29. The art of mimicry or imitation.

30. Reading, including chanting and intoning.

31. Study of sentences difficult to pronounce. It is played as a game chiefly by women and children, and consists of a difficult sentence being given, and when repeated quickly, the words are often transposed or badly pronounced.

32. Practice with sword, single stick, quarter staff and bow and arrow.

33. Drawing inferences, reasoning or inferring.

34. Carpentry, or the work of a carpenter.

35. Architecture, or the art of building.

36. Knowledge about gold and silver coins, and jewels and gems.

37. Chemistry and mineralogy.

38. Colouring jewels, gems and beads.

39. Knowledge of mines and quarries.

40. Gardening: knowledge of treating the diseases of trees and plants, of nourishing them, and determining their ages.

41. Art of cock fighting, quail fighting and ram fighting.

42. Art of teaching parrots and starlings to speak.

43. Art of applying perfumed ointments to the body, and of dressing the hair with unguents and perfumes and braiding it.

44. The art of understanding writing in cypher, and the writing of words in a peculiar way.

45. The art of speaking by changing the forms of words. It is of various kinds. Some speak by changing the beginning and end of words, others by adding unnecessary letters between every syllable of a word, and so on.

46. Knowledge of language and of the vernacular dialects.

47. Art of making flower carriages.

48. Art of framing mystical diagrams, of addressing spells and charms, and binding armlets.

49. Mental exercises, such as completing stanzas or verses on receiving a part of them; or supplying one, two or three lines when the remaining lines are given indiscriminately from different verses, so as to make the whole an entire verse with regard to its meaning; or arranging the words of a verse written irregularly by separating the vowels from the consonants, or leaving them out altogether; or putting into verse or prose sentences represented by signs or symbols. There are many other such exercises.

50. Composing poems.

51. Knowledge of dictionaries and vocabularies.

52. Knowledge of ways of changing and disguising the appearance of persons.

53. Knowledge of the art of changing the appearance of things, such as making cotton to appear as silk, coarse and common things to appear as fine and good.

54. Various ways of gambling.

55. Art of obtaining possession of the property of others by means of muntras or incantrations.

56. Skill in youthful sports.

57. Knowledge of the rules of society, and of how to pay respects and compliments to others.

58. Knowledge of the art of war, of arms, of armies, etc.

59. Knowledge of gymnastics.

60. Art of knowing the character of a man from his features.

61. Knowledge of scanning or constructing verses.

62. Arithmetical recreations.

63. Making artificial flowers.

64. Making figures and images in clay.

A public woman, endowed with a good disposition, beauty and other winning qualities, and also versed in the above arts, obtains the name of a Ganika, or public woman of high quality, and receives a seat of honour in an assemblage of men. She is, moreover, always respected by the king, and praised by learned men, and her favour being sought for by all, she becomes an object of universal regard. The daughter of a king too, as well as the daughter of a minister, being learned in the above arts, can make their husbands favourable to them, even though these may have thousands of other wives besides themselves. And in the same manner, if a wife becomes separated from her husband, and falls into distress, she can support herself easily, even in a foreign country, by means of her knowledge of these arts. Even the bare knowledge of them gives attractiveness to a woman, though the practice of them may be only possible or otherwise according to the circumstances of each case. A man who is versed in these arts, who is loquacious and acquainted with the arts of gallantry, gains very soon the hearts of women, even though he is only acquainted with them for a short time.

IV

The life of a citizen

Having thus acquired learning, a man, with the wealth that he may have gained by gift, conquest, purchase, deposit, or inheritance from his ancestors, should become a householder, and pass the life of a citizen. He should take a house in a city, or large village, or in the vicinity of good men, or in a place which is the resort of many persons. This abode should be situated near some water, and divided into different compartments for different purposes. It should be surrounded by a garden, and also contain two rooms, an outer and an inner one. The inner room should be occupied by the females, while the outer room, balmy with rich perfumes, should contain a bed, soft, agreeable to the sight, covered with a clean white cloth, low in the middle part, having garlands and bunches of flowers upon it, and a canopy above it, and two pillows, one at the top, another at the bottom. There should be also a sort of couch besides, and at the head of this a sort of stool, on which should be placed the fragrant ointments for the night, as well as flowers, pots containing collyrium and other fragrant substances, things used for perfuming the mouth, and the bark of the common citron tree. Near the couch, on the ground, there should be a pot for spitting, a box containing ornaments, and also a lute hanging from a peg made from the tooth of an elephant, a board for drawing, a pot containing perfume, some books, and some garlands of the yellow amaranth flowers. Not far from the couch and on the ground, there should be a round seat, a toy cart, and a board for playing with dice; outside the outer room there should be cages of birds, and a separate place for spinning, carving and such like diversions. In the gardens there should be a whirling swing and a common swing, as also a bower of creepers covered with flowers, in which a raised parterre should be made for sitting.

Now the householder having got up in the morning and performed his necessary duties, should wash his teeth, apply a limited quantity of ointments and perfumes to his body, put some ornaments on his person and collyrium on his eyelids and below his eyes, colour his lips with alacktaka, and look at himself in the glass. Having then eaten betel leaves, with other things that give fragrance to the mouth, he should perform his usual business. He should bathe daily, anoint his body with oil every other day, apply a lathering substance to his body every three days, get his head (including face) shaved every four days, and the other parts of his body every five or ten days. All these things should be done without fail, and the sweat of the armpits should also be removed. Meals should be taken in the forenoon, in the afternoon, and again at night, according to Charayana. After breakfast, parrots and other birds should be taught to speak, and the fighting of cocks, quails and rams should follow. A limited time should be devoted to diversions with Pithamardas, Vitas, and Vidushakas, and then should be taken the midday sleep. After this the householder, having put on his clothes and ornaments, should, during the afternoon, converse with his friends. In the evening there should be singing, and after that the householder, along with his friend, should await in his room, previously decorated and perfumed, the arrival of the woman that may be attached to him, or he may send a female messenger for her, or go for her himself. After her arrival at his house, he and his friend should welcome her, and entertain her with a loving and agreeable conversation. Thus end the duties of the day. The following are the things to be done occasionally as diversions or amusements.

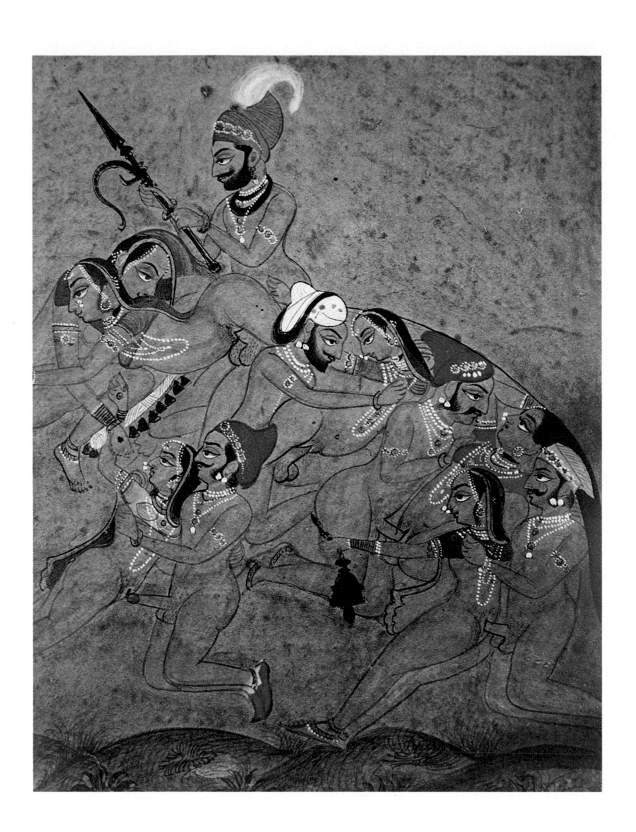

1. Holding festivals in honour of different Deities.
2. Social gatherings of both sexes.
3. Drinking parties.
4. Picnics.
5. Other social diversions.

Festivals

On some particular auspicious day, an assembly of citizens should be convened in the temple of Saraswati. There the skill of singers, and of others who may have come recently to the town, should be tested, and on the following day they should always be given some rewards. After that they may either be retained or dismissed, according as their performances are liked or not by the assembly. The members of the assembly should act in concert, both in times of distress as well as to strangers who may have come to the assembly. What is said above should be understood to apply to all the other festivals which may be held in honour of the different Deities, according to the present rules.

Social Gatherings

When men of the same age, disposition and talents, fond of the same diversions and with the same degree of education, sit together in company with public women, or in an assembly of citizens, or at the abode of one among themselves, and engage in agreeable discourse with each other, such is called a sitting in company or a social gathering. The subjects of discourse are to be the completion of verses half composed by others, and the testing the knowledge of one another in the various arts. The women who may be the most beautiful, who may like the same things that the men like, and who may have power to attract the minds of others, are here done homage to.

Drinking Parties

Men and women should drink in one another's houses. And here the men should cause the public women to drink, and should then drink themselves, liqours such as the Madhu, Aireya, Sara, and Asawa, which are of bitter and sour taste; also drinks concocted from the barks of various trees, wild fruits and leaves.

Going to Gardens or Picnics

In the forenoon, men, having dressed themselves should go to gardens on horseback, accompanied by public women and followed by servants. And having done there all the duties of the day, and passed the time in various agreeable diversions, such as the fighting of quails, cocks and rams, and other spectacles, they should return home in the afternoon in the same manner, bringing with them bunches of flowers, etc.
The same also applies to bathing in summer in water from which wicked or dangerous animals have previously been taken out, and which has been built in on all sides.

Other Social Diversions

Spending nights playing with dice. Going out on moonlight nights. Keeping the festive day in honour of spring. Plucking the sprouts and fruits of the mangoe trees. Eating the fibres of lotuses. Eating the tender ears of corn. Picnicing in the forests, when the trees get their new foliage. The Udakakashvedika or sporting in the water. Decorating each other with the flowers of some trees. Pelting each other with the flowers of the Kadamba tree, and many other sports which may either be known to the whole country, or may be peculiar to particular parts of it. These and similar other amusements should always be carried on by citizens.

The above amusements should be followed by a person who diverts himself alone in company with a courtesan, as well as by a courtesan who can do the same in company with her maid servants or with citizens.

A Pithamada is a man without wealth, alone in the world, whose only property consists of his Mallika, some lathering substance and a red cloth, who comes from a good country, and who is skilled in all the arts; and by teaching these arts is received in the company of citizens, and in the abode of public women.

A Vita is a man who has enjoyed the pleasure of fortune, who is a compatriot of citizens with whom he associates, who is possessed of the qualities of a householder, who has his wife with him, and who is honoured in the assembly of citizens and in the abodes of public women, and lives on their means and on them.

A Vidushaka (also called a Vaihaska, i.e., one who provokes laughter) is a person only acquainted with some of the arts, who is a jester, and who is trusted by all.

These persons are employed in matters of quarrels and reconciliations between citizens and public women.

This remark applies also to female beggars, to women with their heads shaved, to adulterous women, and to old public women skilled in all the various arts.

Thus a citizen living in his town or village, respected by all, should call on the persons of his own caste who may be worth knowing. He should converse in company and gratify his friends by his society, and obliging others by his assistance in various matters, he should cause them to assist one another in the same way.

There are some verses on the subject as follows: –

A citizen discoursing, not entirely in the Sanscrit language, nor wholly in the dialects of the country, on various topics in society, obtains great respect. The wise should not resort to a society disliked by the public, governed by no rules, and intent on the destruction of others. But a learned man living in a society which acts according to the wishes of the people, and which has pleasure for its only object is highly respected in this world.

V

About the kinds of women resorted to by the citizens, and of friends and messengers

When Kama is practised by men of the four castes according to the rules of the Holy Writ (i.e., by lawful marriage) with virgins of their own caste, it then becomes a means of acquiring lawful progeny and good fame, and it is not also opposed to the customs of the world. On the contrary the practice of Kama with women of the higher castes, and with those previously enjoyed by others, even though they be of the same caste, is prohibited. But the practice of Kama with women of the lower castes, with women excommunicated from their own caste, with public women, and with women twice married, is neither enjoined nor prohibited. The object of practising Kama with such women is pleasure only. Nayikas, therefore, are of three kinds, viz., maids, women twice married, and public women. Gonikaputra has expressed on opinion that there is a fourth kind of Nayika, viz., a woman who is resorted to on some special occasion even though she be previously married to another. These special occasions are when a man thinks thus: —

a) This woman is self-willed, and has been previously enjoyed by many others beside myself. I may, therefore, safely resort to her as a public woman though she belongs to a higher caste than mine, and, in so doing I shall not be violating the ordinances of Dharma.

Or thus: –

b) This is a twice-married woman and has been enjoyed by others before me, there is, therefore, no objection to my resorting to her.

Or thus: –

c) This woman has gained the heart of her great and powerful husband, and exercises a mastery over him, who is a friend of my enemy; if, therefore, she becomes united with me she will cause her husband to abandon my enemy.

Or thus: –

d) This woman will turn the mind of her husband, who is very powerful, in my favour, he being at present disaffected towards me, and intent on doing me some harm.

Or thus: –

e) By making this woman my friend I shall gain the object of some friend of mine, or shall be able to effect the ruin of some enemy, or shall accomplish some other difficult purpose.

Or thus: –

f) By being united with this woman, I shall kill her husband, and so obtain his vast riches which I covet.

Or thus: –

g) The union of this woman with me is not attended with any danger, and will bring me wealth, of which, on account of my poverty and inability to support myself, I am very much in need. I shall, therefore obtain her vast riches in this way without any difficulty.

Or thus: –

h) This woman loves me ardently, and knows all my weak points, if therefore, I am unwilling to be united with her, she will make my faults public and thus tarnish my character and reputation. Or she will bring some gross accusation against me, of which it may be hard to clear myself, and I shall be ruined. Or perhaps she will detach from me her husband who is powerful, and yet under her control, and will unite him to my enemy, or will herself joint the latter.

Or thus: –

i) The husband of this woman has violated the chastity of my wives, I shall therefore return that injury by seducing his wives.

Or thus: –

j) By the help of this woman I shall kill an enemy of the king who has taken shelter with her, and whom I am ordered by the king to destroy.

Or thus: –

k) The woman whom I love is under the control of this woman. I shall, through the influence of the latter, be able to get at the former.

Or thus: –

l) This woman will bring to me a maid, who possesses wealth and beauty, but who is hard to get at, and under the control of another.

Or lastly thus: –

m) My enemy is a friend of this woman's husband, I shall therefore cause her to join him, and will thus create an enmity between her husband and him.

For these and similar other reasons the wives of other men may be resorted to, but it must be distinctly understood that is only allowed for special reasons, and not for mere carnal desire.

Charayana thinks that under these circumstances there is also a fifth kind of Nayika, viz., a woman who is kept by a minister, or who repairs to him occasionally; or a widow who accomplishes the purpose of a man with the person to whom she resorts.

Suvarnanabha adds that a woman who passes the life of an ascetic and in the condition of a widow may be considered as a sixth kind of Nayika.

Ghotakamukha says that the daughter of a public woman, an a female servant, who are still virgins, form a seventh kind of Nayika.

Gonardiya puts forth his doctrine that any woman born of good family, after she has come of age, is an eighth kind of Nayika.

But these four latter kinds of Nayikas do not differ much from the first four kinds of them, as there is no separate object in resorting to them. Therefore, Vatsyayana is of opinion that there are only four kinds of Nayikas, i.e., the maid, the twice-married woman, the public woman, and the woman resorted to for a special purpose.

The following women are not to be enjoyed: —

A leper.

A lunatic.

A woman turned out of caste.

A woman who reveals secrets.

A woman who publicly expresses desire for sexual intercourse.

A woman who is extremely white.

A woman who is extremely black.

A bad-smelling woman.

A woman who is a near relation.

A woman who is a female friend.

A woman who leads the life of an ascetic.

And, lastly the wife of a relation, of a friend, of a learned Brahman, and of the king.

The followers of Babhravya say that any woman who has been enjoyed by five men is a fit and proper person to be enjoyed. But Gonikaputra is of opinion that even when this is the case, the wives of a relation, of a learned Brahman and of a king should be excepted.

The following are of the kind of friends: —

One who has played with you in the dust, i.e., in childhood.

One who is bound by an obligation.

One who is of the same disposition and fond of the same things.

One who is a fellow student.

One who is acquainted with your secrets and faults, and whose faults and secrets are also known to you.

One who is a child of your nurse.

One who is brought up with you.

One who is an hereditary friend.

These friends should possess the following qualities: –

They should tell the truth.

They should not be changed by time.

They should be firm.

They should be free from covetousness.

They should not be capable of being gained over by others.

They should not reveal your secrets.

Charayana says that citizens form friendship with washermen, barbers, cow-herds, florists, druggists, betelleaf sellers, tavern keepers, beggars, Pitharmardas, Vitas and Vidushekas, as also with the wives of all these people.

A messenger should possess the following qualities: –

Skilfulness.

Boldness.

Knowledge of the intention of men by their outward signs.

Absence of confusion, i.e., no shyness.

Knowledge of the exact meaning of what others do or say.

Good manners.

Knowledge of appropriate times and places for doing different things.

Ingenuity in business.

Quick comprehension.

Part II
Of Sexual Union

I

Kinds of Sexual Union According to Dimensions, Force and Desire, and Time

Quick application of remedies, i.e., quick and ready resources.

And this part ends with a verse: —

The man who is ingenious and wise, who is accompanied by a friend, and who knows the intentions of others, as also the proper time and place for doing everything, can gain over, very easily, even a woman who is very hard to be obtained.

Kinds of Union

Man is divided into three classes, viz., the hare man, the bull man, and the horse man, according to the size of his lingam.

Women also, according to the depth of her yoni, is either a female deer, a mare, or a female elephant.

There are thus three equal unions between persons of corresponding dimensions, and there are six unequal unions, when the dimensions do not correspond, or nine in all, as the following table shows:

Equal		Unequal	
Men	Women	Men	Women
Hare	Deer	Hare	Mare
Bull	Mare	Hare	Elephant
Horse	Elephant	Bull	Deer
		Bull	Elephant
		Horse	Deer
		Horse	Mare

In these unequal unions, when the male exceeds the female in point of size, his union with a woman who is immediately next to him in size is called high union, and is of two kinds; while his unions with the woman most remote from him in size is called the highest union, and is of one kind only. On the other hand, when the female exceeds the male in point of size, her union with a man immediately next to her in size is called low union, and is of two kinds; while her union with a man most remote from her in size is called the lowest union, and is of one kind only.

In other words, the horse and mare, the bull and deer, form the high union, while the horse and deer form the highest union. On the female side, the elephant and bull, the mare und hare, form low unions, while the elephant and the hare make the lowest unions.

There are then, nine kinds of union according to dimensions. Amongst all these, equal unions are the best, those of a superlative degree, i.e., the highest and the lowest, are the worst, and the rest are middling, and with them the high are better than the low.

There are also nine kinds of union according to the force of passion or carnal desire, as follows:

Men	Women	Men	Women
Small	Small	Small	Middling
Middling	Middling	Small	Intense
Intense	Intense	Middling	Small
		Middling	Intense
		Intense	Small
		Intense	Middling

A man is called a man of small passion whose desire at the time of sexual union is not great, whose semen is scanty, and who cannot bear the warm embraces of the female.

Those who differ from this temperament are called men of middling passion, while those of intense passion are full of desire.

In the same way, women are supposed to have the three degrees of feeling as specified above.

Lastly, according to time there are three kinds of men and women, viz., the short-timed, the moderate-timed, and the long-timed, and of these as in the previous statements, there are nine kinds of union.

But on this last heard there is a difference of opinion about the female which should be stated.

Auddalika says, "Females do not emit as males do. The males simply remove their desire, while the females, from their consciousness of desire, feel a certain kind of pleasure, which gives them satisfaction, but it is imposible for them to tell you what kind of pleasure they feel. The fact from which this becomes evident is, that males, when engaged in coition, cease of themselves after emission, and are satisfied, but it is not so with females."

The opinion is however objected to on the grounds, that if a male be a long-timed, the female loves him the more, but if he be short-timed, she is dissatisfied with him. And this circumstance, some say, would prove that the female emits also.

But this opinion does not hold good, for if it takes a long time to allay a woman's desire, and during this time she is enjoying great pleasure, it is quite natural then that she should wish for its continuation. And on this subject there is a verse as follows:

"By union with men the lust, desire, or passion of women is satisfied, and the pleasure derived from the consciousness of it is called their satisfaction."

The followers of Babhravya, however, say that the semen of women continues to fall from the beginning of the sexual union to its end, and it is right that it should be so, for if they had no semen there would be no embryo.

To this there is an objection. In the beginning of coition the passion of the woman is middling, and she cannot bear the vigorous thrusts of her lover, but by degrees her passion increases until she ceases to think about her body, and then finally she wishes to stop from further coition.

This objection, however, does not hold good, for even in ordinary things that revolve with great force, such as a potter's wheel, or a top, we find that the motion at first is slow, but by degrees it becomes very rapid. In the same way the passion of the woman having gradually increased, she has a desire to discontinue coition, when all the semen has fallen away. And there is a verse with regard to this as follows:

"The fall of the semen of the man takes place only at the end of coition, while the semen of the woman falls continually, and after the semen of both has all fallen away then they wish for the discontinuance of coition."

Lastly, Vatsyayana is of opinion that the semen of the female falls in the same way as that of the male.

Now some may ask here: If men and women are beings of the same kind, and are engaged in bringing about the same results, why should they have different works to do.

Vatsya says that this is so, because the ways of working as well as the consciousness of pleasure in men and women are different. The difference in the ways of working, by which men are the actors, and women are the persons acted upon, is owing to the nature of the male and the female, otherwise the actor would be sometimes the person acted upon, and vice versa. And from this difference in the

ways of working follows the difference in the consciousness of pleasure, for a man thinks, "this woman is united with me", and a woman thinks, "I am united with this man."

It may be said that if the ways of working in men and women are different, why should not there be a difference, even in the pleasure they feel, and which is the result of those ways.

But this objection is groundless, for the person acting and the person acted upon being of different kinds, there is a reason for the difference in their ways of working; but there is no reason for any difference in the pleasure they feel, because they both naturally derive pleasure from the act they perform.

On this again some may say that when different persons are engaged in doing the same work, we find that they accomplish the same end or purpose; while, on the contrary, in the case of men and women we find that each of them accomplishes his or her own end separately, and this is inconsistent. But this is a mistake, for we find that sometimes two things are done at the same time, as for instance in the fighting of rams, both the rams receive the shock at the same time on their heads. Again, in throwing one wood apple against another, and also in a fight or struggle of wrestlers. If it be said that in these cases the things employed are of the same kind, it is answered that even in the case of men and women, the nature of the two persons is the same. And as the difference in their ways of working arises from the difference of their conformation only, it follows that men experience the same kind of pleasure as women do.

There is also a verse on this subject as follows: "Men and women being of the same nature, feel the same kind of pleasure, and therefore a man should marry such a woman as will love him ever afterwards."

The pleasure of men and women being thus proved to be of the same kind, it follows that in regard to time, there are nine kinds of sexual intercourse, in the same way as there are nine kinds, according to the force of passion.

There being thus nine kinds of union with regard to dimensions, force of passion, and time, respectively, by making combinations of them, innumerable kinds of union would be produced. Therefore in each particular kind sexual of union, men should use such means as they may think suitable for the occasion.

At the first time of sexual union the passion of the male is intense, and his time is short, but in subsequent unions on the same day the reverse of this is the case. With the female, however, it is the contrary, for at the first time her passion is weak, and then her time long, but on subsequent occasions on the same day, her passion is intense and her time short, until her passion is satisfied.

On the different Kinds of Love

Men learned in the humanities are of the opinion that love is of four kinds, viz.:
1. Love acquired by continual habit.
2. Love resulting from the imagination.
3. Love resulting from belief.
4. Love resulting from the perception of external objects.

1). Love resulting from the constant and continual performance of some act, is called love acquired by constant practice and habit, as for instance the love of sexual intercourse, the love of hunting, the love of drinking, the love of gambling, etc., etc.

2). Love which is felt for things to which we are not habituated, and which proceeds entirely from ideas, is called love resulting from imagination, as for instance, that love which some men and women and eunuchs feel for the Auparishataka or mouth congress, and that which is felt by all for such things as embracing, kissing, etc., etc.

3). The love which is mutual on both sides, and proved to be true, when each looks upon the other as his or her very own, such is called love resulting from belief by the learned.

4). The love resulting from the perception of external objects is quite evident and well known to the world, because the pleasure which it affords is superior to the pleasure of the other kinds of love, which exists only for its sake.

What has been said in this chapter upon the subject of sexual union is sufficient for the learned; but for the edification of the ignorant, the same will now be treated of at length and in detail.

II

Of the embrace

This part of the Kama Shastra, which treats of sexual union, is also called "Sixty-four", (Chatushshashti). Some old authors say that it is called so, because it contains sixty-four chapters. Others are of opinion that the author of this part being a person named Panchala, and the person who recited the part of the Rig Veda called Dashatapa, which contains sixty-four verses, being also called Panchala, the name "sixty-four" has been given to the part of the work in honour of the Rig Vedas. The followers of Babhravya say on the other hand that this part contains eight subjects, viz., the embrace, kissing, scratching with the nails or fingers, biting, lying down, making various sounds, playing the part of man, and the Auparishtaka, or mouth congress. Each of these subjects being of eight kinds, and eight multiplied by eight being sixty-four, this part is therefore named "sixty-four." But Vatsyayana affirms that as this part contains also the following subjects, viz., striking, crying, the acts of man during congress, the various kinds of congress, and other subjects, the name "sixty-four" is given to it only accidentally. As, for instance, we say this tree is "Saptaparna", or seven-leaved, this offering of rice is "Panchavarna", or five-coloured, but the tree has not seven leaves, neither has the rice five colours.

However the part sixty-four is now treated of, and the embrace, being the first subject, will now be considered.

Now the embrace which indicates the mutual love of a man and woman who have come together is of four kinds, viz:

Touching.
Piercing.
Rubbing.
Pressing.

The action in each case is denoted by the meaning of the word which stands for it.

1). When a man under some pretext or other goes in front or alongside of a woman and touches her body with his own, it is called the "touching embrace."

2). When a woman in a lonely place bends down, as if to pick up something, and pierces, as it were, a man sitting or standing, with her breasts, and the man in return takes hold of them, it is called a "piercing embrace."

The above two kinds of embrace takes place only between persons who do not, as yet, speak freely with each other.

3). When two lovers are walking slowly together, either in the dark, or in a place of public resort, or in a lonely place, and rub their bodies against each other, it is called a "rubbing embrace."

4). When on the above occasion one of them presses the other's body forcibly against a wall or pillar, it is called a "pressing embrace."

These two last embraces are peculiar to those who know the intentions of each other.

At the time of the meeting the four following kinds of embrace are used, viz.:
Jataveshitaka, or the twining of a creeper.
Vrikshadhirudhaka, or climbing a tree.
Tila-Tandulaka, or the mixture of sesamum seed with rice.
Kshiraniraka, or milk and water embrace.

1). When a woman, clinging to a man as a creeper twines round a tree, bends his head down to hers with the desire of kissing him and slightly makes the sound of sut sut, embraces him, and looks lovingly towards him, it is called an embrace like the "twining of a creeper."

2). When a woman, having placed one of her feet on the foot of her lover, and other on one of his thighs, passes one of her arms round his back, and the other on his shoulders, makes slightly the sounds of singing and cooing, and wishes, as it were, to climb up to him in order to have a kiss, it is called an embrace like the "climbing of a tree."

These two kinds of embrace take place when the lover is standing.

3). When lovers lie on a bed, and embrace each other so closely that the arms and thighs of the one are encircled by the arms and thighs of the other, and are, as it were, rubbing up against them, this is called an embrace like "the mixture of sesamum seed with rice."

4). When a man and a woman are very much in love with each other, and, not thinking of any pain or hurt, embrace each other as if they were entering into each other's bodies either while the woman is sitting on the lap of the man, or in front of him, or on a bed, then it is called an embrace like a "mixture of milk and water."

These two kinds of embrace take place at the time of sexual union.

Babhravya has thus related to us the above eight kinds of embraces.

Suvarnanabha moreover gives us four ways of embracing simple members of the body, which are:

The embrace of the thighs.

The embrace of the jaghana, i.e., the part of the body from the navel downwards to the thighs.

The embrace of the breasts.

The embrace of the forehead.

1). When one of two lovers presses forcibly one or both of the thighs of the other between his or her own it is called the "embrace of thighs."

2). When a man presses the jaghana or middle part of the woman's body against his own, and mounts upon her to practice, either scratching with the nail or finger, or biting, or striking, or kissing, the hair of the woman being loose and flowing, it is called the "embrace of the jaghana."

3). When a man places his breast between the breasts of a woman and presses her with it, it is called the "embrace of the breasts."

4). When either of the lovers touches the mouth, the eyes and the forehead of the other with his or her own, it is called the "embrace of the forehead."

Some say that even shampooing is a kind of embrace, because there is a touching of bodies in it. But Vatsyayana thinks that shampooing is performed at a different time, and for a different purpose, and it is also of a different character, it cannot be said to be included in the embrace.

There are also some verses on the subject as follows: "The whole subject of embracing is of such a nature that men who ask questions about it, or who hear about it, or who talk about it, acquire thereby a desire for enjoyment. Even those embraces that are not mentioned in the Kama Shastra should be practised at the time of sexual enjoyment, if they are in any way conducive to the increase of love or passion. The rules of the Shastra apply so long as the passion of man is middling, but when the wheel of love is once set in motion, there is then no Shastra and no order."

III

On kissing

It is said by some that there is no fixed time or order between the embrace, the kiss, and the pressing or scratching with the nails or fingers, but that all these things should be done generally before sexual union takes place, while striking and making the various sounds generally takes place at the time of the union. Vatsyayana however, thinks that anything may take place at any time, for love does not care for time or order.

On the occasion of the first congress, kissing and the other things mentioned above should be done moderately, they should not be continued for a long time, and should be done alternately. On subsequent occasions however the reverse of all this may take place, and moderation will not be necessary, they may continue for a long time, and for the purpose of kindling love, they may be all done at the same time.

The following are the places for kissing, riz., the forehead, the eyes, the cheeks, the throat, the bosom, the breasts, the lips, and the interior of the mouth. Moreover the people of the Lat country kiss also on the following places, viz., the joints of the thighs, the arms and the navel. But Vatsyayana thinks that though kissing is practised by these people in the above places on account of the intensity of their love, and the customs of their country, it is not fit to be practised by all.

Now in a case of a young girl there are three sorts of kisses, viz.:

The nominal kiss.

The throbbing kiss.

The touching kiss.

1). When a girl only touches the mouth of her lover with her own, but does not herself do anything, it is called the "nominal kiss."

2). When a girl, setting aside her bashfulness a little, wishes to touch the lip that is pressed into her mouth, and with that object moves her lower lip, but not the upper one, it is called the "throbbing kiss."

3). When a girl touches her lover's lip with her tongue, and having shut her eyes, places her hands on those of her lover, it is called the "touching kiss."

Other authors describe four other kinds of kisses, viz.:

The straight kiss.

The bent kiss.

The turned kiss.

The pressed kiss.

1). When the lips of two lovers are brought into direct contact with each other, it is called a "straight kiss."

2). When the heads of two lovers are bent towards each other, and when so bent, kissing takes place, it is called a "bent kiss."

3). When one of them turns up the face of the other by holding the head and chin, and then kissing, it is called a "turned kiss."

4). Lastly when the lower lip is pressed with much force, it is called a "pressed kiss."

There is also a fifth kind of kiss called the "greatly pressed kiss", which is effected by taking hold of the lower lip between two fingers, and then after touching it with the tongue, pressing it with great force with the lip.

As regards kissing, a wager may be laid as to which will get hold of the lips of the other first. If the woman loses, she should pretend to cry, should keep her lover off by shaking her hands, and turn away from him and dispute with him saying, "let another wager be laid." If she loses this a second time, she should appear doubly distressed, and when her lover is off his guard or asleep, she should get hold of his lower lip, and hold it in her teeth, so that it should not slip away, and then she should laugh, make a loud noise, deride him, dance about, and say whatever she likes in a joking way, moving her eyebrows, and rolling her eyes. Such are the wagers and quarrels as far as kissing is concerned, but the same may be applied with regard to the pressing or scratching with the nails and fingers, biting and striking. All these however are only peculiar to men and women of intense passion.

When a man kisses the upper lip of a woman, while she in return kisses his lower lip, it is called the "kis of the upper lip."

When one of them takes both the lips of the other between his or her own, it is called a "clasping kiss." A woman, however, only takes this kind of kiss from a man who has no moustache. And on the occasion of the kiss, if one of them touches the teeth, the tongue, and the palate of the other, with his or her tongue, it is called the "fighting of the tongue." In the same way, the pressing of the teeth of the one against the mouth of the other is to be practised.

Kissing is of four kinds, viz., moderate, contracted, pressed, and soft, according to the different parts of the body which are kissed, for different kinds of kisses are appropriate for different parts of the body.

When a woman looks at the face of her lover while he is asleep, and kisses it to show her intention or desire, it is called a "kiss that kindles love."

When a woman kisses her lover while he is engaged in business, or while he is quarrelling with her, or while he is looking at something else, so that his mind may be turned away, it is called a "kiss that turns away."

When a lover coming home late at night kisses his beloved, who is asleep on her bed, in order to show her his desire, it is called a "kiss that awakens." On such an occasion the woman may pretend to be asleep at the time of her lover's arrival, so that she may know his intention and obtain respect from him.

When a person kisses the reflection of the person he loves in a mirror, in water, or on a wall, it is called a "kiss showing the intention."

When a person kisses a child sitting on his lap, or a picture, or an image, or figure, in the presence of the person beloved by him, it is called a "transferred kiss." When at night at a theatre, or in an assembly of caste men, a man coming up to a woman kisses a finger of her hand if she be standing, or a toe of her foot if she be sitting, or when a woman is shampooing her lover's body, places her face on his thigh (as if she was sleepy) so as to inflame his passion, and kisses his thigh or great toe, it is called a "demonstrative kiss."

There is also a verse on this subject as follows:

"Whatever things may be done by one of the lovers to the other, the same should be turned by the other, ie., if the woman kisses him he should kiss her in return, if she strikes him he should also strike her in return".

VI

On pressing, or marking, or scratching with the nails

When love becomes intense, pressing with the nails or scratching the body with them is practised, and it is done on the following occasions: On the first visit; at the time of setting out on a journey; on the return from a journey; at the time when an angry lover is reconciled; and lastly when a woman is intoxicated.

But pressing with the nails is not a usual thing except with those who are intensely passionate, i.e., full of passion. It is employed together with biting, by those to whom the practice is agreeable.

Pressing with the nails is of the eight following kinds, according to the forms of the marks which are produced, viz.:

1. Sounding.
2. Half moon.
3. A circle.
4. A line.
5. A tiger's nail or claw.
6. A peacock's foot.

7. The jump of a hare.

8. The leaf of a blue lotus.

The places that are to be pressed with the nails are as follows: the arm pit, the throat, the breasts, the lips, the jaghana, or middle parts of the body, and the thighs. But Suvarnanabha is of opinion that then the impetuosity of passion is excessive, then the places need not be considered.

The qualities of good nails are that they should be bright, well set, clean, entire, convex, soft, and glossy in appearance. Nails are of three kinds according to their size, viz.:

Small.

Middling.

Large.

Large nails, which give grace to the hands, and attract the hearts of women from their appearance, are possessed by the Bengalees.

Small nails, which can be used in various ways, and are to be applied only with the object of giving pleasure, are possessed by the people of the southern districts.

Middling nails, which contain the properties of both the above kinds, belong to the people of the Maharashtra.

1). When a person presses the chin, the breasts, the lower lip, or the jaghana of another so softly that no scratch or mark is left, but only the hair on the body becomes erect from the touch of the nails, and the nails themselves make a sound, it is called a "sounding or pressing with the nails."

This pressing is used in the case of a young girl when her lover shampoos her, scratches her head, and wants to trouble or frighten her.

2). The curved mark with the nails, which is impressed on the neck and the breasts, is called "the half moon."

3). When the half moons are impressed opposite to each other, it is called a "circle." This mark with the nails is generally made on the navel, the small cavities about the buttocks, and on the joints of the thigh.

4). A mark in the form of a small line, and which can be made on any part of the body, is called a "line."

5). This same line, when it is curved, and made on the breast, is called a "tiger's nail."

6). When a curved mark is made on the breast by means of the five nails, it is called a "peacock's foot." This mark is made with the object of being praised, for it requires a great deal of skill to make it properly.

7). When five marks with the nails are made close to one another near the nipple of the breast, it is called "the jump of a hare."

8). A mark made on the breast or on the hips in the form of a leaf of the blue lotus, is called the "leaf of a blue lotus."

When a person is going on a journey, and makes a mark on the thighs, or on the breast, it is called a "token of remembrance." On such an occasion three or four lines are impressed close to one another with the nails.

Here ends the marking with the nails. Marks of other kinds than the above may also be made with the nails, for the ancient authors say, that as there are innumerable degrees of skill among men (the practice of this art being known to all), so there are innumerable ways of making these marks. And as pressing or marking with the nails is independent of love, no one can say with certainty how many different kinds of marks with the nails do actually exist. The reason of this is, Vatsyayana says, that as variety is necessary in love, so love is to be produced by means of variety. It is on this account that courtezans, who are well acquainted with various ways and means, become so desirable, for if variety is sought in all the arts and amusements, such as archery and others, how much more should it be sought after in the present case.

The marks of the nails should not be made on married women, but particular kinds of marks may be made on their private parts for the remembrance and increase of love.

There are also some verses on the subject, are follows:

"The love of a woman who sees the marks of nails on the private parts of her body, even though they are old and almost worn out, becomes again fresh and new. If there be no marks of nails to remind a person of the passages of love, then love is lessened in the same way as when no union takes place for a long time."

Even when a stranger sees at a distance a young woman with the marks of nails on her breast, he is filled with love and respect for her.

A man, also, who carries the marks of nails and teeth on some parts of his body, influences the mind of a woman, even though it be ever so firm. In short, nothing tends to increase love so much as the effects of marking with the nails, and biting.

V

On biting, and the means to be employed with regard to women of different countries

All the places that can be kissed, are also the places that can be bitten, except the upper lip, the interior of the mouth, and the eyes.

The qualities of good teeth are as follows: They should be equal, possessed of a pleasing brightness, capable of being coloured, of proper proportions, unbroken, and with sharp ends.

The defects of teeth on the other hand are, that they are blunt, protruding from the gums, rough, soft, large, and loosely set.

The following are the different kinds of biting, viz.

The hidden bite.

The swollen bite.

The point.

The line of points.

The coral and the jewel.

The line of jewels.

The broken cloud.

The biting of the boar.

1). The biting which is shown only by the excessive redness of the skin that is bitten, is called the "hidden bite."

2). When the skin is pressed down on both sides, it is called the "swollen bite."

3). When a small portion of the skin is bitten with two teeth only, it is called the "point."

4). When such small portions of the skin are bitten with all the teeth, it is called the "line of points."

5). The biting which is done by bringing together the teeth and the lips, is called the "coral and the jewel." The lip is the coral, and the teeth the jewel.

6). When biting is done by all the teeth, it is called the "line of jewels."

7). The biting which consists of unequal risings in a circle, and which comes from the space between the teeth, is called the "broken cloud." This is impressed on the breasts.

8). The biting which consists of many broad rows of marks near to one another, and with red intervals, is called the "biting of a boar." This is impressed on the breasts and the shoulders; and these two last modes of biting are peculiar to persons of intense passion.

The lower lip is the place on which the "hidden bite", the "swollen bite", and the "point" are made; again the "swollen bite", and the "coral and the jewel" bite are done on the cheek. Kissing, pressing with the nails, and biting are the ornaments of the left cheek, and when the word cheek is used it is to be understood as the left cheek. Both the "line of points" and the "line of jewels" are to be impressed on the throat, the arm pit, and the joints of the thighs; but the "line of points" alone is to be impressed on the forehead and the thighs.

The marking with the nails, and the biting of the following things, viz., an ornament of the forehead, an ear ornament, a bunch of flowers, a betel leaf, or a tamala leaf, which are worn by, or belong to the woman that is beloved, are signs of the desire of enjoyment.

Here end the different kinds of biting.

In the affairs of love a man should do such things as are agreeable to the women of different countries.

The women of the central countries, (i.e., between the Ganges and Jumna) are noble in their character, not accustomed to disgraceful practices, and dislike pressing the nails and biting.

The women of the Balhika country are gained over by striking.

The women of Avantika are fond of foul pleasures, and have not good manners.

The women of the Maharashtra are fond of practising the sixty-four arts, they utter low and harsh words, ad like to be spoken to in the same way, and have an impetuous desire of enjoyment.

The women of Pataliputra (i.e., the modern Patna) are of the same nature as the women of the Maharashtra, but show their likings only in secret.

The women of the Dravida country, though they are rubbed and pressed about at the time of sexual enjoyment, have a slow fall of semen, that is they are very slow in the act of coition.

The women of Vanavasi are moderately passionate, they go through every kind of enjoyment, cover their bodies, and abuse those who utter low, mean and harsh words.

The women of Avanti hate kissing, marking with the nails, and biting, but they have a fondness for various kinds of sexual union.

The women of Malwa like embracing and kissing, but not wounding, and they are gained over by striking.

The women of Abhira, and those of the country about the Indus and five rivers (i.e., the Punjab), are gained over by the Auparishtaka or mouth congress.

The women of Aparatika are full of passion, and make slowly the sound "Sit".

The women of the Lat country have even more impetuous desire, and also make the sound "Sit."

The women of the Stri Rajya, and of Koshola (Oude), are full of impetuous desire, their semen falls in large quantities, and they are fond of taking medicine to make it do so.

The women of the Audhra country have tender bodies, they are full of enjoyment, and have a liking for voluptuous pleasures.

The women of Ganda have tender bodies, and speak sweetly.

71

Now Suvarnanabha is of opinion that that which is agreeable to the nature of a particular person, is of more consequence than that which is agreeable to a whole nation, and that therefore the peculiarities of the country should not be observed in such cases. The various pleasures, the dress, and the sports of one country are in time borrowed by another, and in such a case these things must be considered as belonging originally to that country.

Among the things mentions above, viz., embracing, kissing, etc., those which increase passion should be done first, and those which are only for amusement or variety should be done afterwards.

There are also some verses on this subject as follows:

"When a man bites a woman forcibly, she should angrily do the same to him with double force. Thus a 'point' should be returned with a 'line of points', and a 'line of points' with a 'broken cloud', and if she be excessively chafed, she should at once begin a love quarrel with him. At such a time she should take hold of her lover by the hair, and bend his head down, and kiss his lower lip, and then, being intoxicated with love, she should shut her eyes and bite him in various places. Even by day, and in a place of public resort, when her lover shows her any mark that she may have inflicted on his body, she should smile at the sight of it, and turning her face as if she were going to chide him, she should show him with an angry look the marks on her own body that have been made by him. Thus if men and women act according to each other's liking, their love for each other will not be lessened even in one hundred years."

VI

Of the different ways of lying down, and various kinds of congress

On the occasion of a "high congress" the Mrigi (Deer) woman should lie down in such a way as to widen her yoni, while an a "low congress" the Hastine (Elephant) woman should lie down so as to contract hers. But in an "equal congress" they should lie down in the natural position. What is said above concerning the Mrigi and the Hastini applies also to the Vadawa (Mare) woman. In a "low congress" the woman should particularly make use of medicine, to cause her desires to be satisfied quickly.

The Deer-woman has the following threee ways of lying down.

The widely opened position.

The yawning position.

The position of the wife of Indra.

1). When she lowers her head and raises her middle parts, it is called the "widely opened position." At such a time the man should apply some unguent, so as to make the entrance easy.

2). When she raises her thighs and keeps them wide apart and engages in congress, it is called the "yawning position."

3). When she places her thighs with her legs doubled on them upon her sides, and thus engages in congress, it is called the position of Indrani, and this is learnt only by practice. The position is also useful in the case of the "highest congress."

The "clasping position" is used in "low congress", and in the "lowest congress", together with the "pressing position", the "twining position", and the "mare's position."

When the legs of both the male and the female are stretched straight out over each other, it is called the "clasping position." It is of two kinds, the side position and the supine position, according to the way in which they lie down. In the side position the male should invariably lie on his left side, and cause the woman to lie on her right side, and this rule is to be observed in lying down with all kinds of women.

When, after congress has begun in the clasping position, the woman presses her lover with her thighs, it is called the "pressing position."

When the woman places one of her thighs across the thigh of her lover, it is called the "twining position."

When a woman forcibly holds in her yoni the lingam after it is in, it is called the "mare's position." This is learnt by practice only, and is chiefly found among the women of the Andra country.

The above are the different ways of lying down, mentioned by Babhravya; Suvarnanabha, however, gives the following in addition.

When the female raises both of her thighs straight up, it is called the "rising position."

When she raises both of her legs, and places them on her lover's shoulders, it is called the "yawning position."

When the legs are contracted, and thus held by the lover before his bosom, it is called the "pressed position."

When only one of her legs is stretched out, it is called the "half pressed position."

When the woman places one of her legs on her lover's shoulder, and stretches the other out, and then places the latter on his shoulder, and stretches out the other and continues to do so alternately, it is called the „splitting of a bamboo."

When one of her legs is placed on the head, and the other is stretched out, it is called the "fixing of a nail." This is learnt by practice only.

When both the legs of the woman are contracted, and placed on her stomach, it is called the "crab's position."

When the thighs are raised and placed one upon the other, it is called the "packed position."

When the shanks are placed one upon the other, it is called the "lotus-like position."

When a man, during congress, turns round, and enjoys the woman without leaving her, while she embraces him round the back all the time, it is called the "turning position", and is learnt only by practice.

Thus says Suvarnanabha, these different ways of lying down, sitting, and standing should be practised in water, because it is easy to do so therein. But Vatsyayana is of opinion that congress in water is improper, because it is prohibited by the religious law. When a man and a woman support themselves on each other's bodies, or on a wall, or pillar, and thus while standing engage in congress, it is called the "supported congress."

When a man supports himself against a wall, and the woman, sitting on his hands joined together and held underneath her, throws her arms round his neck, and putting her thighs alongside his waist, moves herself by her feet, which are touching the wall against which the man is leaning, it is called the "suspended congress."

When a woman stands on her hands and feet like a quadruped, and her lover mounts her like a bull, it is called the "congress of a cow." At this time everything that is ordinarily done on the bosom should be done on the back.

In the same way can be carried on the congress of a dog, the congress of a goat, the congress of a deer, the forcible mounting of an ass, the congress of a cat, the jump of a tiger, the pressing of an elephant, the rubbing of a boar, and the mounting of a horse. And in all these cases the characteristics of these different animals should be manifested by acting like them.

When a man enjoys two women at the same time, both of whom love him equally, it is called the "united congress."

When a man enjoys many women altogether, it is called the "congress of a herd of cows."

The following kinds of congress, viz., sporting in water, or the congress of an elephant with many female elephants which is said to take place only in the water, the congress of a collection of goats, the congress of a collection of deer, take place in imitation of these animals.

In Gramaneri many young men enjoy a woman that may be married to one of them, either one after the other, or at the same time. Thus one of them holds her, another enjoys her, a third uses her mouth, a fourth holds her middle part, and in this way they go on enjoying her several parts alternately.

The same things can be done when several men are sitting in company with one courtesan, or when one courtesan is alone with many men. In the same way this can be done by the women of the King's harem when they accidentally get hold of a man.

The people in the Southern countries have also a congress in the anus, that is called the "lower congress."

Thus ends the various kinds of congress. There are also two verses on the subject as follows.

"An ingenious person should multiply the kinds of congress after the fashion of the different kinds of beasts and of birds. For these different kinds of congress, performed according to the usage of each country, and the liking or each individual, generate love, friendship, and respect in the hearts of women."

VII

Of the various modes of striking, and of the sounds appropriate to them

Sexual intercourse can be compared to a quarrel, on account of the contrarieties of love and its tendency to dispute. The place of striking with passion is the body, and on the body the special places are:

> The shoulders.
> The head.
> The space between the breasts.
> The back.
> The jaghana, or middle part of the body.
> The sides.

Striking is of four kinds, viz.:

> Striking with back of the hand.
> Striking with the fingers a little contracted.
> Striking with the fist.
> Striking with the open palm of the hand.

On account of its causing pain, striking gives rise to the hissing sound, which is of various kinds, and to the eight kinds of crying, viz.:
The sound of Hin.

The thundering sound.

The cooing sound.

The weeping sound.

The sound Phut.

The sound Phât.

The sound Sût.

The sound Plât.

Besides these, there are also words having a meaning, such as "mother", and those that are expressive of prohibition, sufficiency, desire of liberation, pain or praise, and to which may be added sounds like those of the dove, the cuckoo, the green pigeon, the parrot, the bee, the sparrow, the flamingo, the duck, and the quail, which are all occasionally made use of.

Blows with the fist should be given on the back of the woman, while she is sitting on the lap of the man, and she should give blows in return, abusing the man as if she were angry, and making the cooing and the weeping sounds. While the woman is engaged in congress the space between the breasts should be struck with the back of the hand, slowly at first, and then proportionately to the increasing excitement, until the end.

At this time the sounds Hin and others may be made, alternately or optionally, according to habit. When the man, making the sound Phât, strikes the woman on the head, with the fingers of his hand a little contracted, it is called Prasritaka, which means striking with the fingers of the hand a little contracted. In this case the appropriate sounds are the cooing sound, the sound Phât, and the sound Phut in the interior of the mouth, and at the end of congress the sighing and weeping sounds. The sound Phât is an imitation of the sound of a bamboo being split, while the sound Phut is like the sound made by something falling into water. At all times when kissing and such like things are begun, the woman should give a reply with a hissing sound. During the excitement when the woman is not accustomed to striking, she continually utters words expressive of prohibition, sufficiently, or desire of liberation, as well as the words "father", "mother", intermingled with the sighing, weeping and thundering sounds. Towards the conclusion of the congress, the breasts, the jaghana, and the sides of the woman should be pressed with the open palms of the hand, with some force, until the end of it, and then sounds like those of the quail, or the goose should be made.

There are also two verses on the subject as follows:

"The characteristics of manhood are said to consist of roughness and impetuosity, while weakness, tenderness, sensibility, and an inclination to turn away from unpleasant things are the distinguishing marks of womanhood. The excitement of passion, and peculiarities of habit may sometimes cause contrary results to appear, but these do not last long, and in the end the natural state is resumed."

The wedge on the bosom, the scissors on the head, the piercing instrument on the cheeks, and the pinchers on the breasts and sides, may also be taken into consideration with the other four modes of striking, and thus give eight ways altogether. But these four ways of striking with instruments are peculiar to the people of the southern countries, and the marks caused by them are seen on the breasts of their women. They are local peculiarities, but Vatsyayana is of opinion that the practice of them is painful, barbarous, and base, and quite unworthy of imitation.

In the same way anything that is a local peculiarity should not always be adopted elsewhere, and even in the place where the practice is prevalent, excess of it should always be avoided. Instances of the dangerous use of them may be given as follows. The King of the Panchalas killed the courtezan Madhavasena by means of the wedge during congress. King Shatakarni Shatavahana of Kuntalas deprived his great Queen Malayavati of her life by a pair of scissors, and Naradeva, whose hand was deformed, blinded a dancing girl by directing a piercing instrument in a wrong way.

There are also two verses on the subject as follows:

"About these things there cannot be either enumeration or any definite rule. Congress having once commenced, passion alone gives birth to all the acts of the parties."

Such passionate actions and amorous gesticulations or movements, which arise on the spur of the moment, and during sexual intercourse, cannot be defined, and are as irregular as dreams. A horse having once attained the fifth degree of motion goes on with blind speed, regardless of pits, ditches, and posts in his way; and in the same manner a loving pair become blind with passion in the heat of congress, and go on with great impetuosity, paying not the least regard to excess. For this reason one who is well acquainted with the science of love, and knowing his own strength, as also the tenderness, impetuosity, and strength of the young women, should act accordingly. The various modes of enjoyment are not for all times or for all persons, but they should only be used at the proper time, and in the proper countries and places.

VIII

About women acting the part of a man; and of the work of a man

When a woman sees that her lover is fatigued by constant congress, without having his desire satisfied, she should, with his permission, lay him down upon his back, and give him assistance by acting his part. She may also do this to satisfy the curiosity of her lover, or her own desire of novelty.

There are two ways of doing this, the first is when during congress she turns round, and gets on the top of her lover, in such a manner as to continue the congress, without obstructing the pleasure of it; and the other is when she acts the man's part from the beginning. At such a time, with flowers in her hair hanging loose, and her smiles broken by hard breathings, she should press upon her lover's bosom with her own breasts, and lowering her head frequently, should do in return the same actions which he used to do before, returning his blows and chaffing him, should say, "I was laid down by you, and fatigued with hard congress, I shall now therefore lay you down in return." She should then again manifest her own bashfulness, her fatigue, and her desire for stopping the congress. In this way she should do the work of a man, which we shall presently relate.

Whatever is done by a man for giving pleasure to a woman is called the work of a man, and is as follows: —

While the woman is lying on his bed, and is as it were abstracted by his conversa-

81

tion, he should loosen the knot of her under garments, and when she begins to dispute with him, he should overwhelm her with kisses. Then when his lingam is erect he should touch her with his hands in various places, and gently manipulate various parts of the body. If the woman is bashful, and if it is the first time that they have come together, the man should place his hands between her thighs, which she would probably keep close together, and if she is a very young girl, he should first get his hands upon her breasts, which she would probably cover with her own hands, and under her armpits and on her neck. If however she is a seasoned woman, he should do whatever is agreeable either to him or to her, and whatever is fitting for the occasion. After this he should take hold of her hair, and hold her chin in his fingers for the purpose of kissing her. On this, if she is a young girl, she will become bashful and close her eyes. Anyhow he should gather from the action of the woman what things would be pleasing to her during congress.

Here Suvarnanabha says that while a man is doing to the woman what he likes best during congress, he should always make a point of pressing those parts of her body on which she turns her eyes.

The signs of the enjoyment and satisfaction of the woman are as follows: her body relaxes, she closes her eyes, she puts aside all bashfullness, ans shows increased willingness to unite the two organs as closely together as possible. On the other hand, the signs of her want of enjoyment and of failing to be satisfied are as follows: she shakes her hands, she does not let the men get up, feels dejected, bites the man, kicks him, and continues to go on moving after the man has finished. In such cases the man should rub the yoni of the woman with his hand and fingers (as the elephant rubs anything with his trunk) before engaging in congress, until it is softened, and after that is done he should proceed to put his lingam into her.

The acts to be done by the man are:

Moving forward.

Friction or churning.

Piercing.

Rubbing.

Pressing.

Giving a blow.

The blow of a boar.

The blow of a bull.

The sporting of a sparrow.

1). When the organs are brought together properly and directly it is called "moving the organ forward."

2). When the lingam is held with the hand, and turned all round in the yoni, it is called "churning."

3). When the yoni is lowered, and the upper part of it is struck with the lingam, it is called "piercing."

4). When the same thing is done on the lower part of the yoni, it is called "rubbing."

5). When the yoni is pressed by the lingam for a long time, it is called "pressing."

6). When the lingam is removed to some distance from the yoni, and then forcibly strikes it, it is called "giving a blow."

7). When only one part of the yoni is rubbed with the lingam, it is called the "blow of a boar."

8). When both sides of the yoni are rubbed in this way, it is called the "blow of a bull."

9). When the lingam is in the yoni, and moved up and down frequently, and without being taken out, it is called the "sporting of a sparrow." This takes place at the end of congress.

When a woman acts the part of a man, she has the following things to do in addition to the nine given above, viz.

The pair of tongs.

The top.

The swing.

1). When the woman holds the lingam in her yoni, draws it in, presses it, and keeps it thus in her for a long time, it is called the "pair of tongs."

2). When, while engaged in congress, she turns round like a wheel, it is called the "top." This is learnt by practice only.

3). When, on such an occasion, the man lifts up the middle part of his body, and the woman turns round her middle parts, it is called the "swing."

When the woman is tired, she should place her forehead on that of her lover, and should thus take rest without disturbing the union of the organs, and when the woman has rested herself the man should turn round and begin the congress again.

There are also some verses on the subject as follows:

"Though a woman is reserved, and keeps her feelings concealed, yet when she gets on the top of a man, she then shows all her love and desire. A man should gather from the actions of the woman of what disposition she is, and in what way she likes to be enjoyed. A woman during her monthly courses, a woman who has been lately confined, and a fat woman should not be made to act the part of a man."

IX

Of the Auparishtaka or mouth congress

There are two kinds of eunuchs, those that are disguised as males, and those that are disguised as females. Eunuchs disguised as females imitate their dress, speech, gestures, tenderness, timidity, simplicity, softness and bashfulness. The acts that are done on the jaghana or middle parts of women, are done in the mouth of these eunuchs, and this is called Auparishtaka. These eunuchs derive their imaginable pleasure, and their livelihood from this kind of congress, and they lead the life of courtezans. So much concerning eunuchs disguised as females.

Eunuchs disguised as males keep their desires secret, and when they wish to do anything they lead the life of shampooers. Under the pretence of shampooing, an eunuch of this kind embraces and draws towards himself the thighs of the man whom he is shampooing, and after this he touches the joints of his thighs and his jaghana, or central portions of his body. Then, if he finds the lingam of the man erect, he presses it with his hands, and chaffs him for getting into that state. If after this, and after knowing his intention, the man does not tell the eunuch to proceed, then the latter does it of his own accord and begins the congress. If however he is ordered by the man to do it, then he disputes with him, and only consents at last with difficulty.

The following eight tings are then done by the eunuch one after the other, viz.

The nominal congress.
Biting the sides.
Pressing outside.
Pressng inside.
Kissing.
Rubbing.
Sucking a mangoe fruit.
Swallowing up.

At the end of each of these, the eunuch express his wish to stop, but when one of them is finished, the man desires him to do another, and after that is done, then the one that follows it, and so on.

1). When, holding the man's lingam with his hand, and placing it between his lips, the eunuch moves about his mouth, it is called the "nominal congress."

2). When, covering the end of the lingam with his fingers collected together like the bud of a plant or flower, the eunuch presses the sides of it with his lips, using his teeth also, it is called "biting the sides."

3). When, being desired to proceed, the eunuch presses the end of the lingam with his lips closed together, and kisses it as if he were drawing it out, it is called the "outside pressing."

4). When, being asked to go on, he puts the lingam further into his mouth, and presses it with his lips and then takes it out, it is called the "inside pressing."

5). When, holding the lingam in his hand, the eunuch kisses it as if he were kissing the lower, it is called "kissing".

6). When, after kissing it, he touches it with his tongue everywhere, and passes the tongue over the end of it, it is called "rubbing".

7). When, in the same way, he puts the half of it into his mouth, and forcibly kisses and sucks it, this is called "sucking a mangoe fruit."

8). And lastly, when, with the consent of the man, the eunuch puts the whole lingam into his mouth, and presses it to the very end, as if he were going to swallow it up, it is called "swallowing up."

Striking, scratching, and other things may also be done during this kind of congress.

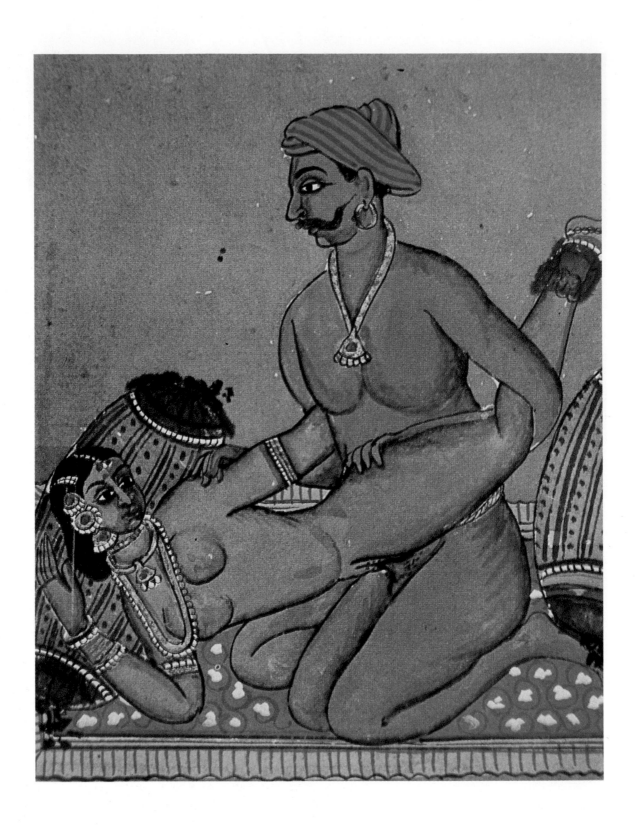

The Auparishtaka is practised also by unchaste and wanton women, female attendants and serving maids, i.e., those who are not married to anybody, but who live by shampooing.

The Acharyas (i.e., ancient and venerable authors) are of opinion that this Auparishtaka is the work of a dog and not of a man, because it is a low practice, and opposed to the orders of the Holy Writ, and because the man himself suffers by bringing his lingam into contact with the mouth of eunuchs and women. But Vatsyayana says that the orders of the Holy Writ do not affect those who resort to courtezans, and the law prohibits the practice of the Auparishtaka with married women only. As regards the injury to the male, that can be easily remedied.

The people of Eastern India do not resort to women who practice the Auparishtaka.

The people of Ahichhatra resort to such women, but do nothing with them, so far as the mouth is concerned.

The people of Saketa do with these women every kind of mouth congress, while the people of Nagara do not practice this, but do every other thing.

The people of the Shurasena country, on the southern bank of the Jumna, do everything without any hesitation, for they say that women being naturally unclean, no one can be certain about their character, their purity, their conduct, their practices, their confidences, or their speech. They are not however on this account to be abandoned, because religious law, on the authority of which they are reckoned pure, lays down that the udder of a cow is clean at the time of milking, though the mouth of a cow, and also the mouth of her calf, are considered unclean by the Hindoos. Again a dog is clean when he seizes a deer in hunting, though food touched by a dog is otherwise considered very unclean. A bird is clean when it causes a fruit to fall from a tree by pecking at it, though things eaten by crows and other birds are considered unclean. And the mouth of a woman is clean for kissing and such like things at the time of sexual intercourse. Vatsyayana moreover thinks that in all these things connected with love, everybody should act according to the custom of his country, and his own inclination. There are also the following verses on the subject.

"The male servants of some men carry on the mouth congress with their masters. It is also practised by some citizens who know each other well, among themselves. Some women of the harem, when they are amorous, do the acts of the mouth on the yonis of one another, and some men do the same thing with women. The way of doing this (i.e., of kissing the yoni) should be known from kissing the mouth. When a man and woman lie down in an inverted order, i.e., with the head of the one towards the feet of the other and carry on this congress, it is called the 'congress of crow'."

For the sake of such things courtezans abandon men possessed of good qualities, liberal and clever, and become attached to low persons, such as slaves and elephant drivers. The Auparishtaka, or mouth congress, should never be done by a lerned Brahman, by a minister that carries on the business of a state, or by a man of good reputation, because though the practice is allowed by the Shastras, there is no reason why it should be carried on, and need only be practised in particular cases. As for instance, the taste, and the strength, and digestive qualities of the flesh of dogs are mentioned in works on medicine, but it does not therefore follow that it should be eaten by the wise. In the same way there are some men, some places and some times, with respect to which these practices can be made use of. A man should therefore pay regard to the place, to the time, and to the practice which is to be carried out, as also as to whether it is agreeable to his nature and to himself, and then he may or may not practice these things according to circumstances. But after all, these things being done secretly, and the mind of the man being fickle, how can it be known what any person will do at any particular time and for any particular purpose.

X

Of the way how to begin and how to end the congress

Different kinds of congress and love quarrels

In the pleasure-room, decorated with flowers, and fragrant with perfumes, attended by his friends and servants, the citizen should receive the woman, who will come bathed and dressed, and will invite her to take refreshment and to drink freely. He should then seat her on his left side, and holding her hair, and touching also the end and knot of her garment, he should gently embrace her with his right arm. They should then carry on an amusing conversation on various subjects, and may also talk suggestively of things which would be considered as coarse, or not to be mentioned generally in society. They may then sing, either with or without gesticulations, and play on musical instruments, talk about the arts, and persuade each other to drink. At last when the woman is overcome with love and desire, the citizen should dismiss the people that may be with him, giving them flowers, ointments, and betel leaves, and then when the two are left alone, they should proceed as has been already described in the previous chapters.

Such is the beginning of sexual union. At the end of the congress, the lovers with modesty, and not looking at each other, should go separately to the washing-room. After this, sitting in their own places, they should eat some betel leaves, and the citizen should apply with his own hand to the body of the woman some pure sandal wood ointment, or ointment of some other kind. He should then embrace her with his left arm, and with agreeable words should cause her to drink from a cup held in his own hand, or he may give her water to drink. They can then eat sweetmeats, or anything else, according to their likings, and may drink fresh juice, soup, gruel, extracts of meat, sherbet, the juice of mangoe fruits, the extract of the juice of the citron tree mixed with sugar, or anything that may be liked in different countries, and known to be sweet, soft, and pure. The lovers may also sit on the terrace of the palace or house, and enjoy the moonlight, and carry on an agreeable conversation. At this time, too, while the woman lies in his lap, with her face towards the moon, the citizen should show her the different planets, the morning star, the polar star, and the seven Rishis, or Great Bear.

This is the end of sexual union.

Congress is of the following kinds, viz.:

> Loving congress.
> Congress of subsequent love.
> Congress of artificial love.
> Congress of transferred love.
> Congress like that of eunuchs.
> Deceitful congress.
> Congress of spontaneous love.

1). When a man and a woman, who have been in love with each other for some time, come together with great difficulty, or when one of the two returns from a journey, or is reconciled after having been separated on account of a quarrel, then congress is called the "loving congress." It is carried on according to the liking of the lovers, and as long as they choose.

2). When two persons come together, while their love for each other is still in its infancy, their congress is called the "congress of subsequent love."

3). When a man carries on the congress by exciting himself by means of the sixty-four ways, such as kissing, etc., etc., or when a man and a woman come together, though in reality they are both attached to different persons, their congress is then called "congress of artificial love." At this time all the ways and means mentioned in the Kama Shastra should be used.

4). When a man, from the beginning to the end of the congress, though having connection with the woman, thinks all the time that he is enjoying another one whom he loves, it is called the "congress of transferred love."

5). Congress between a man and a female water carrier, or a female servant of a caste lower than his own, lasting only until the desire is satisfied, is called "congress like that of eunuchs." Here external touches, kisses, and manipulations are not to be employed.

6). The congress between a courtezan and a rustic, and that between citizens and the women of villages, and bordering countries, is called "deceitful congress."

7). The congress that takes place between two persons who are attached to one another, and which is done according to their own liking is called "spontaneous congress."

Thus ends the kinds of congress.

We shall now speak of love quarrels.

A woman who is very much in love with a man cannot bear to hear the name of her rival mentioned, or to have any conversation regarding her, or to be addressed by her name through mistake. If such takes place, a great quarrel arises, and the woman cries, becomes angry, tosses her hair about, strikes her lover, falls from her bed or seat, and, casting aside her garlands and ornaments, throws herself down on the ground.

At this time, the lover should attempt to reconcile her with conciliatory words, and should take her up carefully and place her on her bed. But she, not replying to his questions, and with increased anger, should bend down his head by pulling his hair, and having kicked him once, twice, or thrice on his arms, head, bosom or back, should then proceed to the door of the room. Dattaka says that she should then sit angrily near the door and shed tears, but should not go out, because she would be found falt with for going away. After a time, when she thinks that the conciliatory words and actions of her lover have reached their utmost, she should then embrace him, talking to him with harsh and reproachful words, but at the same time showing a loving desire for congress.

When the woman is in her own house, and has quarrelled with her lover, she should go to him and show how angry she is, and leave him. Afterwards the citizen having sent the Vita, the Vidushaka or the Pithamurda, to pacify her, she should accompany them back to the house, and spend the night with her lover. Thus ends the love quarrels.

In conclusion.

A man, employing the sixty-four means mentioned by Babhravya, obtains his object, and enjoys the woman of the first quality. Though he may speak well on other subjects, if he does not know the sixty-four divisions, no great respect is paid to him in the assembly of the learned. A man, devoid of other knowledge, but well acquainted with the sixty-four divisions, becomes a leader in any society of men and women. What man will not respect the sixty-four parts, considering they are respected by the learned, by the cunning, and by the courtezans. As the sixty-four parts are respected, are charming, and add to the talent of women, they are called by the Acharvas dear to women. A man skilled in the sixty-four parts is looked upon with love by his own wife, by the wives of others, and by courtezans.

Part III

About the acquisition of a wife

I

On marriage

When a girl of the same caste, and a virgin, is married in accordance with the precepts of Holy Writ, the results of such a union are: the acquisition of Dharma and Artha, offspring, affinity, increase of friends, and untarnished love. For this reason a man should fix his affections upon a girl who is of good family, whose parents are alive, and who is three years or more younger than himself. She should be born of a highly respectable family, possessed of wealth, well connected, and with many relations and friends. She should also be beautiful, of a good disposition, with lucky marks on her body, and with good hair, nails, teeth, ears, eyes, and breasts, neither more nor less than they ought to be, and no one of them entirely wanting, and not troubled with a sickly body. The man should, of course, also possess these qualities himself. But at all events, says Ghotakamukha, a girl who has been already joined with others (i.e., no longer a maiden) should never be loved, for it would be reproachable to do such a thing. Now in order to bring about a marriage with such a girl as described above, the parents and relations of the man should exert themselves, as also such friends on both sides as may desired to assist in the matter. These friends should bring to the notice of the girl's parents, the faults, both present and future, of all the other men that may wish to marry her, and should at the same time extol even to exaggeration all the excellencies, ancestral, and paternal, of their friend, so as to endear him to them, and particularly to those that may be liked by the girl's mother. One of the friends should also disguise himself as an astrologer, and declare the future good fortune and wealth of his friend by showing the existence of all the lucky omens and signs, the good influence of planets, the auspicious entrance of the sun into a sign of the Zodiac, propitious stars and fortunate marks on his body. Others again should rouse the jealousy of the girl's mother by telling her that their friend has a chance of getting from some other quarter even a better girl than hers.

A girl should be taken as a wife, as also given in marriage, when fortune, signs, omen, and the words of others are favourable, for, says Ghotakamukha, a man should not marry at any time he likes. A girl who is asleep, crying, or gone out of the house when sought in marriage, or who is betrothed to another, should not be married. The following also should be avoided:

One who is kept concealed.
One who has an ill-sounding name.
One who has her nose depressed.
One who has her nostril turned up.
One who is formed like a male.
One who is bent down.
One who has crooked thighs.
One who has a projecting forehead.
One who had a bald head.
One who does not like purity.
One who has been polluted by another.
One who is affected with the Gulma.
One who is disfigured in any way.
One who has fully arrived at puberty.
One who is a friend.
One who is a younger sister.
One who is a Varshakari.

In the same way a girl who is called by the name of one of the twenty-seven stars, or by the name of a tree, or of a river, is considered worthless, as also a girl whose name ends in "r" or "l". But some authors say that prosperity is gained only by marrying that girl to whom one becomes attached, and that therefore no other girl but the one who is loved should be married by anyone.

When a girl becomes marriageable her parents should dress her smartly, and should place her where she can be easily seen by all. Every afternoon, having dressed her and decorated her in a becoming manner, they should send her with her female companions to sports, sacrifices, and marriage ceremonies, and thus show her to advantage in society, because she is a kind of merchandise. They should also receive with kind words and signs of friendliness those of an auspicious appearance who may come accompanied by their friends and relations for the purpose of marrying their daughter, and under some pretext or other having first dressed her becomingly, should then present her to them. After this they should await the pleasure of fortune, and with this object should appoint a future day on which a determination could be come to with regard to their daughter's marriage. On this occasion when the persons have come, the parents of the girl should ask them to bathe and dine, and should say "Everything will take place at the proper time", and should not then comply with the request, but should settle the matter later.

When a girl is thus acquired, either according to the custom of the country, or according to his own desire, the man should marry her in accordance with the precepts of the Holy Writ, according to one of the four kinds of marriage.

Thus ends marriage.

There are also some verses on the subject as follows:

Amusement in society, such as completing verses begun by others, marriages, and auspicious ceremonies should be carried on neither with superiors, nor inferiors, but with our equals. That should be known as a high connection when a man, after marrying a girl, has to serve her and her relations afterwards like a servant, and such a connection is censured by the good. On the other hand, that reproachable connection, where a man together with his relations, lords it over his wife, is called a low connection by the wise. But when both the man and the woman afford mutual pleasure to each other, and when the relatives on both sides pay respect to one another, such is called a connection on the proper sense of the word. Therefore a man should contract neither a high connection by which he is obliged to bow down afterwards to his kinsmen, nor a low connection, which is universally reprehended by all.

II

Of creating confidence in the girl

For the first three days after marriage, the girl and her husband should sleep on the floor, abstain from sexual pleasures, and eat their food without seasoning it either with alkali or salt. For the next seven days they should bathe amidst the sounds of auspicious musical instruments, should decorate, themselves, dine together, and pay attention to their relations as well as to those who may have come to witness their marriage. This is applicable to persons of all caste. On the night of the tenth day the man should begin in a lonely place with soft words, and thus create confidence in the girl. Some authors say that for the purpose of winning her over he should not speak to her for three days, but the followers of Babhravya are of opinion that if the man does not speak with her for three days, the girl may be discouraged by seeing him spiritless like a pillar, and, becoming dejected, she may begin to despise him as a eunuch. Vatsyayana says that the man should begin to win her over, and to create confidence in her, but should abstain at first from sexual pleasures. Women being of a tender nature, want tender beginnings, and when they are forcibly approached by men with whom they are but slightly acquainted, they sometimes suddenly become haters of sexual connection, and sometimes even haters of the male sex. The man should therefore approach the girl according to her liking, and should make use of those devices by which he may be able to establish himself more and more into her confidence. These devices are as follows:—

He should embrace her first of all in a way she likes most, because it does not last for a long time.

He should embrace her with the upper part of his body because that is easier and simpler. If the girl is grown up, or if the man has known her for some time, he may embrace her by the light of a lamp, but if he is not well acquainted with her, or if she is a young girl, he should then embrace her in darkness.

When the girl accepts the embrace, the man should put a "tambula" or screw of betel nut and betel leaves in her mouth, and if she will not take it, he should induce her to do so by conciliatory words, entreaties, oaths, and kneeling at her feet, for it is a universal rule that however bashful or angry a woman may be, she never disregards a man's kneeling at her feet. At the time of giving this "tambula" he should kiss her mouth softly and gracefully without making any sound. When she is gained over in this respect he should then make her talk, and so that she may be induced to talk he should ask her questions about things of which he knows or pretends to know nothing, and which can be answered in a few words. If she does not speak to him, he should not frighten her, but should ask her the same thing again and again in a conciliatory manner. If she does not then speak he should urge her to give a reply, because as Ghotakamukha says, "all girls hear everything said to them by men, but do not themselves sometimes say a single word." When she is thus importuned, the girl should give replies by shakes of the head, but if she quarrelled with the man she should not even do that. When she is asked by the man whether she wishes for him, and whether she likes him, she should remain silent for a long time, and when at last importuned to reply, should give him a favourable answer by a nod of her head. If the man is previously acquainted with the girl he should converse with her by means of a female friend, who may be favourable to him, and in the confidence of both, and carry on the conversation on both sides. On such an occasion the girl should smile with her head bent down, and if the female friend say more on her part

102

than she was desired to do, she should chide her and dispute with her. The female friend should say in jest even what she is not desired to say by the girl, and add, "she says so", on which the girl should say indistinctly and prettily, "O no! I did not say so", and she should then smile and throw an occasional glance towards the man.

If this girl is familiar with the man, she should place near him, without saying anything, the tambula, the ointment, or the garland that he may have asked for, or she may tie them up in his upper garment. While she is engaged in this, the man should touch her young breasts in the sounding way of pressing with the nails, and if she prevents him doing this he should say to her, "I will not do it again if you will embrace me", and should in this way cause her to embrace him. While he is being embraced by her should pass his hand repeatedly over and about her body. By and bye he should place her in his lap, and try more and more to gain her consent, and if she will not yield to him he should frighten her by saying "I shall impress marks of my teeth and nails on your lips and breasts, and then make similar marks on my own body and shall tell my friends that you did them. What will you say then?" In this and other ways, as fear and confidence are created in the minds of children, so should the man gain her over to his wishes.

On the second and third nights, after her confidence has increased still more, he should feel the whole of her body with his hand, and kiss her all over; he should also place his hands upon her thighs and shampoo them, and if he succeeds in this he should then shampoo the joints of her thighs. If she tries to prevent him doing this he should say to her, "What harm is there in doing it?" and should persuade her to let him do it. After gaining this point he should touch her private parts, should loosen her girdle and the knot of her dress, and turning up her lower garment should shampoo the joints of her naked thighs. Under various pretences he should do all these things, but he should not at that time begin actual congress. After this he should teach her the sixty-four arts, should tell her how much he loves her, and describe to her the hopes which he formerly entertained regarding her. He should also promise to be faithful to her in future, and should dispel all her fears with respect to rival women, and, at last, after hav-

103

ing overcome her bashfulness, he should begin to enjoy her in a way so as not to frighten her. So much about creating confidence in the girl; and there are, moreover, some verses on the subject as follows: —

A man acting according to the inclinations of a girl should try and gain her over so that she may love him and place her confidence in him. A man does not succeed either by implicitly following the inclination of a girl, or by wholly opposing her, and he should therefore adopt a middle course. He who knows how to make himself beloved by women, as well as to increase their honour and create confidence in them, this man becomes an object of their love. But he, who neglects a girl thinking she is too bashful, is despided by her as a beast ignorant of the working of the female mind. Moreover, a girl forcibly enjoyed by one who does not understand the hearts of girls becomes nervous, uneasy, and dejected, and suddenly begins to hate the man who has taken advantage of her; and then, when her love is not understood or returned, she sinks into despondency and becomes either a hater of mankind altogether, or, hating her own man, she has recourse to other men.

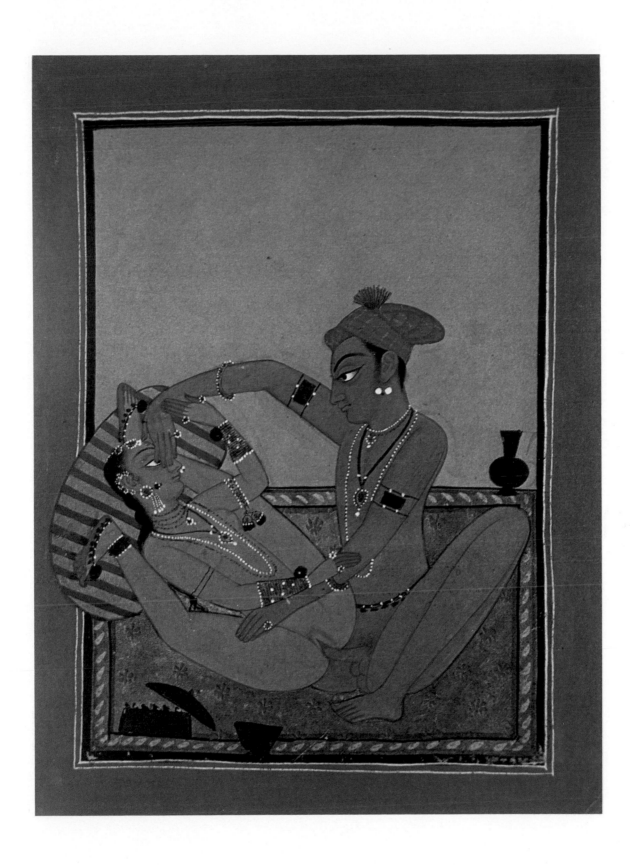

III

On courtship, and the manifestation of the feelings by outward signs and deeds

A poor man possessed of good qualities, a man born of a low family possessed of mediocre qualities, a neighbour possessed of wealth, and one under the control of his father, mother or brothers, should not marry without endeavouring to gain over the girl from her childhood to love and esteem them. Thus a boy separated from his parents, and living in the house of his uncle, should try to gain over the daughter of his uncle, or some other girl, even though she be previously betrothed to another. And this way of gaining over a girl, says Ghotakamukha, is unexceptional, because Dharma can be accomplished by means of it, as well as by any other way of marriage.

When a boy has thus begun to woo the girl he loves, he should spend his time with her and amuse her with various games and diversions fitted for their age and acquaintanceship, such as picking and collecting flowers, making garlands of flowers, playing the parts of members of a fictitious family, cooking food, playing with dice, playing with cards, the game of odd and even, the game finding out the middle finger, the game of six pebbles, and such other games as may be prevalent in the country, and agreeable to the disposition of the girl. In addition to this, he should carry on various amusing games played by several persons together, such as hide and seek, playing with seeds, hiding things in several small heaps of wheat and looking for them, blind-man's buff, gymnastic exercises, and other games of the same sort, in company with the girl, her friends and female attendants. The man should also show great kindness to any woman whom the girl thinks fit to be trusted, and should also make new acquaintances, but above all he should attach to himself by kindness and little services the daughter of the girl's nurse, for if she be gained over, even though she comes to know of his design, she does not cause any obstruction, but is sometimes even able to effect an union between him and the girl. And though she knows the true character of the man, she always talks of his many excellent qualities to the parents and relations of the girl, even though she may not be desired to do so by him.

In this way the man should do whatever the girl takes most delight in, and he should get for her whatever she may have a desire to possess. Thus he should procure for her such playthings as may be hardly known to other girls. He may also show her a ball dyed with various colours, and other curiosities of the same sort; and should give her dolls made of cloth, wood, buffalo-horn ivory, wax, flour, or earth; also utensils for cooking food, and figures in wood, such as a man and woman standing, a pair of rams, or goats, or sheep; also temples made of earth, bamboo, or wood, dedicated to various goddesses; and cages for parrots, cuckoos, starlings, quails, cocks, and partridges; water-vessels of different sorts and of elegant forms, machines for throwing water about, guitars, stands for putting images upon, stools, lac, red arsenic, yellow ointment, vermilion and collyrium, as well as sandal-wood, saffron, betel nut and betel leaves. Such things should be given at different times whenever he gets a good opportunity of meeting her, and some of them should be given in private, and some in public, according to circumstances. In short, he should try in every way to make her look upon him as one who would do for her everything that she wanted to be done.

In the next place he should get her to meet him in some place privately, and should then tell her that the reason of his giving presents to her in secret was the fear that the parents of both of them might be displeased, and then he may add that the things which he had given her had been much desired by other people. When her love begins to show signs of increasing he should relate to her agreeable stories if she expresses a wish to hear such narratives. Or if she takes delight in legerdemain, he should amaze her by performing various tricks of jugglery; or if she feels a great curiosity to see a performance of the various arts, he should show his own skill in them. When she is delighted with singing he should entertain her with music, and on certain days, and at the time of going together to moonlight fairs and festivals, and at the time of her return after being absent from home, he should present her with bouquets of flowers, and with chaplets for the head, and with ear ornaments and rings, for these are the proper occasions on which such things should be presented.

He should also teach the daughter of the girl's nurse all the sixty-four means of pleasure practised by men, and under this pretext should also inform her of his great skill in the art of sexual enjoyment. All this time he should wear a fine dress, and make as good an appearance as possible, for young women love men who live with them, and who are handsome, good looking and well dressed. As for he sayings that though women may fall in love, they still make no effort themselves to gain over the object of their affections, that is only a matter of idle talk.

Now a girl always shows her love by outward signs and actions, such as the following: – She never looks the man in the face, and becomes abashed when she is looked at by him; she looks secretly at him though he has gone away from her side; hangs down her head when she is asked some question by him, and answers in indistinct words and unfinished sentences, delights to be in his company for a long time, speaks to her attendants in a peculiar tone with the hope of attracting his attention towards her when she is at a distance from him, does not wish to go from the place where he is, under some pretext or other she makes him look at different things, narrates to him tales and stories very slowly so that she may continue conversing with him for a long time, kisses and embraces before him a child sitting in her lap, draws ornamental marks on the foreheads of her female servants, performs sportive and graceful movements when her attendants speak jestingly to her in the presence of her lover, confides in her lover's friends, and respects and obeys them, shows kindness to his servants, converses with them, and engages them to do her work as if she were their mistress, and listens attentively to them when they tell stories about her lover to somebody else, enters his house when induced to do so by the daughter of her nurse, and by her assistance manages to converse and play with him, avoids being seen by her lover when she is not dressed and decorated, gives him by the hand of her female friend her ear ornament, ring, or garland of flowers that he may have asked to see, always wears anything that he may have presented to her, becomes dejected when any other bridegroom is mentioned by her parents, and does not mix with those who may be of his party, or who may support his claims.

There are also some verses on the subject as follows: —

A man, who has seen and perceived the feelings of the girl towards him, and who has noticed the outward signs and movements by which those feelings are expressed, should do everything in his power to effect an union with her. He should gain over a young girl by childlike sports, a damsel come of age by his skill in the arts, and a girl that loves him by having recourse to persons in whom she confides.

IV

About things to be done only by the man, and the acquisition of the girl thereby. Also what is to be done by a girl to gain over a man, and subject him to her

Now when the girl begins to show her love by outward signs and motions, as described in the last chapter, the lover should try to gain her over entirely by various ways and means, such as the following: –

When engaged with her in any game or sport he should intentionally hold her hand. He should practise upon her the various kinds of embraces, such as the touching embrace, and others already described in a preceding chapter (Part II. Chapter 2). He should show her a pair of human beings cut out of the leaf of a tree, and such like things, at intervals. When engaged in water sports, he should dive at a distance from her, and come up close to her. He should show an increased liking for the new foliage of trees and such like things. He should describe to her the pangs he suffers on her account. He should relate to her the beautiful dream that he has had with reference to other women. At parties and assemblies of his caste he should sit near her, and touch her under some pretence or other, and having placed his foot upon her's, he should slowly touch each of her toes, and press the ends of the nails; if successful in this, he should get hold of her foot with his hand and repeat the same thing. He should also press a finger of her hand between his toes when she happens to be washing his feet; and whenever he gives anything to her or takes anything from her, he should show her by his manner and look how much he loves her.

He should sprinkle upon her the water brought for rinsing his mouth; and when alone with her in a lonely place, or in darkness, he should make love to her, and tell her the true state of his mind without distressing her in any way. Whenever he sits with her on the some seat or bed he should say to her, "I have something to tell you in private", and then, when she comes to hear it in a quiet place, he should express his love to her more by manner and signs than by words. When he comes to know the state of her feelings towards him he should pretend to be ill, and should make her come to his house to speak to him. There he should intentionally hold her hand, place it on his eyes and forehead, and under the pretence of preparing some medicine for him he should ask her to do the work for his sake in the following words: "This work must be done by you, and by nobody else." When she wants to go away he should let her go, with an earnest request to come and see him again. This device of illness should be continued for three days and three nights. After this, when she begins coming to see him, frequently, he should carry on long conversations with her, for, says Ghotakamukha, "though a man loves a girl ever so much, he never succeeds in winning her without a great deal of talking." At last when the man finds the girl completely gained over, he may then begin to enjoy her. As for the saying that women grow less timid than usual during the evening, and in darkness, and are desirous of congress at those times, and do not oppose men then, and should only be enjoyed at these hours, it is matter of talk only.

When it is impossible for the man to carry on his endeavours alone, he should, by means of the daughter of her nurse, or of a female friend in whom she confides, cause the girl to be brought to him without making known to her his design, and he should then proceed with her in the manner above described. Or he should in the beginning send his own female servant to live with the girl as her friend, and should then gain her over by her means.

112

At last, when he knows the state of her feelings by her outward manner and conduct towards him at religious ceremonies, marriage ceremonies, fairs, festivals, theatres, public assemblies, and such like occasions, he should begin to enjoy her when she is alone, for Vatsyayana lays it down, that women, when resorted to at proper times and in proper places, do not turn away from their lovers.

When a girl, possessed of good qualities and well-bred, though born in a humble family, or destitute of wealth and not therefore desired by her equals, or an orphan girl, or one deprived of her parents, but observing the rules of her family and caste, should wish to bring about her own marriage when she comes of age, such a girl should endeavour to gain over a strong and good looking young man, or a person whom she thinks would marry her on account of the weakness of his mind, and even without the consent of his parents. She should do this by such means as would endear her to the said person, as well as by frequently seeing and meeting him. Her mother also should constantly cause them to meet by means of her female friends, and the daughter of her nurse. The girl herself should try to get alone with her beloved in some quiet place, and at odd times should give him flowers, betel nut, betel leaves and perfumes. She should also show her skill in the practice of the arts, in shampooing, in scratching and in pressing with the nails. She should also talk to him on the subjects he likes best, and discuss with him the ways and means of gaining over and winning the affections of a girl. But old authors say that although the girl loves the man ever so much, she should not offer herself, to make the first overtures, for a girl who does this loses her dignity, and is liable to be scorned and rejected. But when the man shows his wish to enjoy her, she should be favourable to him and should show no change in her demeanour when he embraces her, and should receive all the manifestations of his love as if she were ignorant of the state of his mind. But when he tries to kiss her she should oppose him; when he begs to be allowed to have sexual intercourse with her she should let him touch her private parts only and with considerable difficulty: and though importuned by him, she should not yield herself up to him as if of her own accord, but should resist his attempts to have her. It is only, moreover, when she is certain that she is truly loved, and that her lover is indeed devoted to her, and will not change his mind, that she should

113

then give herself up to him, and persuade him to marry her quickly. After losing her virginity she should tell her confidential friends about it.

Here ends the efforts of a girl to gain over a man.

There are also some verses on the subject as follows: A girl who is much sought after should marry the man that she likes, and whom she thinks would be obedient to her, and capable of giving her pleasure. But when from the desire of wealth a girl is married by her parents to a rich man without taking into consideration the character or looks of the bridegroom, or when given to a man who has several wives, she never becomes attached to the man, even though he be endowed with good qualities, obedient to her will, active, strong, and healthy, and anxious to please her in every way. A husband who is obedient but yet master of himself, though he be poor and not good looking, is better than one who is common to many women, even though he be handsome and attractive. The wives of rich men, where there are many wives, are not generally attached to their husbands, and are not confidential with them, and even though they possess all the external enjoyments of life, still have recourse to other men. A man who is of a low mind, who has fallen from his social position, and who is much given to travelling, does not deserve to be married; neither does one who has many wives and children, or one who is devoted to sport and gambling, and who comes to his wife only when he likes. Of all the lovers of a girl he only is her true husband who possesses the qualities that are liked by her, and such a husband only enjoys real superiority over her, because he is the husband of love.

V

On certain forms of marriage

When a girl cannot meet her lover frequently in private, she should send the daughter of her nurse to him, it being understood that she has confidence in her, and had previously gained her over to her interests. On seeing the man, the daughter of the nurse should, in the course of conversation, describe to him the noble birth, the good disposition, the beauty, talent, skill, knowledge of human nature and affection of the girl in such a way as not to let him suppose that she had been sent by the girl, and should thus create affection for the girl in the heart of the man. To the girl also she should speak about the excellent qualities of the man, especially of those qualities which she knows are pleasing to the girl. She should, moreover, speak with disparagement of the other lovers of the girl, and talk about the avarice and indiscretion of their parents, and the fickleness of their relations. She should also quote samples of many girls of ancient times, such as Sakuntala and others, who, having united themselves with lovers of their own caste and their own choice, were happy ever afterwards in their society. And she should also tell of other girls who married into great families, and being troubled by rival wives, became wretched and miserable, and were finally aband-

115

oned. She should further speak of the good fortune, the continual happiness, the chastity, obedience, and affection of the man, and if the girl gets amorous about him, she should endeavour to allay her shame and her fear as well as her suspicions about any disaster that might result from her marriage. In a word, she should act the whole part of a female messenger by telling the girl all about the man's affection for her, the places he frequented, and the endeavours he made to meet her, and by frequently repeating, "It will be all right if the man will take you away forcibly and unexpectedly."

The forms of marriage

When the girl is gained over, and acts openly with the man as his wife, he should cause fire to be brought from the house of a Brahman, and having spread the Kusha grass upon the ground, and offered an oblation to the fire, he should marry her according to the precepts of the religious law. After this he should inform his parents of the fact, because it is the opinion of ancient authors that a marriage solemnly contracted in the presence of fire cannot afterwards be set aside.

After the consummation of the marriage, the relations of the man should gradually be made acquainted with the affair, and the relations of the girl should also be apprised of it in such a way that they may consent to the marriage, and overlook the manner in which it was brought about, and when this is done they should afterwards be reconciled by affectionate presents and favourable conduct. In this manner the man should marry the girl according to the Gandharva form of marriage.

When the girl cannot make up her mind, or will not express her readiness to marry, the man should obtain her in any one of the following ways: —

1). On a fitting occasion, and under some excuse, he should, by means of a female friend with whom he is well acquainted and whom he can trust, and who also is well known to the girl's family, get the girl brought unexpectedly to his house, and he should then bring fire from the house of a Brahman, and proceed as before described.

2). When the marriage of the girl with some other person draws near, the man should disparage the future husband to the utmost in the mind of the mother of the girl, and then having got the girl to come with her mother's consent to a neighbouring house, he should bring fire from the house of a Brahman, and proceed as above.

3). The man should become a great friend of the brother of the girl, the said brother being of the same age as himself, and addicted to courtesans, and to intrigues with the wives of other people, and should give him assistance in such matters, and also give him occasional presents. He should then tell him about his great love for his sister, as young men will sacrifice even their lives for the sake of those who may be of the same age, habits, and dispositions as themselves. After this the man should get the girl brought by means of her brother to some secure place, and having brought fire from the house of a Brahman should proceed as before.

4). The man should on the occasion of festivals get the daughter of the nurse to give the girl some intoxicating substance, and then cause her to be brought to some secure place under the pretence of some business, and there having enjoyed her before she recovers from her intoxication, should bring fire from the house of a Brahman, and proceed as before.

5). The man should, with the connivance of the daughter of the nurse, carry off the girl from her house while she is asleep, and then, having enjoyed her before she recovers from her sleep, should bring fire from the house of a Brahman, and proceed as before.

6). When the girl goes to a garden, or to some village in the neighbourhood, the man should, with his friends, fall on her guards, and having killed them, or frightened them away, forcibly carry her off, and proceed as before.

There are verses on this subject as follows: – In all the forms of marriage given in this chapter of this work, the one that precedes is better than the one that follows it, on account of its being more in accordance with the commands of religion, and therefore it is only when it is impossible to carry the former into

117

practice that the latter should be resorted to. As the fruit of all good marriages is love, the Gandharva form of marriage is respected, even though it is formed under unfavourable circumstances, because it fulfils the object sought for. Another cause of the respect accorded to the Gandharva form of marriage is, that it brings forth happiness, causes less trouble in its performance than the other forms of marriage, and is above all the result of previous love.

Part IV

About a wife

I

On the manner of living of a virtuous woman, and of her behaviour during the absence of her husband

A virtuous woman, who has affection for her husband, should act in conformity with his wishes as if he were a divine being, and with his consent should take upon herself the whole care of his family. She should keep the whole house well cleaned, and arrange flowers of various kinds in different parts of it, and make the floor smooth and polished so as to give the whole a neat and becoming appearance. She should surround the house with a garden, and place ready in it all the materials required for the morning, noon and evening sacrifices. Moreover she should herself revere the sanctuary of the Household Gods, for says Gonardiya, "nothing so much attracts the heart of a householder to his wife as a careful observance of the things mentioned above."

Towards the parents, relations, friends, sisters, and servants of her husband she should behave as they deserve. In the garden she should plant beds of green vegetables, bunches of the sugar cane, and clumps of the fig tree, the mustard plant, the parsley plant, the fennel plant, and the xanthochymus pictorius. Clusters of various flowers such as the trapa bispinosa, the jasmine, the gas-

minum grandiflorum, the yellow amaranth, the wild jasmine, the tabernamontana coronaria, the nadyaworta, the china rose and others, should likewise be
planted, together with the fragrant grass andropogon schænanthus, and the
fragrant root of the plant andropogon miricatus. She should also have seats and
arbours made in the garden, in the middle of which a well, tank, or pool should
be dug.

The wife should always avoid the company of female beggars, female buddish
medicants, unchaste and roguish women, female fortune tellers and witches. As
regards meals she should always consider what her husband likes and dislikes,
and what things are good for him, and what are injurious to him. When she
hears the sounds of his footsteps coming home she should at once get up, and be
ready to do whatever he may command her, and either order her female servant
to wash his feet, or wash them herself. When going anywhere with her husband,
she should put on her ornaments, and without his consent she should not either
give or accept invitations, or attend marriages and sacrifices, or sit in the company of female friends, or visit the temples of the Gods. And if she wants to
engage in any kind of games or sports, she should not do it against his will. In the
same way she should always sit down after him, and get up before him, and
should never awaken him when he is asleep. The kitchen should be situated in a
quiet and retired place, so as not to be accessible to strangers, and should always
look clean.

In the event of any misconduct on the part of her husband, she should not
blame him excessively, though she be a little displeased. She should not use
abusive language towards him, but rebuke him with conciliatory words, whether
he be in the company of friends or alone. Moreover, she should not be a scold,
for says Gonardiya, "there is no cause of dislike on the part of a husband so great
as this characteristic in a wife." Lastly she should avoid bad expressions, sulky
looks, speaking aside, standing in the doorway, and looking at passers-by,
conversing in the pleasure groves, and remaining in a lonely place for a long
time; and finally she should always keep her body, her teeth, her hair and
everything belonging to her tidy, sweet, and clean.

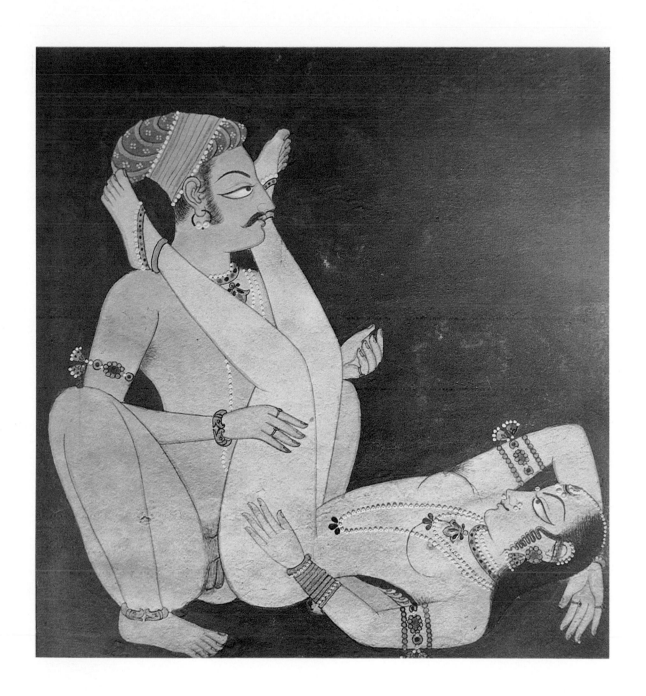

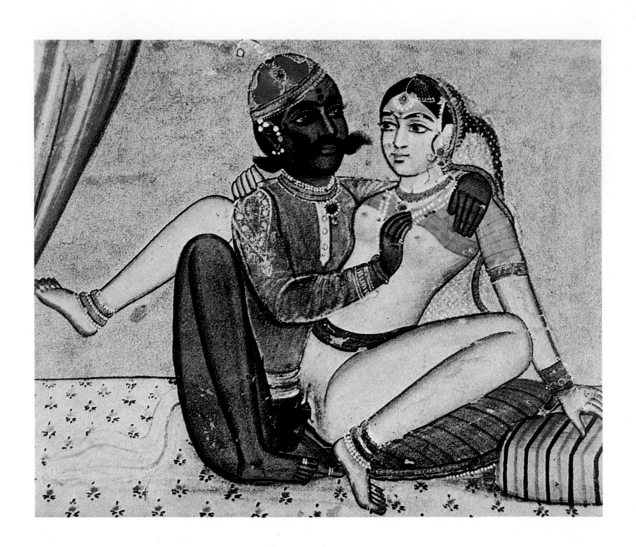

When the wife wants to approach her husband in private her dress should consist of many ornaments, various kinds of flowers, and a cloth decorated with different colours, and some sweet-smelling ointments or unguents. But her everyday dress should be composed of a thin close-textured cloth, a few ornaments and flowers, and a little scent, not too much. She should also observe the fasts and vows of her husband, and when he tries to prevent her doing this, she should persuade him to let her do it.

At appropriate times of the year, and when they happen to be cheap, she should buy earth, bamboos, firewood, skins, and iron pots, as also salt and oil. Fragrant substances, vessels made of the fruit of the plant wrightea antidysenterica, or oval leaved wrightea, medicines, and other things which are always wanted, should be obtained when required and kept in a secret place of the house. The seeds of the radish, the potato, the common beet, the Indian wormwood, the mangoe, the cucumber, the egg plant, the kushmanda, the pumpkin gourd, the surana, the bignonia indica, the sandal wood, the premna spinosa, the garlic plant, the onion, and other vegetables, should be bought and sown at the proper seasons.

The wife, moreover, should not tell to strangers, the amount of her wealth, nor the secrets which her husband has confided to her. She should surpass all the women of her own rank in life in her cleverness, her appearance, her knowledge of cookery, her pride, and her manner of serving her husband. The expenditure of the year should be regulated by the profits. The milk that remains after the meals should be turned into ghee or clarified butter. Oil and sugar should be prepared at home; spinning and weaving should also be done there; and a store of ropes and cords, and barks of trees for twisting into ropes should be kept. She should also attend to the pounding and cleaning of rice, using its small grain and chaff in some way or other. She should pay the salaries of the servants, look after the tilling of the fields, and keeping of the flocks and herds, superintend the making of vehicles, and take care of the rams, cocks, quails, parrots, starlings, cuckoos, peacocks, monkeys, and deer; and finally adjust the income and expenditure of the day. The worn-out clothes should be given to those servants who have done good work, in order to show them that their services have been appreciated, or they may be applied to some other use. The vessels in which wine is prepared, as well as those in which it is kept, should be carefully looked after, and put away at the proper time. All sales and purchases should also be well attended to. The friends of her husband she should welcome by presenting them with flowers, ointment, incense, betel leaves, and betel nut. Her father-in-law and mother-in-law she should treat as they deserve, always remaining dependant on their will, never contradicting them, speaking to them in few and not harsh words, not laughing loudly in their presence, and acting with their friends and enemies as with her own. In addition to the above she should not be vain, or too much taken up with her enjoyments. She should be liberal towards her servants, and reward them on holidays and festivals; and not give away anything without first making it known to her husband.

Thus ends the manner of living of a virtuous woman.

During the absence of her husband on a journey the virtuous woman should wear only her auspicious ornaments, and observe the fasts in honour of the Gods. While anxious to hear the news of her husband, she should still look after her household affairs. She should sleep near the elder women of the house, and make herself agreeable to them. She should look after and keep in repair the things that are liked by her husband, and continue the works that have been begun by him. To the abode of her relations should not go except on occasions of joy and sorrow, and then she should go in her usual travelling dress, accompanied by her husband's servants, and not remain there for a long time. The fasts and feasts should be observed with the consent of the elders of the house. The resources should be increased by making purchases and sales according to the practice of the merchants, and by means of honest servants, superintended by herself. The income should be increased, and the expenditure diminished as much as possible. And when her husband returns from his journey, she should receive him at first in her ordinary clothes, so that he may know in what way she has lived during his absence, and should bring to him some presents, as also materials for the worship of the Deity.

Thus ends the part relating to the behaviour of a wife during the absence of her husband on a journey.

There are also some verses on the subject as follows.

"The wife, whether she be a woman of noble family, or a virgin widow remarried, or a concubine should lead a chaste life, devoted to her husband, and doing every thing for his welfare. Women acting thus, acquire Dharma, Artha, and Kama, obtain a high position, and generally keep their husbands devoted to them.

II

On the conduct of the elder wife towards the other wives of her
husband, and on that of a younger wife towards the elder ones.
Also on the conduct of a virgin widow re-married; of a wife disliked
by her husband; of the women in the King's harem; and lastly on
the conduct of a husband towards many wives

The causes of re-marrying during the lifetime of the wife are as follows;

1. The folly or ill temper of the wife.
2. Her husband's dislike to her.
3. The want of offspring.
4. The continual birth of daughters.
5. The incontinence of the husband.

From the very beginning a wife should endeavour to attract the heart of her husband, by showing to him continually her devotion, her good temper, and her wisdom. If however she bears him no children, she should herself tell her husband to marry another woman. And when the second wife is married, and brought to the house, the first wife should give her a position superior to her own, and look upon her as a sister. In the morning the elder wife should forcibly make the younger one decorate herself in the presence of their husband, and should not mind all the husband's favour being given to her. If the younger wife does anything to displease her husband the elder one should not neglect her, but should always be ready to give her most careful advice, and should teach her to do various things in the presence of her husband. Her children she should treat as her own, her attendants she should look upon with more regard, even than on her own servants, her friends she should cherish with love and kindness, and her relations with great honour.

When there are many other wives besides herself, the elder wife should associate with the one who is immediately next to her in rank and age, and should instigate the wife who has recently enjoyed her husband's favour to quarrel with the present favourite. After this she should sympathize with the former, and having collected all the other wives together, should get them to denounce the favourite as a scheming and wicked woman, without however committing herself in any way. If the favourite wife happens to quarrel with the husband, then the elder wife should take her part and give her false encouragement, and thus cause the quarrel to be increased. If there be only a little quarrel between the two, the elder wife should do all she can to work it up into a large quarrel. But if after all this she finds the husband still continues to love his favourite wife she should then change her tactics, and endeavour to bring about a conciliation between them, so as to avoid her husband's displeasure.

Thus ends the conduct of the elder wife.

The younger wife should regard the elder wife of her husband as her mother, and should not give anything away, even to her own relations, without her knowledge. She should tell her everything about herself, and not approach her husband without her permission. Whatever is told to her by the elder wife she should not reveal to others, and she should take care of the children of the senior even more than of her own. When alone with her husband she should serve him well, but should not tell him of the pain she suffers from the existence of a rival wife. She may also obtain secretly from her husband some marks of his particular regard for her, and may tell him that she lives only for him, and for the regard that he has for her. She should never reveal her love for her husband, nor her husband's love for her to any person, either in pride or in anger, for a wife that

130

reveals the secrets of her husband is despised by him. As for seeking to obtain the regard of her husband, Gonardiya says, that is should always be done in private, for fear of the elder wife. If the elder wife be disliked by her husband, or be childless, she should sympathize with her, and should ask her husband to do the same, but should surpass her in leading the life of a chaste woman.

Thus ends the conduct of the younger wife towards the elder.

A widow in poor circumstances, or of a weak nature, and who allies herself again to a man, is called a widow re-married.

The followers of Babhravya say that a virgin widow should not marry a person whom she may be obliged to leave on account of his bad character, or of his being destitute of the excellent qualities of a man, she thus being obliged to have recourse to another person. Gonardya is of opinion that as the cause of a widow's marrying again is her desire for happiness, and as happiness is secured by the possession of excellent qualities in her husband, joined to love of enjoyment, it is better therefore to secure a person endowed with such qualities in the first instance. Vatsyayana however thinks that a widow may marry any person that she likes, and that she thinks will suit her.

At the time of her marriage the widow should obtain from her husband the money to pay the costs of drinking parties, and picnics with her relations, and of giving them and her friends kindly gifts and presents; or she may do these things at her own cost if she likes. In the same way she may wear either her husband's ornaments or her own. As to the presents of affection mutually exchanged between the husband and herself there is no fixed rule about them. If she leaves her husband after marriage of her own accord, she should restore to him whatever he may have given her, with the exception of the mutual presents. If however she is driven out of the house by her husband she should not return anything to him.

After her marriage she should live in the house of her husband like one of the chief members of the family, but should treat the other ladies of the family with kindness, the servants with generosity, and all the friends of the house with familiarity and good temper. She should show that she is better acquainted with the sixty-four arts than the other ladies of the house, and in any quarrels with

131

her husband she should not rebuke him severely, but in private do everything that he wishes, and make use of the sixty-four ways of enjoyment. She should be obliging to the other wives of her husband, and to their children she should give presents, behave as their mistress, and make ornaments and play-things for their use. In the friends and servants of her husband she should confide more than in his other wives, and finally she should have a liking for drinking parties, going to picnics, attending fairs and festivals, and for carrying out all kinds of games and amusements.

Thus ends the conduct of a virgin widow re-married.

A woman who is disliked by her husband, and annoyed and distressed by his other wives, should associate with the wife who is liked most by her husband, and who serves him more than the others, and should teach her all the arts with which she is acquainted. She should act as the nurse of her husband's children, and having gained over his friends to her side, should through them make him acquainted of her devotion to him. In religious ceremonies she should be a leader, as also in vows and fasts, and should not hold too good an opinion of herself. When her husband is lying on his bed she should only go near him when it is agreeable to him, and should never rebuke him, or show obstinacy in any way. If her husband happens to quarrel with any of his other wives, she should reconcile them to each other, and if he desires to see any woman secretly, she should manage to bring about the meeting between them. She should moreover, make herself acquainted with the weak points of her husband's character, but always keep them secret, and on the whole behave herself in such a way as may lead him to look upon her as a good and devoted wife.

Here ends the conduct of a wife disliked by her husband.

The above sections will show how all the women of the King's seraglio are to behave, and therefore we shall now speak separately about the king.

The female attendants in the harem (called severally Kanchukiyas, Mahallarikas, and Mahallikas,) should bring flowers, ointments and clothes from the King's wives to the King, and he having received these things should give them as presents to the servants, along with the things worn by him the previous day. In

132

the afternoon the King, having dressed and put on his ornaments, should interview the women of the harem, who should also be dressed and decorated with jewels. Then having given to each of them such a place and such respect as may suit the occasion, and as they may deserve, he should carry on with them a cheerful conversation. After that he should see such of his wives as may be virgin widows re-married, and after them the concubines and dancing girls. All of these should be visited in their own private rooms.

When the King rises from his noonday sleep, the woman whose duty it is to inform the King regarding the wife who is to spend the night with him should come to him accompanied by the female attendants of that wife whose turn may have arrived in the regular course, and of her who may have been accidentally passed over as her turn arrived, and of her who may have been unwell at the time of her turn. Theses attendants should place before the King the ointments and unguents sent by each of these wives, marked with the seal of her ring, and their names and their reasons for sending the ointments should be told to the King. After this the King accepts the ointment of one of them, who then is informed that her ointment has been accepted, and that her day has been settled.

At festivals, singing parties and exhibitions, all the wives of the King should be treated with respect and served with drinks.

But the women of the harem should not be allowed to go out alone, neither should any woman outside the harem be allowed to enter it except those whose character is well known. And lastly the work which the King's wives have to do should not be too fatiguing.

Thus ends the conduct of the King towards the women of the harem, and of their own conduct.

A man marrying many wives should act fairly towards them all. He should neither disregard nor pass over their faults, and should not reveal to one wife the love, passion, bodily blemishes, and confidential reproaches of the other. No opportunity should be given to any one of them of speaking to him about their rivals, and if one of them should begin to speak ill of another, he should chide her and tell her that she has exactly the same blemishes in her character. One of them should please by secret confidence, another by secret respect, and another by secret flattery, and he should please them all by going to gardens, by amusements, by presents, by honouring their relations, by telling them secrets, and lastly by loving unions. A young woman who is of a good temper, and who conducts herself according to the precepts of the Holy Writ, wins her husband's attachment, and obtains a superiority over her rivals.

Part V

About the wives of other men

I

Of the characteristics of men and women. – The reasons why women reject the addresses of men. – About men who have success with women, and about women who are easily gained over

The wives of the other people may be resorted to on the occasions already described in Part I, Chapter 5, of fitness for cohabitation, the danger to oneself in uniting with them, and the future effect of these unions, should first of all be examined. A man may resort to the wife of another, for the purpose of saving his own life, when he perceives that his love for her proceeds from one degree of intensity to another. These degrees are ten in number, and are distinguished by the following marks: –

1. Love of the eye.
2. Attachment of the mind.
3. Constant reflection.
4. Destruction of sleep.
5. Emaciation of the body.
6. Turning away from objects of enjoyment.
7. Removal of shame.

8. Madness.

9. Fainting.

10. Death.

Ancient authors say that a man should know the disposition, truthfulness, purity, and will of a young woman, as also the intensity, or weakness of her passions, from the form of her body, and from her characteristic marks and signs. But Vatsyayana is of opinion that the forms of bodies, and the characteristic marks or signs are but erring tests of character, and that women should be judged by their conduct, by the outward expression of their thoughts, and by the movements of their bodies.

Now as a general rule Gonikaputra says that a woman falls in love with every handsome man she sees, and so frequently they do not take any further steps, owing to various considerations. In love the following circumstances are peculiar to the woman. She loves without regard to right or wrong, and does not try to gain over a man simply for the attainment of some particular purpose. Moreover, when a man first makes up to her willing to unite herself with him. But when the attempts to gain her are repeated and renewed, she at last consents. But with a man, even though he may have begun to love, he conquers his feelings from a regard for morality and wisdom, and although his thoughts are often on the woman, he does not yield, even though an attempt be made to gain him over. He sometimes makes an attempt or effort to win the object of his affections, and having failed, he leaves her alone for the future. In the same way, when a woman is once gained, he often becomes indifferent about her. As for the saying that a man does not care for what is easily gained, and only desires a thing which cannot be obtained without difficulty, it is only a matter of talk.

The causes of a woman rejecting the addresses of a man are as follows:

1. Affection for her husband.

2. Desire of lawful progeny.

3. Want of opportunity.

4. Anger at being addressed by the man too familiarly.

5. Difference in rank of life.

6. Want of certainty on account of the man being devoted to travelling.

7. Thinking that the man may be attached to some other person.

8. Fear of the man's not keeping his intentions secret.

9. Thinking that the man is too devoted to his friends, and has too great a regard for them.

10. The apprehension that he is not in earnest.

11. Bashfulness on account of his being an illustrious man.

12. Fear on account of his being powerful, or possessed of too impetuous passion, in the case of the deer woman.

13. Bashfulness on account of his being too clever.

14. The thought of having once lived with him on friendly terms only.

15. Contempt of his want of knowledge of the world.

16. Distrust of his low character.

17. Disgust at his want of perception of her love for him.

18. In the case of an elephant woman, the thought that he is a hare man, or a man of weak passion.

19. Compassion lest anything should befall him on account of his passion.

20. Despair at her own imperfections.

21. Fear of discovery.

22. Disilluion at seeing his grey hair or shabby appearance.

23. Fear that he may be employed by her husband to test her chastity.

24. The thought that he has too much regard for morality.

Whichever of the above causes a man may detect, he should endeavour to remove it from the very beginning. Thus, the bashfulness that may arise from his greatness or his ability, he should remove by showing his great love and affection for her. The difficulty of the want of opportunity, or if his inaccessibility, he should remove by showing her some easy way of access. The excessive respect entertained by the woman for him should be removed by making himself very familiar. The difficulties that arise from his being thought a low character he should remove by showing his valour and his wisdom; those that come from neglect by extra attention; and those that arise from fear by giving her proper encouragement.

The following are the men who generally obtain success with women.

1. Men well versed in the science of love.
2. Men skilled in telling stories.
3. Men acquainted with women from their childhood.
4. Men who have secured their confidence.
5. Men who send presents to them.
6. Men who talk well.
7. Men who do things that they like.
8. Men who have not loved other women previously.
9. Men who act as messengers.
10. Men who knew their weak points.
11. Men who are desired by good women.
12. Men who are united with their female friends.
13. Men who are good looking.
14. Men who have been brought up with them.
15. Men who are their neighbours.
16. Men who are devoted to sexual pleasures, even though these be their own servants.
17. The lovers of the daughters of their nurse.
18. Men who have been lately married.
19. Men who like picnics and pleasure parties.
20. Men who are liberal.
21. Men who are celebrated for being very strong (Bull men).
22. Enterprising and brave men.
23. Men who surpass their husbands in learning and good looks, in good qualities, and in liberality.
24. Men whose dress and manner of living are magnificent.

The following are the women who are easily gained over: —

1. Women who stand at the doors of their houses.
2. Women who are always looking out on the street.
3. Women who sit conversing in their neighbour's house.
4. A woman who is always staring at you.

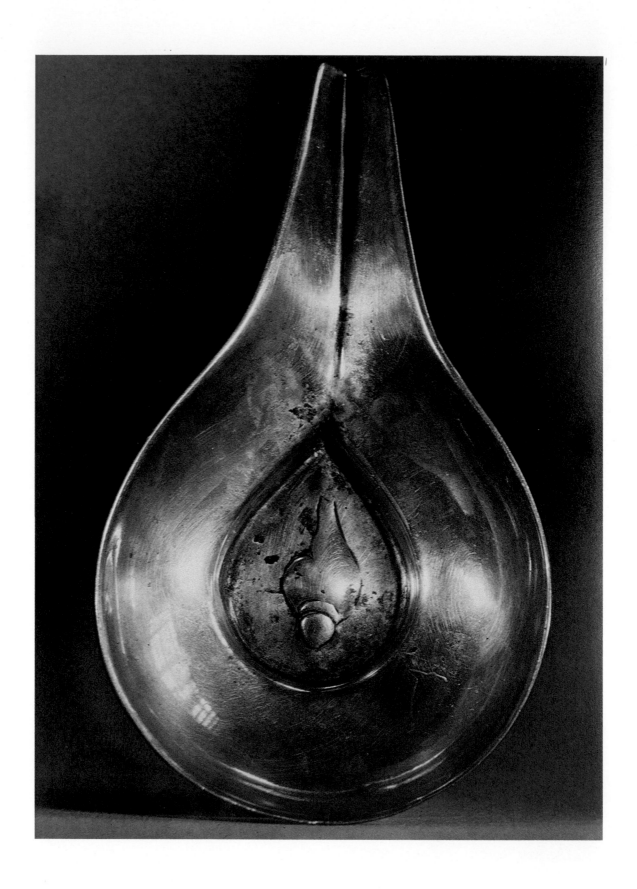

5. A female messenger.

6. A woman who looks sideways at you.

7. A woman whose husband has taken another wife without any just cause.

8. A woman who hates her husband, or who is hated by him.

9. A woman who has nobody to look after her, or keep her in check.

10. A woman who has not had any children.

11. A woman whose family or caste is not well known.

12. A woman whose children are dead.

13. A woman who is very fond of society.

14. A woman who is apparently very affectionate with her husband.

15. The wife of an actor.

16. A widow.

17. A poor woman.

18. A woman fond of enjoyments.

19. The wife of a man with many younger brothers.

20. A vain woman.

21. A woman whose husband is inferior to her in rank or abilities.

22. A woman who is proud of her skill in the arts.

23. A woman disturbed in mind by the folly of her husband.

24. A woman who has been married in her infancy magnificent.

To a rich man, and not liking him when she grows up, desires a man possessing a disposition, talents, and wisdom suitable to her own tastes.

25. A woman who is slighted by her husband without any cause.

26. A woman who ist not respected by other women of the same rank or beauty as herself.

27. A woman whose husband is devoted to travelling.

28. The wife of a jeweller.

29. A jealous woman.

30. A covetous woman.

31. An immoral woman.

32. A barren woman.

33. A lazy woman.

34. A cowardly woman.
35. A humpbacked woman.
36. A dwarfish woman.
37. A deformed woman.
38. A vulgar woman.
39. An ill-smelling woman.
40. A sick woman.
41. An old woman.

There are also two verses on the subject as follows:

"Desire which springs from nature, and which is increased by art, and from which all danger is taken away by wisdom, becomes firm and secure. A clever man, depending on his own ability, and observing carefully the ideas and thoughts of women, and removing the causes of their turning away from men, is generally successful with them."

II

About making acquaintance with the woman, and of the efforts to gain her over

Ancient authors are of opinion that girls are not so easily seduced by employing female messengers as by the efforts of the man himself, but that the wives of others are more easily got at by the aid of female messengers than by the personal efforts of the man. But Vatsyayana lays it down that whenever it is possible a man should always act himself in these matters, and it is only when such is impracticable, or impossible, that female messengers should be employed. As for the saying that women who act and talk boldly and freely are to be won by the personal efforts of the man, and that women who do not possess those qualities are to be got at by female messengers, it is only a matter of talk.

Now when a man acts himself in the matter he should first of all make the acquaintance of the woman he loves in the following manner.

1st. He should arrange to be seen by the woman either on a natural or special opportunity. A natural opportunity is when one of them goes to the house of the other, and a special opportunity is when they meet either at the house of a friend, or a caste-fellow, or a minister, or a physician, as also on the occasion of marriage ceremonies, sacrifices, festivals, funerals, and garden parties.

145

2nd. When they do meet, the man should be careful to look at her in such a way as to cause the state of his mind to be made known to her; he should pull about his moustache, make a sound with his nails, cause his own ornaments to tinkle, bite his lower lip, and make various other signs of that description. When she is looking at him he should speak to his friends about her and other women, and should show to her his liberality and his appreciation of enjoyments. When sitting by the side of a female friend he should yawn and twist his body, contract his eyebrows, speak very slowly as if he was weary, and listen to her indifferently. A conversation having two meanings should also be carried on with a child or some other person, apparently having regard to a third person, but really having reference to the woman he loves, and in this way his love should be made manifest under the pretext of referring to others rather than to herself. He should make marks that have reference to her, on the earth with his nails, or with a stick, and should embrace and kiss a child in her presence, and give it the mixture of betel nut and betel leaves with his tongue, and press its chin with his fingers in a caressing way. All these things should be done at the proper time and in proper places.

3rd. The man should fondle a child that may be sitting on her lap, and give it something to play with, and also take the same back again. Conversation with respect to the child may also be held with her, and in this manner he should gradually become well acquainted with her, and he should also make himself agreeable to her relations. Afterwards, this acquaintance should be made a pretext for visiting her house frequently, and on such occasions he should converse on the subject of love in her absence, but with her hearing. As his intimacy with her increases he should place in her charge some kind of deposit or trust, and take away from it a small portion at a time; or he may give her some fragrant substances, or betel nuts to be kept for him by her. After this he should endeavour to make her well acquainted with his own wife, and get them to carry on confidential conversations, and to sit together in lonely places. In order to see her frequently he should arrange so that the same goldsmith, the same jeweller, the same basket maker, the same dyer, and the same washerman should be employed by the two families. And he should also pay her long visits openly under the pretence of being engaged with her on business, and one business should lead to another, so as to keep up the intercourse between them. Whenever she wants anything, or is in need of money, or wishes to acquire skill in one of the arts, he should cause her to understand that he is willing and able to do anything that she wants, to give her money, or teach her one of the arts, all these things being quite within his ability and power. In the same way he should hold discussions with her in company with other people, and they should talk of the doings and sayings of other persons, and examine different things, like jewellery, precious stones, etc. On such occasions he should show her certain things with the values of which she may be acquainted, and if she begins to dispute with him about the things or their value, he should not contradict her, but point out that he agrees with her in every way.

Thus ends the ways of making the acquaintance of the woman desired.

Now after a girl has become acquainted with the man as above described, and has manifested her love to him by the various outward signs; and by the motions of her body, the man should make every effort to gain her over. But as girls are not acquainted with sexual union, they should be treated with the greatest delicacy, and the man should proceed with considerable caution, though in the case of other women, accustomed to sexual intercourse, this is not necessary. When the intentions of the girl are known, and her bashfulness put aside, the man should begin to make use of her money, and an interchange of clothes, rings, and flowers should be made. In this the man should take particular care that the things given by him are handsome and valuable. He should moreover receive from her a mixture of betel nut and betel leaves, and when he is going to a party he should ask for the flower in her hair, or for the flower in her hand. If he himself gives her a flower it should be a sweet smelling one, and marked with marks made by his nails or teeth. With increasing assiduity he should dispel her fears, and by degrees get her to go with him to some lonely place, and there he should embrace and kiss her. And finally at the time of giving her some betel nut, or of receiving the same from her, or at the time of making an exchange of flowers, he should touch and press her private parts, thus bringing his efforts to a satisfactory conclusion.

When a man is endeavouring to seduce one woman, he should not attempt to seduce any other at the same time. But after he has succeeded with the first, and enjoyed her for a considerable time, he can keep her affections by giving her presents that she likes, and then commence making up to another woman. When a man sees the husband of a woman going to some place near his house, he should not enjoy the woman then, even though she may be easily gained over at that time. A wise man having a regard for his reputation should not think of seducing a woman who is apprehensive, timid, not to be trusted, well guarded, or possessed of a father-in-law, or mother-in-law.

III

Examination of the state of a woman's mind

When a man is trying to gain over a woman he should examine the state of her mind, and act as follows.

If she listens to him, but does not manifest to him in any way her own intentions, he should then try to gain her over by means of a go-between.

If she meets him once, and again comes to meet him better dressed than before, or comes to him in some lonely place, he should be certain that she is capable of being enjoyed by the use of a little force. A woman who lets a man make up to her, but does not give herself up, even after a long time, should be considered as a trifler in love, but owing to the fickleness of the human mind, even such a woman can be conquered by always keeping up a close acquaintance with her.

When a women avoids the attentions of a man, and on account of respect for him, and pride in herself, will not meet him or approach him, she can be gained over with difficulty, either by endeavouring to keep on familiar terms with her, or else by an exceedingly clever go-between.

When a man makes up to a woman, and she reproaches him with harsh words, she should be abandoned at once.

When a woman reproaches a man, but at the same time acts affectionately towards him, she should be made love to in every way.

A woman, who meets a man in lonely places, and puts up with the touch of his foot, but pretends, on account of the indecision of her mind, not to be aware of it, should be conquered by patience, and by continued efforts as follows:

If she happens to go to sleep in his vicinity he should put his left arm round her, and see when she awakes whether she repulses him in reality, or only repulses him in such a way as if she was desirous of the same thing being done to her again. And what is done by the arm can also be done by the foot. If the man succeeds in this point he should embrace her more closely, and if she will not stand the embrace her more closely, and if she will not stand the embrace and gets up, but behaves with him as usual the next day, he should consider then that she is not unwilling to be enjoyed by him. If however she does not appear again, the man should try to get over her by means of a go-between; and if, after having disappeared for some time she again appears, and behaves with him as usual, the man should then consider that she would not object to be united with him.

When a woman gives a man an opportunity, and makes her own love manifest to him, he should proceed to enjoy her. And the signs of a woman manifesting her love are these:

1. She calls out to a man without being addressed by him in the first instance.
2. She shows herself to him in secret places.
3. She speaks to him tremblingly and inarticulately.
4. She has the fingers of her hand, and the toes of her feet moistened with perspiration, and her face blooming with delight.
5. She occupies herself with shampooing his body and pressing his head.
6. When shampooing him she works with one hand only, and with the other she touches and embraces parts of his body.
7. She remains with both hands placed on his body motionless as if she had been surprised by something, or was overcome by fatigue.
8. She sometimes bends down her face upon his thighs, and when asked to shampoo them does not manifest any unwillingness to do so.

9. She places one of her hands quite motionless on his body, and even though the man should press it between two members of his body, she does not remove it for a long time.

10. Lastly, when she has resisted all the efforts of the man to gain her over, she returns to him next day to shampoo his body as before.

When a woman neither gives encouragement to a man, nor avoids him, but hides herself and remains in some lonely place, she must be got at by means of the female servant who may be near her. If when called by the man she acts in the same way, then she should be gained over by means of a skilful go-between. But if she will have nothing to say to the man, he should consider well about her before he begins any further attempts to gain her over.

Thus ends the examination of the state of the woman's mind.

A man should first get himself introduced to a woman, and then carry on a conversation with her. He should give her hints of his love for her, and if he finds from her replies that she receives these hints favourably, he should then set to work to gain her over without any fear. A woman who shows her love by outward signs to the man at his first interview should be gained over very easily. In the same way a lascivious woman, who when addressed in loving words replies openly in words expressive of her love, should be considered to have been gained over at that very moment. With regard to all women, whether they be wise, simple, or confiding, this rule is laid down that those who make an open manifestation of their love are easily gained over.

IV

About the business of a go-between

If a woman has manifested her love or desire, either by signs or by motions of the body, and is afterwards rarely or never seen anywhere, or if a woman is met for the first time, the man should get a go-between to approach her.

Now the go-between, having wheedled herself into the confidence of the woman by acting according to her disposition, should try to make her hate or despise her husband by holding artful conversations with her, by telling her about medicines for getting children, by talking to her about other people, by tales of various kinds, by stories about the wives of other men, and by praising her beauty, wisdom, generosity and good nature, and then saying to her: "It is indeed a pity that you, who are so excellent a woman in every way, should be possessed of a husband of this kind. Beautiful lady, he is not fit even to serve you." The go-between should further talk to the woman about the weakness of the passion of her husband, his jealousy, his roguery, his ingratitude, his aversion to enjoyments, his dulness, his meanness, and all the other faults that he may have, and with which she may be acquainted. She should particularly harp upon that fault or that failing by which the wife may appear to be the most affected. If the wife be

153

a deer woman, and the husband a hare man, then there would be no fault in that direction, but in the event of his being a hare man, and she a mare woman or elephant woman, then this fault should be pointed out to her.

Gonikaputra is of opinion that when it is the first affair of the woman, or when her love has only been very secretly shown, the man should then secure and send to her a go-between, with whom she may be already acquainted, and in whom she confides.

But to return to our subject. The go-between should tell the woman about the obedience and love of the man, and as her confidence and affection increase, she should then explain to her the thing to be accomplished in the following way. "Hear this, oh beautiful lady, that this man, born of a good family, having seen you, has gone mad on your account. The poor young man, who is tender by nature, has never been distressed in such a way before, and it is highly probably that he will succumb under his present affliction, and experience the pains of death." If the woman listens with a favourable ear, then on the following day the go-between, having observed marks of good spirits in her face, in her eyes, and in her manner of conversation, should again converse with her on the subject of the man, and should tell her the stories of Ahalya and Indra, of Sakoontala and Dushyanti, and such others as may be fitted for the occasion. She should also describe to her the strength of the man, his talents, his skill in the sixty-four sorts of enjoyments mentioned by Babhravya, his good looks, and his liaison with some praiseworthy woman, no matter whether this last ever took place or not.

In addition to this, the go-between should carefully note the behaviour of the woman, which if favourable would be, as follows: She would address her with a smiling look would seat herself close beside her, and ask her, "Where have you been? What have you been doing? Where did you dine? Where did you sleep? Where have you been sitting?" Moreover the woman would meet the go-between in lonely places and tell her stories there, would yawn contemplatively, draw long sighs, give her presents, remember her on occasions of festivals, dismiss her with a wish to see her again, and say to her jestingly, "Oh, well-speaking woman, why do you speak these bad words to me?" would discourse on the sin of her union with the man, would not tell her about any previous visits or conversations that she may have had with him, but wish to be asked about these, and lastly would laugh at the man's desire, but would not reproach him in any way. Thus ends the behaviour of the woman with the go-between.

When the woman manifests her love in the manner above described, the go-between should increase it by bringing to her love tokens from the man. But if the woman be not acquainted with the man personally, the go-between should win her over by extolling and praising his good qualities, and by telling stories about his love for her. Here Auddalaka says that when a man or woman are not personally acquainted with each other, and have not shown each other any signs of affection, the employment of a go-between is useless.

The followers of Babhravya on the other hand affirm that even though they be personally unacquainted, but have shown each other signs of affection there is an occasion for the employment of a go-between. Gonikaputra asserts that a go-between should be employed, provided they are acquainted with each other, even though no signs of affection may have passed between them. Vatsyayana however lays it down that even though they may not be personally acquainted with each other, and may not have shown each other any signs of affection still they are both capable of placing confidence in a go-between.

Now the go-between should show the woman the presents, such as the betel nut and betel leaves, the perfumes, the flowers, and the rings which the man may have given to her for the sake of the woman, and on these presents should be impressed the marks of the man's teeth, and nails, and other signs. On the cloth that he may send he should draw with saffron both his hand joined together as if in earnest entreaty.

The go-between should also show to the woman ornamental figures of various kinds cut in leaves, together with ear ornaments, and chaplets made of flowers containing love letters expressive of the desire of the man, and she should cause her to send affectionate presents to the man in return. After they have mutually accepted each other's presents, then a meeting should be arranged between them on the faith of the go-between.

The followers fo Babhravya say that this meeting should take place at the time

155

of going to the temple of a Deity, or on occasions of fairs, garden parties, theatrical performances, marriages, sacrifices, festivals and funerals, as also at the time of going to the river to bathe, or at times of natural calamities, fear of robbers or hostile invasions of the country.

Gonikaputra is of opinion however that these meetings had better be brought about in the abodes of female friends, mendicants, astrologers, and ascetics. But Vatsyayana decides that that place is only well suited for the purpose which has proper means of ingress and egress, any accidental occurrence, and when a man who has once entered the house, can also leave it at the proper time without any disagreeable encounter.

Now go-betweens or female meesengers are of the following different kinds, viz.:

1). A go-between who takes upon herself the whole burden of the business.

2). A go-between who does only a limited part of the business.

3). A go-between who is the bearer of a letter only.

4). A go-between acting on her own account.

5). The go-between of an innocent young woman.

6). A wife serving as a go-between.

7). A mute go-between.

8). A go-between who acts the part of the wind.

1). A woman who, having observed the mutual passion of a man and woman, brings them together and arranges it by the power of her own intellect, such a one is called a go-between who takes upon herself the whole burden of the business. This kind of go-between is chiefly employed when the man and the woman are already acquainted with each other, and have conversed together, and in such cases she is sent not only by the man (as is always done in all other cases) but by the woman also. — The above name is also given to a go-between who, perceiving that the man and the woman are suited to each other, tries to bring about a union between them, even though they be not acquainted with each other.

2). A go-between who, perceiving that some part of the affair is already done, or that the advances on the part of the man are already made, completes the rest of

156

the business, is called a go-between who performs only a limited part of the business.

3). A go-between, who simply carries messages between a man and a woman, who love each other, but who cannot frequently meet, is called the bearer of a letter or message.

This name is also given to one who is sent by either of the lovers to acquaint either the one or the other with the time and place of their meeting.

4). A woman who goes herself to a man, and tells him of her having enjoyed sexual union with him in a dream, and expresses her anger at his wife having rebuked him for calling her by the name of the rival instead of by her own name, and gives him something bearing the marks of her teeth and nails, and informs him that she knew she was formerly desired by him, and asks him privately whether she or his wife is the best looking, such a person is called a woman who is a go-between for herself. Now such a woman should be met and interviewed by the man in private and secretly.

The above name is also given to a woman who having made an agreement with some other woman to act as her go-between, gains over the man to herself, by the means of making him personally acquainted with herself, and thus causes the other woman to fail. The same applies to a man who, acting as a go-between for another, and having no previous connection with the woman, gains her over for himself, and thus causes the failure of the other man.

5). A woman, who has gained the confidence of the innocent young wife of any man, and who has learned her secrets without exercising any pressure on her mind, and found out from her how her husband behaves to her, if this woman then teaches her the art of securing his favour, and decorates her so as to show her love, and instructs her how and when to be angry, or to pretend to be so, and then, having herself made marks of the nails and teeth on the body of the wife, gets the latter to send for her husband to show these marks to him, and thus excite him for enjoyment, such is called the go-between of an innocent young woman. In such cases the man should send replies to his wife through the same woman.

6). When a man gets his wife to gain the confidence of a woman whom he want

157

to enjoy, and to call on her and talk to her about the wisdom and ability of her husband, that wife is called a wife serving as a go-between. In this case the feelings of the woman with regard to the man should also be made known through the wife.

7). When any man sends a girl or a female servant to any woman under some pretext or other, and places a letter in her bouquet of flowers, or in her ear ornaments, or marks something about her with his teeth or nails, that girl or female servant is called a mute go-between. In this case the man should expect an answer from the woman through the same person.

8). A person, who carries a message to a woman, which has a double meaning, or which relates to some past transactions, or which is unintelligible to other people, is called a go-between who acts the part of the wind. In this case the reply should be asked for through the same woman.

Thus end the different kinds of go-betweens.

A female astrologer, a female servant, a female beggar, or a female artist are well acquainted with the business of a go-between, and very soon gain the confidence of other women. Any one of them can raise enmity between any two persons if she wishes to do so, or extol the loveliness of any woman that she wishes to praise, or describe the arts practised by other women in sexual union. They can also speak highly of the love of a man, of his skill in sexual enjoyment, and of the desire of other women, more beautiful even than the woman they are addressing, for him, and explain the restraint under which he may be at home. Lastly a go-between can, by the artfulness of her conversation unite a woman with a man, even though he may not have been thought of by her, or may have been considered beyond his aspirations. She can also bring back a man to a woman, who, owing to some cause or other, has separated himself from her.

V

About the love of persons in authority for the wives of other men

Kings und their ministers have no access to the abodes of others, and moreover their mode of living is constantly watched and observed and imitated by the people at large just as the animal world, seeing the sun rise, get up after him, and when he sits in the evening, lie down again in the same way. Persons in authority should not therefore do any improper act in public, as such are impossible from their position, and would be deserving of censurc. But if they find that such an act is necessary to be done, they should make use of the proper means as described in the following paragraphs.

The head man of the village, the King's officer employed there, and the man whose business it is to glean corn, can gain over female villagers simply by asking them. It is on this account that this class of woman are called unchaste women by voluptuaries.

The union of the above mentioned men with this class of woman takes place on the occasions of unpaid labour, of filling the granaries in their houses, of taking things in and out of the house, of cleaning the houses, of working in the fields, and of purchasing cotton, wool, flax, hemp and thread, and at the season of the purchase, sale, and exchange of various other articles, as well as at the time of doing various other works. In the same way the superintendents of cow pens enjoy the women in the cowpens; and the officers, who have the superintendence of widows, of the women who are without supporters, and of women who have left their husbands, have sexual intercourse with these women. The intelligent accomplish their object by wandering at night in the village, and while villagers also unite with the wives of their sons, being much alone with them. Lastly the superintendents of markets have a great deal to do with the female villagers at the time of their making purchases in the market.

During the festival of the eighth moon. *i.e.*, during the bright half of the month of Nargashirsha, as also during the moonlight festival of the month of Kartika, and the spring festival of Chaitra, the woman of cities and towns generally visit the women of the Kings's harem in the royal palace. These visitors go to the several apartments of the women of the harem, as they are acquainted with them and pass the night in conversation, and in proper sports, and amusement, and go away in the morning. On such occasions a female attendant of the King, (previously acquainted with the woman whom the King desires), should loiter about, and accost this woman when she sets out to go home, and induce her to come and see the amusing things in the palace. Previous to these festivals even, she should have caused it to be intimated to this woman that on the occasion of this festival she would show her all the interesting things in the royal palace. Accordingly she should show her the bower of the coral creeper, the garden house with its floor inlaid with precious stones, the bower of grapes, the building on the water, the secret passages in the walls of the palace, the pictures, the sporting animals, the machines, the birds, and the cages of the lions and the tigers. After this, when alone with her, she should tell her about the love of the King for her, and should describe to her the good fortune which would attend upon her union with the King, giving her at the time a strict promise of secrecy. If the woman does not accept the offer, she should conciliate and please her with handsome presents befitting the position of the King, and having accompanied her for some distance should dismiss her with great affection.

2). Or, having made the acquaintance of the husband of the woman whom the

King desires, the wives of the King should get the wife to pay them a visit in the harem, and on this occasion a female attendant of the King, having been sent thither, should act as above described.

3). Or, one of the King's wives should get acquainted with the woman that the King desires, by sending one of the female attendants to her, who should, on their becoming more intimate, induce her to come and see the royal abode. Afterwards when she has visited the harem, and acquired confidence, a female confidante of the King, sent thither, should act as before described.

4). Or, the King's wife should invite the woman, whom the King desires, to come to the royal palace, so that she might see the practice of the art in which the King's wife may be skilled, and after she has come to the harem, a female attendant of the King, sent thither, should act as before described.

5). Or, a female beggar, in league with the King's wife, should say to the woman desired by the King, and whose husband may have lost his wealth, or may have some cause of fear from the King: "This wife of the King has influence over him, and she is, moreover, naturally king-hearted, we must therefore go to her in this matter. I shall arrange for your entrance into the harem, and she will do away with all cause of danger and fear from the King." If the woman accepts this offer, the female beggar should take her two or three times to the harem, and the King's wife there should give her a promise of protection. After this, when the woman, delighted with her reception and promise of protection, again goes to the harem, then a female attendant of the King, sent thither, should act as directed.

6). What has been said above regarding the wife of one who has some cause of fear from the King applies also to the wives of those who seek service under the King, or who are oppressed by the King's ministers, or who are poor, or who are not satisfied with their position, or who are desirous of gaining the King's favour, or who wish to become famous among the people, or who are oppressed by the members of their own caste, or who want to injure their caste fellows, or who are spies of the King, or who have any other object to attain.

7). Lastly, if the woman desired by the King be living with some person who is not her husband, then the King should cause her to be arrested, and having made her a slave, on account of her crime, should place her in the harem. Or the King should cause his ambassador to quarrel with the husband of the woman desired by him, and should then imprison her as the wife of an enemy of the King, and by this means should place her in the harem.

Thus end the means of gaining over the wives of others secretly.

The above mentioned ways of gaining over the wives of other men are chiefly practised in the palaces of Kings. But a King should never enter the abode of another person, for Abhira, the King of the Kottas was killed by a washerman while in the house of another, and in the same way Jayasana the King of the Kashis was slain by the commandant of his cavalry.

But according to the customs of some countries there are facilities for Kings to make love to the wives of other men. Thus in the country of the Andras the newly married daughters of the people therof enter the King's harem with some presents on the tenth day of their marriage, and having been enjoyed by the King are then dismissed. In the country of the Vatsagulmas the wives of the chief ministers approach the King at night to serve him. In the country of the Vaidarbhas the beautiful wives of the inhabitants pass a month in the King's harem under the pretence of affection for the King. In the country of the Aparatakas the people gave their beautiful wives as presents to the ministers and the Kings. And lastly in the country of the Saurashtras the women of the city and the country enter the royal harem for the King's pleasure either together or separately.

There are also two verses on the subject as follows:

"The above and other ways are the means employed in different countries by Kings with regard to the wives of other persons. But a King, who has the welfare of his people at heart, should not on any account put them into practice."

"A King, who has conquered the six enemies of mankind, becomes the master of the whole earth."

VI

About the women of the royal harem; and of the keeping of one's own wife

The women of the royal harem cannot see or meet any men on account of their being strictly guarded, neither do they have their desires satisfied, because their only husband is common to many wives. For this reason among themselves they give pleasure to each other in various ways as now described.

Having dressed the daughters of their nurses, or their female friends, or their female attendants, like men, they accomplish their object by means of bulbs, roots, and fruits having the form of the Lingam, or they lie down upon the statue of a male figure, in which the Lingam is visible and erect.

Some Kings, who are compassionate, take or apply certain medicines to enable them to enjoy many wives in one night, simply for the purpose of satisfying the desire of their women, though they perhaps have no desire of their own. Others enjoy with great affection only those wives that they particularly like, while others only take them, according as the turn of each wife arrives in due course. Such are the ways of enjoyment prevalent in Eastern countries, and what is said about the means of enjoyment of the female is also applicable to the male.

By means of their female attendants the ladies of the royal harem generally get men into their apartments in the disguise or dress of women. Their female attendants, and the daughters of their nurses, who are acquainted with their secrets, should exert themselves to get men to come to the harem in this way by telling them of the good fortune attending it, and by describing the facilities of entering and leaving the palace, the large size of the premises, the carelessness of the sentinels, and the irregularities of the attendants about the persons of the royal wives. But these women should never induce a man to enter the harem by telling him falsehoods, for that would probably lead to his destruction.

As for the man himself he had better not enter a royal harem, even though it may be easily accessible, on account of the numerous disasters to which he may be exposed there. If however he wants to enter it, he should first ascertain whether there is an easy way to get out, whether it is closely surrounded by the pleasure garden, whether it has separate enclosures belonging to it, whether the sentinels are careless, whether the King has gone abroad, and then, when he is called by the women of the harem, he should carefully observe the localities, and enter by the way pointed out by them. If he is able to manage it, he should hang about the harem every day, and, under some pretext or other, make friends with the sentinels, and show himself attached to the female attendants of the harem, who may have become acquainted with his design, and to whom he should express his regret at not being able to obtain the object of his desire. Lastly he should cause the whole business of a go-between to be done by the woman who may have access to the harem, and he should be careful to be able to recognize the emissaries of the King.

When a go-between has no access to the harem, then the man should stand in some place where the lady, whom he loves, and whom he is anxious to enjoy, can be seen.

If that place is occupied by the King's sentinels, he should then disguise himself as a female attendant of the lady who comes to the place, or passes by it. When she looks at him he should let her know his feelings by outward signs and gestures, and should show her pictures, things with double meanings, chaplets of flowers, and rings. He should carefully mark the answer she gives, whether by word or sign, or by gesture, and should then try and get into the harem. If he is certain of her coming to some particular place he should conceal himself there, and at the appointed time should enter along with her as one of the guards. He may also go in and out, concealed in a folded bed, or bed covering, or with his body made invisible, by means of external applications, a receipt for one of which is as follows:

The heart of an ichneumon, the fruit of the long gourd (Tumbi), and the eyes of a serpent should all be burnt without letting out the smoke, the ashes should then be ground and mixed in equal quantities with water. By putting this mixture upon the eyes a man can go about unseen.

Other means of invisibility are prescribed by Duyana Brahmans and Jogashiras. Again the man may enter the harem during the festival of the eighth moon in the month of Nargashirsha, and during the moonlight festivals when the female attendants of the harem are all busily occupied, or in confusion.

The following principles are laid down on this subject.

The entrance of young men into harems, and their exit from them, generally take place when things are being brought into the palace, or when things are being taken out of it, or when drinking festivals are going on, or when the female attendants are in a hurry, or when the residence of some of the royal ladies is being changed, or when the King's wives go to gardens, or to fairs, or when they enter the palace on their return from them, or lastly, when the King is absent on a long pilgrimage. The women of the royal harem know each other's secrets, and having but one object to attain, they give assistance to each other. A young man, who enjoys all of them, and who is common to them all, can continue enjoying his union with them so long as it is kept quiet, and is not known abroad.

Now in the country of the Aparatakas the royal ladies are not well protected, and consequently many young men are passed into the harem by the women who have access to the royal palace. The wives of the King of the Ahira country accomplish their objects with those sentinels in the harem who bear the name of Kashtriyas. The royal ladies in the country of the Vatsagulmas cause such men as are suitable to enter into the harem along with their female messengers. In the country of the Vaidarbhas the sons of the royal ladies enter harem when they please, and enjoy the women, with the exception of their own mothers. In the

Stri-rajya the wives of the King are enjoyed by his caste fellows and relations. In the Ganda country the royal wives are enjoyed by Brahmans, friends, servants and slaves. In the Samdhava country, servants, foster children, and other persons like them enjoy the women of the harem. In the country of the Haima-vatas adventurous citizens bribe the sentinels and enter the harem. In the country of the Vanayas and the Kalmyas, Brahmans, with the knowledge of the King, enter the harem under the pretence of giving flowers to the ladies, and speak with them from behind a curtain, and from such conversation union afterwards takes place. Lastly the women in the harem of the King of the Prachyas conceal one young man in the harem for every batch of nine or ten of the women.

Thus act the wives of others.

For these reasons a man should guard his own wife. Old authors say that a King should select for sentinels in his harem such men as have their freedom from carnal desires well tested. But such men, though free themselves from carnal desire, by reason of their fear of avarice, may cause other persons to enter the harem, and therefore Gonikaputra says, that Kings should place such men in the harem as may have had their freedom from carnal desires, their fears, and their avarice well tested. Lastly Vatsyayana says, that under the influence of Dharma people might be admitted, and therefore men should be selected who are free from carnal desires, fear, avarice, and Dharma.

The followers of Babhravya say that a man should cause his wife to associate with a young woman who would tell him the secrets of other people, and thus find out from her about his wife's chastity. But Vatsyayana says, a man should not cause his innocent wife to be corrupted by bringing her into the company of a deceitful woman.

The following are the causes of the destruction of a woman's chastity.

Always going into society, and sitting in company.

Absence of restraint.

The loose habits of her husband,

want of caution in her relations with other men.

Continued and long absence of her husband.

Living in a foreign country.

Destruction of her love and feelings by her husband.

The company of loose women.

The jealousy of her husband.

There are also the following verses on the subject.

"A clever man, learning from the Shastras the ways of winning over the wives of other people, is never deceived in the case of his own wives. No one, however, should make use of these ways for seducing the wives of others, because they do not always succeed, and, moreover, often cause disasters, and the destruction of Dhrama and Artha. This book, which is intended for the good of the people, and to teach them the ways of guarding their own wives, should not be made use of merely for gaining over the wives of others."

Part VI

About courtesans

Introductory remarks

This Part VI., about courtesans, was prepared by Vatsyayana, from a treatise on the subject, that was written by Dattaka, for the women of Pataliputra (the modern Patna), some two thousand years ago. Dattaka's work does not apear to be extant now, but this abridgement of it is very clever, and quite equal to any of the productions of Emile Zola, and other writers of the realistic school of to-day. Although a great deal has been written on the subject of the courtesan, nowhere will be found a better description of her, of her belongings, of her ideas, and of the working of her mind, than is contained in the following pages.

The details of the domestic and social life of the early Hindoos would not be complete without mention of the courtesan, and Part VI., is entirely devoted to this subject. The Hindoos have ever had the good sense to recognise courtesans as a part and portion of human society, and so long as they behaved themselves with decency and propriety, they were regarded with a certain respect. Anyhow, they have never been treated in the East with that brutality and contempt so common in the West, while their education has always been of a superior kind to that bestowed upon the rest of womankind in Oriental countries.

In the earlier days the well-educated Hindoo dancing girl and courtesan doubtless resembled the Hetera of the Greeks, and being educated and amusing, were far more acceptable as companions than the generality of the married or unmarried women of that period. At all times and in all countries, there has ever been a little rivalry between the chaste and the unchaste. But while some women are born courtesans, and follow the instincts of their nature in every class of society, it has been truly said by some authors that every woman has got an inkling of the profession in her nature, and does her best, as a general rule, to make herself agreeable to the male sex.

The subtlety of women, their wonderful perceptive powers, their knowledge, and their intuitive appreciation of men and things, are all shown in the following pages, which may be looked upon as a concentrated essence that has been since worked up into detail by many writers in every quarter of the globe.

I

Of the causes of a courtesan resorting to men; of the means of attaching to herself the man desired; and of the kind of man that it is desirable to be acquainted with

By having intercourse with men courtesans obtain sexual pleasure, as well as their own maintainance. Now when a courtesan takes up with a man from love, the action is natural; but when she resorts to him for the purpose of getting money, her action is artificial or forced. Even in the latter case, however, she should conduct herself as if her love were indeed natural, because men repose their confidence on those women who apparently love them. In making known her love to the man, she should show an entire freedom from avarice, and for the sake of her future credit she should abstain from acquiring money from him by unlawful means.

A courtesan, well dressed and wearing her ornaments, should sit or stand at the door of her house, and without exposing herself too much, should look on the public road so as to be seen by the passers by, she being like an object on view for sale. She should form friendships with such persons as would enable her to separate men from other women, and attach them to herself, to repair her own misfortunes, to acquire wealth, and to protect her from being bullied, or set upon by persons with whom she may have dealings of some kind or another. These persons are:

The guards of the town, or the police.

The officers of the courts of justice.

Astrologers.

Powerful men, or men with interest.

Learned men.

Teachers of the sixty-four arts.

Pithamardas or confidants.

Vitas or parasites.

Vidushakas or jesters.

Flower sellers.

Perfumers.

Vendors of spirits.

Washermen.

Barbers.

Beggars.

And such other persons as may be found necessary for the particular object to be acquired.

The following kinds of men may be taken up with, simply for the purpose of getting their money.

Men of independent income.

Young men.

Men who are free from any ties.

Men who hold places of authority under the King.

Men who have secured their means of livelihood without difficulty.

Men possessed of unfailing sources of income.

Men who consider themselves handsome.

Men who are always praising themselves.

One who is an eunuch, but wishes to be thought a man.

One who hates his equals.

One who is naturally liberal.

One who has influence with the King or his ministers.

One who is always fortunate.

One who is proud of his wealth.

One who disobeys the orders of his elders.

One upon whom the members of his caste keep an eye.

An only son whose father is wealthy.

An ascetic who is internally troubled with desire.

A brave man.

A physician of the King.

Previous acquaintances.

On the other hand, those who are possessed of excellent qualities are to be resorted to for the sake of love, and fame. Such men are as follows:

Men of high birth, learned, with a good knowledge of the world, and doing the proper things at the proper times, poets, good story tellers, eloquent men, energetic men, skilled in various arts, far-seeing into the future, possessed of great minds, full of perseverance, of a firm devotion, free from anger, liberal, affectionate to their parents, and with a liking for all social gatherings, skilled in completing verses begun by others and in various other sports, free from all disease, possessed of a perfect body, strong, and not addicted to drinking, powerful in sexual enjoyment, sociable, showing love towards women and attracting their hearts to himself, but not entirely devoted to them, possessed of independent means of livelihood, free from envy, and last of all, free from suspicion.

Such are the good qualities of a man.

The woman also should have the following characterstics, viz.:

She should be possessed of beauty, and aimiability, with auspicious body marks. She should have a liking for good qualities in other people, as also a liking for wealth. She should take delight in sexual unions resulting from love, and should be of a firm mind, and of the same class as the man with regard to sexual enjoyment. She should always be anxious to acquire and obtain experience and knowledge, be free from avarice, and always have a liking for social gatherings, and for the arts.

The following are the ordinary qualities of all women, viz.:

To be possessed of intelligence, good disposition, and good manners; to be straightforward in behaviour, and to be grateful; to consider well the future before doing anything; to possess activity, to be of consistent behaviour, and to have a knowledge of the proper times and places for doing things; to speak always without meanness, loud laughter, malignity, anger, avarice, dullness, or stupidity, to have a knowledge of the Kama Sutra, and to be skilled in all the arts connected with it.

The faults of the women are to be known by the absence of any of the above mentioned good qualities.

The following kinds of men are not fit to be resorted to by courtesans, viz.:

One who is consumptive; one who is sickly; one whose mouth contains worms; one whose wife is dear to him; one who speaks harshly; one who is always suspicious; one who is avaricious; one who is pitiless; one who is a thief; one who is self-conceited; one who has a liking for sorcery; one who does not care for respect or disrespect; one who can be gained over even by his enemies by means of money; and lastly, one who is extremely bashful.

Ancient authors are of opinion that the causes of a courtesan resorting to men are love, fear, money, pleasure, returning some act of enmity, curiosity, sorrow, constant intercourse, Dharma, celebrity, compassion, the desire of having a friend, shame, the likeness of the man to some beloved person, the search after good fortune, the getting rid of the love of somebody else, the being of the same place, constancy, and poverty. But Vatsyayana decides that desire of wealth, freedom from misfortune, and love, are the only causes that affect the union of courtesans with men.

Now a courtesan should not sacrifice money to her love, because money is the chief thing to be attended to. But in cases of fear, etc., she should pay regard to strength and other qualities. Moreover, even though she be invited by any man to join him, she should not at once consent to a union, because men are apt to despise things which are easily acquired. On such occasions she should first send the shampooers, and the singers, and the jesters, who may be in her service, or, in their absence the Pithamardas, or confidants, and others, to find out the state of his feelings, and the condition of his mind. By means of these persons she should ascertain whether the man is pure or impure, affected, or the reverse, capable of attachment, or different, liberal or niggardly; and if she finds him to her liking, she should then employ the Vita and others to attach his mind to her. Accordingly, the Pithamarda should bring the man to her house, under the pretence of seeing the fights of quails, cocks, and rams, of hearing the maina (a kind of starling) talk, or of seeing some other spectacle, or the practice of some art; or he may take the women to the abode of the man. After this, when the man comes to her house the woman shuld give him something capable of producing curiosity, and love in his heart, such as an affectionate present, telling him that it was specially designed for his use. She should also amuse him for a long time by telling him such stories, and doing such things as he may take most delight in. When he goes away she should frequently send to him a female attendant, skilled in carrying on a jesting conversation, and also a small present at the same time. She should also sometimes go to him herself under the pretence of some business, and accompanied by the Pithamarda.

Thus end the means of attaching to herself the man desired.

There are also some verses on the subject as follows:

"When a lover comes to her abode, a courtesan should give him a mixture of betel leaves and betel nut, garlands of flowers, and perfumed ointments, and, showing her skill in arts, should entertain him with a long conversation. She should also give him some loving presents, and make an exchange of her own things with his, and at the same time should show him her skill in sexual enjoyment. When a courtesan is thus united with her lover she should always delight him by affectionate gifts, by conversation, and by the application of tender means of enjoyment."

II

Of living like a wife

When a courtesan is living as a wife with her lover, she should behave like a chaste woman, and do everything to his satisfaction. Her duty in this respect, in short, is, that she should give him pleasure, but should not become attached to him, though behaving as if she were really attached.

Now the following is the manner in which she is to conduct herself, so as to accomplish the above mentioned purpose. She should have a mother dependent on her, one who should be represented as very harsh, and who looked upon money as her chief object in life. In the event of there being no mother, then an old and confidential nurse should play the same role. The mother or nurse, on their part, should appear to be displeased with the lover, and forcibly take her away from him. The woman herself should always show pretended anger, dejection, fear, and shame on this account, but should not disobey the mother or nurse at any time.

She should make out to the mother or nurse that the man in suffering from bad health, and making this a pretext for going to see him, she should go on that account. She is moreover, to do the following things for the purpose of gaining the man's favour, viz.:

Sending her female attendant to bring the flowers used by him on the previous day, in order that she may use them herself as a mark of affection, also asking for the mixture of betel nut and leaves that have remained uneaten by him; expressing wonder at his knowledge of sexual intercourse, and the several means of enjoyment used by him; learning from him the sixty-four kinds of pleasure mentioned by Babhravya; continually practising the ways of enjoyment as taught by him, and according to his liking; keeping his secrets; telling him her own desires and secrets; concealing her anger; never neglecting him on the bed when he turns his face towards her; touching any parts of his body according to his wish; kissing and embracing him when he is asleep; looking at him with apparent anxiety when he is wrapt in thought, or thinking of some other subject than herself; showing neither complete shamelessness, nor excessve bashfulness when he meets her, or sees her standing on the terrace of her house from the public road; hating his enemies; loving those who are dear to him; showing a liking for that which he likes; being in high or low spirits according to the state that he is in himself; expressing a curiosity to see his wives; not continuing her anger for a long time; suspecting even the marks and wounds made by herself with her nails and teeth on his body to have been some other woman; keeping her love for him unexpressed by words, but showing it by deeds, and signs, and hints; remaining silent when he is asleep, intoxicated, or sick; being very attentive when he describes his good actions, and reciting them afterwards to his praise and benefit; giving witty replies to him if he be sufficiently attached to her; listening to all his stories, except those that relate to her rivals; expressing feelings of dejection and sorrow if he sighs, yawns, or falls down; pronouncing the words "live long" when he sneezes; pretending to be ill, or to have the desire of pregnancy, when she feels dejected; abstaining from praising the good qualities of anybody else, and from censuring those who possess the same faults as her own man; wearing anything that may have been given to her by him; abstaining from putting on her ornaments, and from taking food when he is in pain, sick, low spirited, or suffering from misfortune, and condoling and lamenting with him over the same; wishing to accompany him if he happens to leave the country himself or if he be banished from it by the King; expressing a desire not to live after him; telling him that the whole object and desire of her life was to be united with him; offering previously promised sacrifices to the Diety when he acquires wealth, or has some desire fulfilled, or when he has recovered from some illness or disease; putting on ornaments every day; not acting too freely with him; reciting his name and the name of his family in her songs, placing his hand on her loins, bosom and forehead, and falling asleep after feeling the pleasure of his touch; sitting on his lap and falling asleep there; wishing to have a child by him; desiring not to live longer than he does; abstaining from revealing his secrets to others; dissuading him from vows and fasts by saying "let the sin fall upon me"; keeping vows and fasts along with him when it is impossible to change his mind on the subject; telling him that vows and fasts are difficult to be observed, even by herself, when she has any dispute with him about them; looking on her own wealth and his without any distinction; abstaining from going to public assemblies without him, and accompanying hm when he desires her to do so; taken delight in using things previously used by him, and in eating food that he has left uneaten; venerating his family, his disposition, his skill in the arts, his learning, his caste, his complexion, his native country, his friends, his good qualities, his age, and his sweet temper; asking him to sing, and to do other such like things, if able to do them; going to him without paying any regard to fear, to cold, to heat, or to rain; saying with regard to the next world that he should be her lover even there; adapting her tastes, disposition and actions to his liking; abstaining from sorcery; disputing continually with her mother on the subject of going to him, and, when forcibly taken by her mother to some other place, expressing her desire to die by taking poison, by starving herself to death, by stabbing herself with some weapon, or by hanging herself; and lastly assuring the man of her constancy and love by means of her agents, and receiving money herself, but abstaining from any dispute with her mother with regard to pecuniary matters. When the man sets out on a journey, she should make him swear that he will return quickly, and in his absence should put aside her vows of worshipping the Deity, and should wear no ornaments except those that are lucky. If the time fixed for his return has passed, she should endeavour to ascertain the real time of his return from omens, from the reports of the people, and from the positions of

185

the planets, the moon and the stars. On accasions of amusement, and of auspicious dreams, she should say "Let me be soon united to him." If moreover, she feels melancholy, or sees any inauspicious omen, she should perform some rite to appease the Deity.

When the man does return home she should worship the God Kama (i.e., the Indian Cupid), and offer oblations to other Deities, and having caused a pot filled with water to be brought by her friends, she should perform the worship in honour of the crow who eats the offerings which we make to the names of deceased relations. After the first visit is over she should ask her lover also to perform certain rites, and this he will do if he is sufficiently attached to her.

Now a man is said to be sufficiently attached to a woman when his love is disinterested; when he has the same object in view as his beloved one; when he is quite free from any suspicions on her account; and when he is indifferent to money with regard to her.

Such is the manner of a courtesan living with a man like a wife, and set forth here for the sake of guidance from the rules of Dattaka. What is not laid down here should be practised according to the custom of the people, and the nature of each individual man.

There are also two verses on the subject as follows:

"The extent of the love of women is not known, even to those who are the objects of their affection, on account of its subtlety, and on account of the avarice, and natural intelligence of womankind."

"Women are hardly ever known in their true light, though they may love men, or become indifferent towards them; may give them delight or abandon them; or may extract from them all the wealth that they may possess."

III

Of the means of getting money. Of the signs of the change of a lover's feelings, and of the way to get rid of him

Money is got out of a lover in two ways, viz.:

By natural or lawful means, and by artifices. Old authors are of opinion that when a courtesan can get as much money as she wants from her lover, she should not make use of artifice. But Vatsyayana lays down that though she may gets some money from him by natural means, yet when she makes use of artifice he gives her doubly more, and therefore artifice should be resorted to for the purpose of extorting money from him at all events.

Now the artifices to be used for getting money from her lover are as follows:

1st. Taking money from him on different occasions, for the purpose of purchasing various articles, such as ornaments, food, drink, flowers, perfumes and cloths, and either not buying them, or getting from him more than their cost.

2nd. Praising his intelligence to his face.

3rd. Pretending to be obliged to make gifts on occasion of festivals connected with vows, trees, gardens, temples, or tanks.

4th. Pretending that at the time of going to his house, her jewels have been stolen either by the King's guards, or by robbers.

5th. Alleging that her property has been destroyed by fire, by the falling of her house, or by the carelessness of her servants.

6th. Pretending to have lost the ornaments of her lover along with her own.

7th. Causing him to hear through other people of the expenses incurred by her in coming to see him.

8th. Contracting debts for the sake of her lover.

9th. Disputing with her mother on account of some expense incurred by her for her lover, and which was not approved of by her mother.

10th. Not going to parties and festivities in the houses of her friends for the want of presents to make to them, she having previously informed her lover of the valuable presents given to her by these very friends.

11th. Not performing certain festive rites under the pretence that she has no money to perform them with.

12th. Engaging artists to do something for her lover.

13th. Entertaining physicians and ministers for the purpose of attaining some object.

14th. Assisting friends and benefactors both on festive occasions, and in misfortune.

15th. Performing household rites.

16th. Having to pay the expenses of the ceremony of marriage of the son of a female friend.

17th. Having to satisfy curious wishes during her state of pregnancy.

18th. Pretending to be ill, and charging her cost of treatment.

19th. Having to remove the troubles of a friend.

20th. Selling some of her ornaments, so as to give her lover a present.

21st. Pretending to sell some of her ornaments, furniture, or cooking utensils to a trader, who has been already tutored how to behave in the manner.

22nd. Having to buy cooking utensils of greater value than those of other people, so that they might be more easily distinguished, and not changed for others of an inferior description.

23rd. Remembering the former favours of her lover, and causing them always to be spoken of her friends and followers.

24th. Informing her lover of the great gains of other courtesans.

25th. Describing before them, and in the presence of her lover, her own great gains, and making them out to be greater even than theirs, though such may not have been really the case.

26th. Openly opposing her mother when she endeavours to persuade her to take up with men with whom she has been formerly acquainted, on account of the great gains to be got from them.

27th. Lastly, pointing out to her lover the liberality of his rivals.

Thus ends the ways and means of getting money.

*

A woman should always know the state of the mind, of the feelings, and of the disposition of her lover towards her, from the changes of his temper, his manner, and the colour of his face.

The behavior of a waning lover is as follows:

1st. He gives the woman either less than is wanted, or something else than that which is asked for.

2nd. He keeps her in hopes by promises.

3rd. He pretends to do one thing, and does something else.

4th. He does not fulfil her desires.

5th. He forgets his promises, or does something else than that which he has promised.

6th. He speaks with is own servants in a mysterious way.

7th. He sleeps in some other house under the pretence of having to do something for a friend.

8th. Lastly, he speaks in private with the attendants of a woman with whom he was formerly acquainted.

Now when a courtesan finds that her lover's disposition towards her is changing, she should get possession all his best things before he becomes aware of her intentions, and allow a supposed creditor to take them away forcibly from her in satisfaction of some pretended debt. After this, if the lover is rich, and has always behaved well towards her, she should ever treat him with respect; but if he is poor

189

and destitute she should get rid of him as if she had never been acquainted with him in any way before.

The means of getting rid of a lover are as follows:

1st. Describing the habits and vices of the lover as disagreeable and censurable, with the sneer of the lip, and the stamp of the foot.

2nd. Speaking on a subject with which he is not acquainted.

3rd. Showing no admiration for his learning, and passing a censure upon it.

4th. Putting down his pride.

5th. Seeking the company of men who are superior to him in learning and wisdom.

6th. Showing a disregard for him on all occasions.

7th. Censuring men possessed of the same faults as her lover.

8th. Expressing dissatisfaction at the ways and means of enjoyment used by him.

9th. Not giving him her mouth to kiss.

10th. Refusing access to her Jaghana, i.e., the part of the body between the navel and the thighs.

11th. Showing a dislike for the wounds made by his nails and teeth.

12th. Not pressing close up against him at the time when he embraces her.

13th. Keeping her limbs without movement at the time of congress.

14th. Desiring him to enjoy her when he is fatigued.

15th. Laughing at his attachments to her.

16th. Not responding to his embraces.

17th. Turning away from him when he begins to embrace her.

18th. Pretending to be sleepy.

19th. Going out visiting, or into company, when she perceives his desire to enjoy her during the day time.

20th. Misconstructing his words.

21st. Laughing without any joke, or at the time of any joke made by him, laughing under some pretence.

22nd. Looking with side glances at her own attendants, and clapping her hands when he says anything.

23rd. Interrupting him in the middle of his stories, and beginning to tell other stories.

24th. Reciting his faults and his vices, and declaring them to be incurable.

25th. Saying words to her female attendants calculated to cut the heart of her lover to the quick.

26th. Taking care not to look at him when he comes to her.

27th. Asking him what cannot be granted.

28th. And, after all, finally dismissing him.

There are also two verses on this subject as follows:

"The duty of a courtesan consists in forming connections with suitable men after due and full consideration and attaching the person with whom she is united to herself; in obtaining wealth from the person who is attached to her, and then dismissing him after she has taken away all his possessions."

"A courtesan leading in this manner the life of a wife is not troubled with too many lovers, and yet obtains abundance of wealth."

IV

About re-union with a former Lover

When a courtesan abandons her present lover after all his wealth is exhausted, she may then consider about her re-union with a former lover. But she should return to him only if he has acquired fresh wealth, or is still wealthy, and if he is still attached to her. And if this man be living at the time with some other woman she should consider well before she acts.

Now such a man can only be in one of the six following conditions, viz.:

1st. He may have left the first woman of his own accord, and may even have left another woman since then.

2nd. He may have been driven away from both women.

3rd. He may have left the one woman of her own accord, and been driven away by the other.

4th. He may have left the one woman of his own accord, and be living with another woman.

5th. He may have been driven away from the one woman, and left the other of his own accord.

6th. He may have been driven away by the one woman, and may be living with another.

1). Now if the man has left both women of his own accord, he should not be resorted to, on account of the fickleness of his mind, and his indifference to the excellences of both of them.

2). As regard the man who may have been driven away from both women, if he has been driven away from the last one because the woman could get more money from some other man, then he should be resorted to, for if attached to the first woman he would give her more money, through vanity and emulation to spite the othe woman. But if he has been driven away by the woman on account of his poverty, or stinginess, he should not then be resorted to.

3). In the case of the man who may have left the one woman of his own accord, and been driven away by the other, if he agrees to return to the former and give her plenty of money beforehand, then he should be resorted to.

4). In the case of the man who may have left the one woman of his own accord, and be living with another woman, the former, (wishing to take up with him again), should first ascertain if he left her in the first instance in the hope of finding some particular excellence in the other woman, and that not having found any such excellence, he was willing to come back to her, and to give her much money on account of his conduct, and on account of his affection still existing for her.

Or, whether, having discovered many faults in the other woman, he would now see even more excellences in herself than actually exist and would be prepared to give her much money for these qualities.

Or, lastly, to consider whether he was a weak man, or a man fond of enjoying many women, or one who liked a poor woman, or one who never did anything for the woman that he was with. After maturely considering all these things, she should resort to him or not, according to circumstances.

5). As regards the man who may have been driven away from the one woman, and left the other of his own accord, the former woman (wishing to re-unite with him), should first ascertain whether he still has any affection for her, and would consequently spend much money upon her; or whether, being attached to her excellent qualities, he did not take delight in any other woman; or whether, being driven away from her formerly before completely satisfying his sexual desires, he

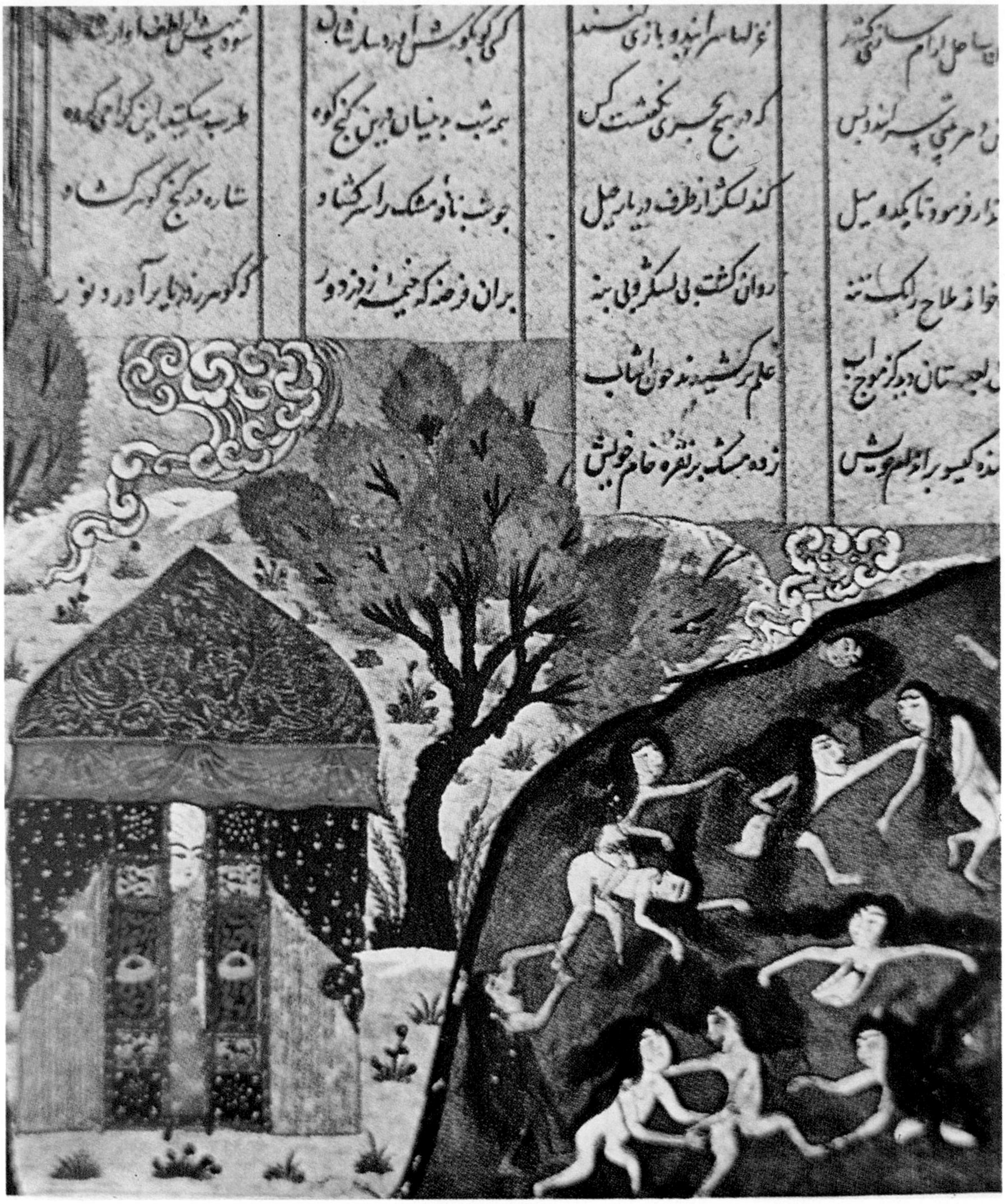

wished to get back to her, so as to be revenged for the injury done to him; or whether he wished to create confidence in her mind, and then take back from her the wealth which she formerly took from him, and finally destroy her; or, lastly, whether he wished first to separate her from her present lover, and then to break away from her himself. If, after considering all these things, she is of opinion that his intentions are really pure and honest, she can re-unite herself with him. But if his mind be at all tainted with evil intentions, he should be avoided.

6). In the case of the man who may have been driven away by one woman, and be living with another, if the man makes overtures to return to the first one, the courtesan should consider well before she acts, and while the other woman is engaged in attracting him to herself, she should try in her turn (though keeping herself behind the scenes) to gain him over, on the grounds of any of the following considerations, viz.:

1st. That he was driven away unjustly and for no proper reason, and now that he has gone to another woman, every effort must be used to bring him back to myself.

2nd. That if he were once to converse with me again, he would break away from the other woman.

3rd. That the pride of my present lover would be put down by means of the former one.

4th. That he has become wealthy, has secured a higher position, and holds a place of authority under the King.

5th. That he is separate from his wife.

6th. That he is now independent.

7th. That he lives apart from his father, or brother.

8th. That by making peace with him, I shall be able to get hold of a very rich man, who is now prevented from coming to me by my present lover.

9th. That as he is not respected by his wife, I shall now be able to separate him from her.

10th. That the friend of this man loves my rival, who hates me cordially, I shall therefore by this means separate the friend from his mistress.

11th. And lastly, I shall bring discredit upon him by bringing him back to me, thus showing the fickleness of his mind.

When a courtesan is resolved to take up again with a former lover, her Pitha-murda and other servants should tell him that his former expulsion from the woman's house was caused by the wickedness of her mother; that the woman loved him just as much as ever at that time, but could not help the occurence on account of her deference to her mother's will; that she hated the union of her present lover, and disliked him excessively. In addition to his, they should create confidence in his mind by speaking to him of her former love for him, and should allude to the mark of that love that she has ever remembered. This mark of her love should be connected with some kind of pleasure that may have been practised by him, such as his way of kissing her, or manner of having connection with her.

Thus end the ways of bringing about a re-union with a former lover.

When a woman has to choose between two lovers, one of whom was formerly united with her, while the other is a stranger, the Acharyas (sages) are of opinion that the first one is preferable, because his disposition and character being already known by previous careful observation, he can be easily pleased and satisfied; but Vatsyayana thinks that a former lover, having already spent a great deal of his wealth, is not able or willing to give much money again, and is not therefore to be relied upon so much as a stranger. Particular cases may however arise differing from this general rule on account of the different natures of men. There are also verses on the subject as follows:

"Re-union with a former lover may be desirable so as to separate some particular woman from some particular man, or some particular man from some particular woman, or to have a certain effect upon the present lover."

"When a man is excessively attached to a woman, he is afraid of her coming into contact with other men; he does not then regard or notice her faults; and he gives her much wealth through fear of her leaving him."

"A courtesan should be agreeable to the man who is attached to her, and despise the man who does not care for her. If while she is living with one man, a messen-

ger comes to her from some other man, she may either refuse to listen to any negotiations on his part, or appoint a fixed time for him to visit her, but she should not leave the man who may be living with her and who may be attached to her."
"A wise woman should only renew her connection with a former lover if she is satisfied that good fortune, gain, love, and friendship, are likely to be the result of such a re-union."

V

Of different kinds of gain

When a courtesan is able to realize much money every day, by reason of many customers, she should not confine herself to a single lover; under such circumstances, she should fix her rate for one night, after considering the place, the season, and the condition of the people, and having regard to her own good qualities and good looks, and after comparing her rates with those of other courtesans. She can inform her lovers, and friends, and aquaintances about these charges. If, however, she can obtain a great gain from a single lover, she may resort to him alone, and live with him like a wife.

Now, the Sages are of opinion, that, when a courtesan has the chance of an equal gain from two lovers at the same time, a preference should be given to the one who would give her the kind of thing which she wants. But Vatsyayana says that the preference should be given to the one who gives her gold, because it cannot be taken back like some other things, it can be easily received, and is also the means of procuring anything that may be wished for. Of such things as gold, silver, copper, bell metal, iron, pots, furniture, beds, upper garments, under vestments, fragrant substances, vessels made of gourds, ghee, oil, corn, cattle, and other things of a like nature, the first, viz., gold, is superior to all the others.

When the same labour is required to gain any two lovers, or when the same kind of thing is to be got from each of them, the choice should be made by the advice of a friend, or it may be made from their personal qualities, or from the signs of good or bad fortune that may be connected with them.

When there are two lovers, one of whom is attached to the courtesan, and the other is simply very generous, the Sages say that the preference should be given to the generous lover, but Vatsyayana is of opinion that the one who is really attached to the courtesan should be preferred, because he can be made to be generous, even as a miser gives money if he becomes fond of a woman, but a man who is simply generous cannot be made to love with real attachment. But among those who are attached to her, if there is one who is poor, and one who is rich, the preference is of course to be given to the latter.

When there are two lovers, one of whom is generous, and the other ready to do any service for the courtesan, some Sages say that the one who is ready to do the service should be preferred, but Vatsyayana is of opinion that a man who does a service thinks that he has gained his object when he has done something once, but a generous man does not care for what he has given before. Even here the choice should be guided by the likelihood of the future good to be derived from her union with either of them.

When one of the two lovers is grateful, and the other liberal, some Sages say that the liberal one should be preferred, but Vatsyayana is of opinion that the former should be chosen, because liberal men are generally haughty, plain spoken, and wanting in consideration towards others. Even though these liberal men have been on friendly terms for a long time, yet if they see any fault in the courtesan, or are told lies about her by some other woman, they do not care for past services, but leave abruptly. On the other hand the grateful man does not at once break off from her, on account of a regard for the pains she may have taken to please him. In this case also the choice is to be guided with respect to what may happen in future.

When an occasion for complying with the request of a friend, and a chance of getting money come together, the Sages say that the chance of getting money should be preferred. But Vatsyayana thinks that the money can be obtained tomorrow as well as to-day, but if the request of a friend be not at once complied with, he may become disaffected. Even here, in making the choice, regard must be paid to future good fortune.

On such an occasion, however, the courtesan might pacify her friend by pretending to have some work to do, and telling him that his request will be complied with next day, and in this way secure the chance of getting the money that has been offered her.

When the chance of getting money, and the chance of avoiding some disaster come at the same time, the Sages are of opinion that the chance of getting money should be preferred, but Vatsyayana says that money has only a limited importance, while a disaster that is once averted may never occur again. Here, however, the choice should be guided by the greatness or smallness of the disaster.

The gains of the wealthiest and best kinds of courtesans are to be spent as follows:

Building temples, tanks, and gardens; giving a thousand cows to different Brahmans; carrying on the worship of the Gods, and celebrating festivals in their honour; and, lastly, performing such vows as may be within their means.

The gains of other courtesans are to be spent as follows:

Having a white dress to wear every day; getting sufficient food and drink to satisfy hunger and thirst; eating daily a perfumed Tambula, *i.e.*, a mixture of betel nut and betel leaves; and wearing ornaments gilt with gold. The Sages say that these represent the gains of all the middle and lower classes of courtesans, but Vatsyayana is of opinion that their gains cannot be calculated, or fixed in any way, as these depend on the influence of the place, the customs of the people, their own appearance, and many other things.

When a courtesan wants to keep some particular man from some other woman; or wishes to get him away from some woman to whom he may be attached; or to deprive some woman of the gains realized by her from him; or if she thinks that she would raise her position; or enjoy some great good fortune; or become desirable to all men by uniting herself with this man; or if she wishes to get his assistance in averting some misfortune; or is really attached to him and loves him; or wishes to injure somebody through his means; or has regard to some former favour conferred upon her by him; or wishes to be united with him merely from desire; for any of the above reasons, she should agree to take from him only a small sum of money in a friendly way.

When a courtesan intends to abandon a particular lover, and take up with another one; or when she has reason to believe that her lover will shortly leave her, and return to his wives; or that having squandered all his money, and become penniless, his guardian, or master, or father would come and take him away; or that her lover is about to lose his position, or lastly, that he is of a very fickle mind, she should, under any of these circumstances, endeavour to get as much money as she can from him as soon as possible.

On the other hand, when the courtesan thinks that her lover is about to receive valuable presents; or get a place of authority from the King; or be near the time of inheriting a fortune; or that his ship would soon arrive laden with merchandise; or that he has large stocks of corn and other commodities; or that if anything was done for him it would not be done in vain; or that he is always true to his word; then she should have regard to her future welfare, and live with the man like a wife.

There are also verses on the subject as follows:

"In considering her present gains, and her future welfare, a courtesan should avoid such persons as have gained their means of subsistence with very great difficulty, as also those who have become selfish and hardhearted by becoming the favourites of Kings."

"She should make every endeavour to unite herself with prosperous and well-to-do people, and with those whom it is dangerous to avoid, or to slight in any way. Even at some cost to herself she should become acquainted with energetic and liberal-minded men, who when pleased would give her a large sum of money, even for very little service, or for some small thing."

VI

Of gains and losses; attendant gains and losses; and doubts; as also of the different kinds of courtesans.

It sometimes happens that while gains are being sought for, or expected to be realised, that losses only are the result of our efforts, the causes of these losses are:

Weakness of intellect.

Excessive love.

Excessive pride.

Excessive self conceit.

Excessive simplicity.

Excessive confidence.

Excessive anger.

Carelessness.

Recklessness.

Influence of evil genius.

Accidental circumstances.

The results of these losses are:

Expense incurred without any result.

Destruction of future good fortune.

Stoppage of gains about to be realized.

Loss of what is already obtained.

Acquisition of a sour temper.

Becoming unamiable to every body.

Injury to health.

Loss of hair and other accidents.

Now gain is of three kinds, viz.: gain of wealth, gain of religious merit, and gain of pleasure; and similarly, loss is of three kinds, viz.: loss of wealth, loss of religious merit, and loss of pleasure. At the time when gains are sought for, if other gains come aong with them, these are called attendant gains. When gain is uncertain, the doubt of its being a gain is called a simple doubt. When there is a doubt whether either of two things will happen or not, it is called a mixed doubt. If while one thing is being done two results take place, it is called a combination of two results, and if several results follow from the same action, it is called a combination of results on every side.

We shall now give examples of the above.

As already stated, gain is of three kinds, and loss, which is opposed to gain, is also of three kinds.

a). When by living with a great man a courtesan acquires present wealth, and in addition to this becomes acquainted with other people, and thus obtains a chance of future fortune, and an accession of wealth, and becomes desirable to all, this is called a gain of wealth attended by other gain.

b). When by living with a man a courtesan simply gets money, this called a gain of wealth not attended by any other gain.

c). When a courtesan receives money from other people besides her lover, the results are: the chance of the loss of future good from her present lover; the chance of disaffection of a man securely attached to her; the hatred of all; and the chance of a union with some low person, tending to destroy her future good. This gain is called a gain of wealth attended by losses.

d). When a courtesan, at her own expense, and without any results in the shape of gain, has connection with a great man, or an avaricious minister, for the sake of diverting some misfortune, or removing some cause that may be threatening the destruction of a great gain, this loss is said to be a loss of wealth attended by gains of the future good which it may bring about.

e). When a courtesan is kind, even at her own expense, to a man who is very stingy, or to a man proud of his looks, or to an ungrateful man skilled in gaining the hearts of others without any good resulting from these connections to her in the end, this loss is called a loss of wealth not attended by any gain.

f). When a courtesan is kind to any such man as described above, but who in addition are favourites of the King, and moreover cruel and powerful, without any good result in the end, and with a chance of her being turned away at any moment, this loss is called a loss of wealth attended by other losses.

In this way gains and losses, and attendant gains and losses in religious merit and pleasures may become known to the reader, and combinations of all of them may also be made.

Thus end the remarks on gains and losses, and attendant gains and losses.

In the next place we come to doubts, which are again of three kinds, viz.: doubts about wealth, doubts about religious merit, and doubts about pleasures.

The following are examples.

a). When a courtesan is not certain how much a man may give her, or spend upon her, this is called a doubt about wealth.

b). When a courtesan feels doubtful whether she is right in entirely abandoning a lover from whom she is unable to get money, she having taken all his wealth from him in the first instance, this doubt is called a doubt about religious merit.

c). When a courtesan is unable to get hold of a lover to her liking, and is uncertain whether she will derive any pleasure from a person surrounded by his family, or from a low person, this called a doubt about pleasure.

d) When a courtesan is uncertain whether some powerful but low principled fellow would cause loss to her on account of her not being civil to him, this is called a doubt about the loss of wealth.

e). When a courtesan feels doubtful whether she would lose religious merit by abandoning a man who is attached to her without giving him the slightest favour, and thereby causing him unhappiness in this world and the next, this doubt is called a doubt about the loss of a religious merit.

f). When a courtesan is uncertain as to whether she might create disaffection by speaking out, and revealing her love and thus not get her desire satisfied, this is called a doubt about the loss of pleasure.

Thus end the remarks on doubts.

Mixed doubts

a). The intercourse or connection with a stranger, whose disposition is unknown, and who may have been introduced by a lover, or by one who possessed authority, may be productive either of gain or loss, and therefore this is called a mixed doubt about the gain and loss of wealth.

b). When a courtesan is requested by a friend, or is impelled by pity to have intercourse with a learned Brahman, a religious student, a sacrificer, a devotee, or an ascetic who may have all fallen in love with her, and who may be consequently at the point of death, by doing this she might either gain or lose religious merit, and therefore this is called a mixed doubt about the gain and loss of religious merit.

c). If a courtesan relies solely upon the report of other people (*i.e.,* hearsay) about a man, and goes to him without ascertaining herself whether he possesses good qualities or not, she may either gain or lose pleasure in proportion as he may be good or bad, and therefore this is called a mixed doubt about the gain and loss of pleasure.

Uddalika has described the gains and losses on both sides as follows.

a). If, when living with a lover, a courtesan gets both wealth and pleasure from him, it is called a gain on both sides.

b). When a courtesan lives with a lover at her own expense without getting any profit out of it, and the lover even takes back from her what he may have formerly given her, it is called a loss on both sides.

c). When a courtesan is uncertain whether a new acquaintance would become attached to her, and moreover, if he became attached to her, whether he would give her anything, it is then called a doubt on both sides about gains.

d). When a courtesan is uncertain whether a former enemy, if made up by her at her own expense, would do her some injury on account of his grudge against her; or, if becoming attached to her, would take away angrily from her anything that he may have given to her, this is called a doubt on both sides about loss.

Babhravya has described the gains and losses on both sides as follows.

a). When a courtesan can get money from a man whom she may go to see, and also money from a man whom she may not go to see, this is called a gain on both sides.

b). When a courtesan has to incur further expense if she goes to see a man, and yet runs the risk of incurring an irremediable loss if she does not go to see him, this is called a loss on both sides.

c). When a courtesan is uncertain, whether a particular-man would give her anything on her going to see him, without incurring expense on her part, or whether on her neglecting him another man would give her something, this is called a doubt on both sides about gain.

d). When a courtesan is uncertain, whether, on going at her own expense to see an old enemy, he would take back from her what he may have given her, or whether by her not going to see him he would cause some disaster to fall upon her, this is called a doubt on both sides about loss.

By combining the above, the following six kinds of mixed results are produced, viz.:

a). Gain on one side, and loss on the other.

b). Gain on one side, and doubt of gain on the other.

c). Gain on one side, and doubt of loss on the other.

d). Loss on one side, and doubt of gain on the other.

e). Doubt of gain on one side, and doubt of loss on the other.

f). Doubt of loss on one side, and loss on the other.

A courtesan, having considered all the above things, and taken counsel with her friends, should act so as to acquire gain, the chances of great gain, and the warding off of any great disaster. Religious merit and pleasure should also be formed into separate combinations like those of wealth, and then all should be combined with each other, so as to form new combinations.

When a courtesan consorts with men she should cause each of them to give her money as well as pleasure. At particular times, such as Spring Festivals, etc., she should make her mother announce to the various men, that on a certain day her daughter would remain with the man who would gratify such and such a desire of hers.

When young men approach her with delight, she should think of what she may accomplish through them.

The combination of gains and losses on all sides are: gain on one side, and loss on all others; loss on one side and gain on all others; gain on all sides, loss on all sides.

A courtesan should also consider doubts about gain and doubts about loss with reference both to wealth, religious merit, and pleasure.

Thus ends the consideration of gain, loss, attendant gains, attendant losses, and doubts.

The different kinds of courtesans are:

A bawd.

A female attendant.

An unchaste woman.

A dancing girl.

A female artisan.

A woman who has left her family.

A woman living on her beauty.

And, finally, a regular courtesan.

All the above kinds of courtesans are acquainted with various kinds of men, and should consider the ways of getting money from them, of pleasing them, of separating themselves from them, and of re-uniting with them. They should also take into consideration particular gains and losses, attendant gains and losses, and doubts in accordance with their several conditions.

Thus end the considerations of courtesans.

There are also two verses on the subject as follows:

"Men want pleasure, while women want money, and therefore this Part, which treats of the means of gaining wealth, should be studied."

"There are some women who seek for love, and there are others who seek for money; for the former the ways of love are told in previous portions of this work, while the ways of getting money, as practised by courtesans, are described in this Part."

Part VII

About the means of attracting others to yourself

I

On personal adornment; on subjugating the hearts of others; and on tonic medicines.

When a person fails to obtain the object of his desires by any of the ways previously related, he should then have recourse to other ways of attracting others to himself.

Now, good looks, good qualities, youth, and liberality are the chief and most natural means of making a person agreeable in the eyes of others. But in the absence of these a man or a woman must have resort to artifical means, or to art, and the following are some recipes that may be found useful.

a). An ointment made of the tabernamontana coronaria, the costus speciosus or arabicus, and the flacourtia cataphracta can be used as an unguent of adornment.

b). If a fine powder is made of the above plants, and applied to the wick of a lamp, which is made to burn with the oil of blue vitrol, the black pigment or lamp black produced therefrom, when applied to the eyelashes, has the effect of making a person look lovely.

c). The oil of the hogweed, the echites putescens, the sarina plant, the yellow amaranth, and the leaf of the nymphæ, if applied to the body, has the same effect.

d). A black pigment from the same plants produces a similar effect.

e). By eating the powder of the nelumbrium speciosum, the blue lotus, and the mesna roxburghii, with ghee and honey, a man becomes lovely in the eyes of others.

f). The above things together with the tabernamontana coronaria, and the xanthochymus pictorius, if used as an ointment, produce the same results.

g). If the bone of a peacock or of an hyena be covered with gold, and tied on the right hand, it makes a man lovely in the eyes of other people.

h). In the same way, if a bead, made of the seed of the jujube, or of the conch shell, be enchanted by the incantations mentioned in the Atharvana Veda, or by the incantations of those well skilled in the science of magic and tied on the hand, it produces the same result as described above.

i). When a female attendant arrives at the age of puberty, her master should keep her secluded, and when men ardently desire her on account of her seclusion, and on account of the difficulty of approaching her, he should then bestow her hand on such a person as may endow her with wealth and happiness.

This is a means of increasing the loveliness of a person in the eyes of others. In the same way, when a daughter of a courtesan arrives at the age of puberty, the mother should get together a lot of young men of the same age, disposition, and knowledge as her daughter, and tell hem that she would give her in marriage to the person who would give her presents of a particular kind.

After this the daughter should be kept in seclusion as far as possible, and the mother should give her in marriage to the man who may be ready to give her the presents agreed upon. If the mother is unable to get so much out of the man she should show some of her own things as having been given to the daughter by the bridegroom.

Or, the mother may allow her daughter to be married to the man privately, as if she was ignorant of the whole affair, and then pretending that it has come to her knowledge, she may give her consent to the union.

The daughter, too, should make herself attractive to the sons of wealthy citizens, unknown to her mother, and make them attached to her, and for this purpose should meet them at the time of learning to sing, and in places where music is played, and at the houses of other people, and then request her mother, through a female friend, or servant, to be allowed to unite herself to the man who is most agreeable to her.

When the daughter of a courtesan is thus given to a man, the ties of marriage should be observed for one year, and after that she may do what she likes. But even after the end of the year, when otherwise engaged, if she should be now and then invited by her first husband to come and see him, she should put aside her present gain, and go to him for the night.

Such is the mode of temporary marriage among courtesans, and of increasing their loveliness, and their value in the eyes of others. What has been said about them should also be understood to apply to the daughters of dancing women, whose mothers should give them only to such persons as are likely to become useful to them in various ways.

Thus end the ways of making oneself lovely in the eyes others.

a). If a man, after anointing his lingam with a mixture of the powders of the white thorn apple, the long pepper, and the black pepper, and honey, engages in sexual union with a woman, he makes her subject to his will.

b). The application of a mixture of the leaf of the plant vatodbhranta, of the flowers thrown on a human corpse when carried out to be burnt, and the powder of the bones of the peacock, and of the jiwanjiva bird produces the same effect.

c). The remains of a kite who has died a natural death, ground into powder, and mixed with cowach and honey, has also the same effect.

d). Anointing oneself with an ointment made of the plant emblica myrabolans has the power of subjecting women to one's will.

e). If a man cuts into small pieces the sprouts of the vajnasunhi plant, and dips them into a mixture of red arsenic and sulphur, and then dries them seven times, and applies this powder mixed with honey to his lingam, he can subjugate a woman to his will directly that he has had sexual union with her, or, if, by burning these very sprouts at nights and looking at the smoke, he sees a golden moon behind, he will then be successful with any woman; of if he throws some of the powder of these same sprouts mixed with the excrement of a monkey upon a maiden, she will not be given in marriage to anybody else.

f). If pieces of the arris root are dressed with the oil of the mango, and placed for six months in a hole made in the trunk of the sisu tree, and are then taken out and made up into an ointment, and applied to the lingam, this is said to serve as the means of subjugating women.

g). If the bone of a camel is dipped into the juice of the plant eclipta prostata, and then burnt, and the black pigment produced from its ashes is placed in a box also made of the bone of a camel, then that pigment is said to be very pure, and wholesome for the eyes, and serves as a means of subjugating others to the person who uses it. The same effect can be produced by black pigment made of the bones of hawks, vultures, and peacocks.

Thus end the ways of subjugating others to one's own will.

Now the means of increasing sexual vigour are as follows:

a). A man obtains sexual vigour by drinking milk mixed with sugar, the root of the uchchata plant, the piper chaba, and liquorice.

b). Drinking milk mixed with sugar, and having the testicle of a ram or a goat boiled in it, is also productive of vigour.

c). The drinking of the juice of the hedysarum gangeticum, the kuili, and the kshirika plant mixed with milk, produces the same effect.

d). The seed of the long pepper along with the seeds of the sanseviera roxburghiana, and the hedysarum gangeticum plant, all pounded together, and mixed with milk, is productive of a similar result.

e). According to ancient authors, if a man pounds the seeds or roots of the trapa bispinosa, the kasurika, the tuscan jasmine, and liquorice, together with the kshirakapoli (a kind of onion), and puts the powder into milk mixed with sugar and ghee, and having boiled the whole mixture on a moderate fire, drinks the paste so formed, he will be able to enjoy innumerable women.

f). In the same way, if a man mixes rice with the eggs of the sparrow, and having boiled this in milk, adds to it ghee and honey, and drinks as much of it as necessary, this will produce the same effect.

g). If a man takes the outer covering of sesamum seeds, and soaks them with the eggs of sparrows, and then, having boiled them in milk, mixed with sugar and ghee, along with the fruits of the trapa bispinosa and the kasurika plant, and adding to it the flour of wheat and beans, and then drinks this composition, he is said to be able to enjoy many women.

h). If ghee, honey, sugar and liquorice in equal quantities, the juice of the fennel plant, and milk are mixed together, this nectar-like composition is said to be holy, and provocative of sexual vigour, a preservative of life, and sweet to the taste.

i). The drinking of a paste composed of the asparagus racemosus, the shvadaushtra plant, the guduchi plant, the long pepper, and liquorice, boiled in milk, honey, and ghee, in the spring, is said to have the same effect as the above.

j). Boiling the asparagus racemosus, and the shvadaushtra plant, along with the pounded fruits of the premna spinosa in water, and drinking the same, is said to act in the same way.

k). Drinking boiled ghee, or clarified butter, in the morning during the spring season, is said to be beneficial to health and strength, and agreeable to the taste.

l). If the powder of the seed of the shvadaushtra plant and the flower or barley are mixed together in equal parts, and a portion of it *i.e.,* two palas in weight, is eaten every morning on getting up, it has the same effect as the preceding recipe. There are also verses on the subject as follows:

"The means of producing love and sexual vigour should be learnt from the science of medicine, from the Vedas, from those who are learned in the arts of magic, and from confidential relatives. No means should be tried which are doubtful in their effects which are likely to cause injury to the body, which involve the death of animals, and which bring us in contact with impure things. Such means should only be used as are holy, acknowledged to be good, and approved of by Brahmans, and friends."

II

Of the ways of exciting desire, and miscellaneous experiments, and recipes

If a man is unable to satisfy a Hastini, or elephant woman, he should have recourse to various means to excite her passion. At the commencement he should rub her yoni with his hand or fingers, and not begin to have intercourse with her until she becomes excited or experiences pleasure. This is one way of exciting a woman.

Or, he may make use of certain Apadravyas, or things which are put on or around the lingam to supplement its length or its thickness, so as to fit it to the yoni. In the opinion of Babhravya, these Apadravyas should be made of gold, silver, copper, iron, ivory, buffalo's horn, various kinds of wood, tin or lead, and should be soft, cool provocative of sexual vigour, and well fitted to serve the intended purpose. Vatsyayana, however, says that they may be made according to the natural liking of each individual.

The following are the different kinds of Apadravyas.

1). "The armlet" (Valaya) should be of the same size as the lingam, and should have its outer surface made rough with globules.

2). "The couple" (Sanghati) is formed of two armlets.

3). "The bracelet" (Chudaka) is made by joining three or more armlets, until they come up to the required length of the lingam.

4). "The single bracelet" is formed by wrapping a single wire around the lingam, according to its dimensions.

5). The Kantuka or Jalaka is a tube open at both ends, with a hole through it, outwardly rough and studded with soft globules, and made to fit the side of the yoni, and tied to the waist.

When such a thing cannot be obtained, then a tube made of the wood apple, or tubular stalk of the bottle gourd, or a reed made soft with oil and extracts of plants, and tied to the waist with strings may be made use of, as also a row of soft pieces of wood tied together.

The above are the things that can be used in connection with or in the place of the lingam.

The people of the southern countries think that true sexual pleasure cannot be obtained without perforating the lingam, and they therefore cause it to be pierced like the lobes of the ears of an infant pierced for earrings.

Now, when a young man perforates his lingam he should pierce it with a sharp instrument, and then stand in water so long as the blood continues to flow. At night he should engage in sexual intercourse, even with vigour, so as to clean the hole. After this he should continue to wash the hole with decoctions, and increase the size by putting into it small pieces of cane, and the wrightia anti-dysenterica, and thus gradually enlarging the orifice. It may also be washed with liquorice mixed with honey, and the size of the hole increased by the fruit stalks of the sima-patra plant. The hole should also be annointed with a small quantity of oil.

In the hole made in the lingam a man may put Apadravyas of various forms, such as the "round", the "round on one side", the "wooden mortar", the "flower", the "armlet", the "bone of the heron", "the goad of the elephant", the "collection of eight balls", the "lock of hair", the "place where four roads meet", and other things named according to their forms and means of using them. All these

224

Apadravyas should be rough on the outside according to their requirements. The ways of enlarging the lingam must now be related.

When a man wishes to enlarge his lingam, he should rub it with the bristles of certain insects that live in trees, and then, after rubbing it for ten nights with oils, he should again rub it with bristles as before. By continuing to do this a swelling will be gradually produced in the lingam, and he should then lie on a cot, and cause his lingam to hang down through a hole in the cot. After this he should take away all the pain from the swelling by using cool concoctions. The swelling, which is called "Suka", and is often brought about among the people of he Dravida country, lasts for life.

If the lingam is rubbed with the following things, viz., the plant physalis flexuosa, the shavara-kandaka plant, the jalasuka plant, the fruit of the egg plant, the butter of a she-buffalo, the hastri-charma plant, and the juice of the vajrarasa plant, a swelling lasting for one month will be produced.

By rubbing it with oil boiled in the concoctions of the above things, the same effect will be produced, but lasting for six months.

The enlargement of the lingam is also effected by rubbing it or moistening it with oil boiled on a moderate fire along with the seeds of the pomegranite, and the cucumber, the juices of the valuka plant, the hastricharma plant, and the egg-plant.

In addition to the above, other means may be learnt from experienced and confidential persons.

The miscellaneous experiments and recipes are as follows:

a). If a man mixes the powder of the milk hedge plant, and the kantaka plant with the excrement of a monkey and the powdered root of the lanjalika plant, and throws this mixture on a woman, she will not love anybody else afterwards.

b). If a man thickens the juice of the fruits of the cassia fistula, and the eugenia jambolana by mixing them with the powder of the soma plant, the vernonia anthelmintica, the eclipta prostata, and the lohopa-jihirka, and applies this composition to the yoni of a woman, and then has sexual intercourse with her, his love for her will be destroyed.

c). The same effect is produced if a man has connection with a woman who has bathed in the butter-milk of a she-buffalo mixed with the powders of the gopalika plant, the banu-padika plant, and the yellow amaranth.

d). An ointment made of the flowers of the nauclea cadamba, the hog plum, and the eugenia jambolana, and used by a woman, causes her to be disliked by her husband.

e). Garlands made of the above flowers, when worn by the woman, produce the same effect.

f). An ointment made of the fruit of the asteracantha longifolia (kokilaksha) will contract the yoni of a Hastini or elephant woman, and this contraction lasts for one night.

g). An ointment made by pounding the roots of the nelumbrium speciosum, and of the blue lotus, and the powder of the plant physalis flexuosa mixed with ghee and honey, will enlarge the yoni of the Mrigi or deer woman.

h). An ointment made of the fruit of the emblica myrabolans soaked in the milky juice of the milk hedge plant, of the soma plant, the calotropis gigantea, and the juice of the fruit of the veronia anthelmintica, will make the hair white.

i). The juice of the roots of the madayantaka plant, the yellow amaranth, the anjanika plant, the clitoria ternateea, and the shlakshnaparni plant, used as a lotion, will make the hair grow.

j). An ointment made by boiling the above roots in oil, and rubbed in, will make the hair black, and will also gradually restore hair that has fallen off.

k). If lac is saturated seven times in the sweat of the testicle of a white horse, and applied to a red lip, the lip will become white.

l). The colour of the lips can be regained by means of the madayantika and other plants mentioned above under i).

m). A woman who hears a man playing on a reed pipe which has been dressed with the juices of the bahupadika plant, tabernamontana coronaria, the costus speciosus or arabicus, the pinus deodora, the euphorbia antiquorum, the vajra and the kantaka plant, becomes his slave.

n). If food be mixed with the fruit of the thorn apple (Dathura) it causes intoxication.

o). If water be mixed with oil and the ashes of any kind of grass except the kusha grass, it becomes the colour of milk.

p). If yellow myrabolans, the hog plum, the shrawana plant, and the priyangu plant be all pounded together, and applied to iron pots, these pots become red.

q). If a lamp, trimmed with oil extracted from the shrawana and priyangu plants, its wick being made of cloth and the slough of the skins of snakes, is lighted, and long pieces of wood placed near it, those pieces of wood will resemble so many snakes.

r). Drinking the milk of a white cow who has a white calf at her foot is auspicious, produces fame, and preserves life.

s). The blessings of venerable Brahmans, well propitiated, have the same effect. There are also some verses in conclusion:

"Thus have I written in a few words the 'Science of love', after reading the texts of ancient authors, and following the ways of enjoyment mentioned in them."

"He who is acquainted with the true principles of this science pays regard to Dharma, Artha, Kama, and to his own experiences, as well as to the teachings of others, and does not act simply on the dictates of his own desire. As for the errors in the science of love which I have mentioned in this work, on my own authority as an author, I have, immediately after mentioning them, carefully censured and prohibited them."

"An act is never looked upon with indulgence for the simple reason that it is authorised by the science, because it ought to be remembered that it is the intention of the science, that the rules which it contains should only be acted upon in particular cases. After reading and considering the works of Babhravya and other ancient authors, and thinking over the meaning of the rules given by them, the Kama Sutra was composed, according to the precepts of Holy Writ, for the benefit of the world, by Vatsyayana, while leading the life of a religious student, and wholly engaged in the contemplation of the Deity."

"This work is not intended to be used merely as an instrument for satisfying our desires. A person acquainted with the true principles of this science, and who preserves his Dharma, Artha, and Kama, and has regard for the practices of the people, is sure to obtain the mastery over his senses."

227

"In short, an intelligent and prudent person, attending to Dharma and Artha, and attending to Kama also, without becoming the slave of his passions, obtains success in everything that he may undertake."

Concluding remarks

Thus ends, in seven parts, the Kama Sutra of Vatsyayana, which might otherwise be called a treatise on men and women, their mutual relationship, and connection with each other.

It is a work that should be studied by all, both old an young; the former will find in it real truths, gathered by experience, and already tested by themselves, while the latter will derive the great advantage of learning things, which some perhaps may otherwise never learn at all, or which they may only learn when it is too late ("too late" those immortal words of Mirabeau) to profit by the learning.

It can also be fairly commended to the student of social science and of humanity, and above all to the student of those early ideas, which have gradually filtered down through the sands of time, and which seem to prove that the human nature of to-day is much the same as the human nature of the long ago. It has been said of Balzac (the great, if not the greatest of French novelists) that he seemed to have inherited a natural and intuitive perception of the feelings of men and women, and has described them with an analysis worthy of a man of science. The author of the present work must also have had a considerable knowledge of humanities. Many of his remarks are so full of simplicity and truth, that they have stood the test of time, and stand out still as clear and true as when they were first written, some eighteen hundred years ago.

As a collection of facts, told in plain and simple language, it must be remembered that in those early days there was apparently no idea of embellishing the work, either with a literary style, a flow of language, or a quantity of superfluous padding. The author tells the world what he knows in very concise language, without any attempt to produce an interesting story. From his facts how many novels could be written! Indeed much of the matter contained in Parts III. IV. V. and VI., has formed the basis of many of the stories and the tales of past centuries.

There will be found in Part VII., some curious recipes. Many of them appear to be as primitive as the book itself, but in later works of the same nature these recipes and prescriptions appear to have increased, both as regards quality and quantity. In the Anunga Runga or "The Stage of Love", mentioned at page 3 of the Preface in Part I., there are found no less than thirty-three different subjects for which one hundred and thirty recipes and prescriptions are given.

As the details may be interesting, these subjects are described as follows:

1. For hastening the paroxysm of the woman.

2. For delaying the orgasm of the man.

3. Aphrodisiacs.

4. For thickening and enlarging the lingam, rendering it sound and strong hard and lusty.

5. For narrowing and contracting the yoni.

6. For perfuming the yoni.

7. For removing and destroying the hair of the body.

8. For removing the sudden stopping of the monthly ailment.

9. For abating the immoderate appearance of the monthly ailment.

10. For purifying the womb.

11. For causing pregnancy.

12. For preventing miscarriage and other accidents.

13. For ensuring easy labour and ready deliverance.

14. For limiting the number of children.

15. For thickening and beautifying the hair.

16. For obtaining a good black colour to it.

17. For whitening and bleaching it.

18. For renewing it.

19. For clearing the skin of the face from eruptions that break out and leave black spots upon it.

20. For removing the black colour of the epidermis.

21. For enlarging the breasts of women.

22. For raising and hardening pendulous breasts.

23. For giving a fragrance to the skin.

24. For removing the evil savour of perspiration.

25. For anointing the body after bathing.

26. For causing a pleasant smell to the breath.

27. Drugs and charms for the purposes of fascinating, overcoming, and subduing either men or women.

28. Recipes for enabling a woman to attract and preserve her husband's love.

29. Magical collyriums for winning love and friendship.

30. Prescriptions for reducing other persons to submission.

31. Philter pills, and other charms.

32. Fascinating incense, or fumigation.

33. Magical verses which have the power of fascination.

Of the one hundred and thirty recipes given, many of them are absurd, but not more perhaps than many of the recipes and prescriptions in use in Europe not so very long ago. Love-philters, charms, and herbal remedies have been, in early days, as freely used in Europe as in Asia, and doubtless some people believe in them still in many places.

And now, one word about the author of the work, the good old sage Vatsyayana. It is much to be regretted that nothing can be discovered about his life, his belongings, and his surroundings. And the end of Part VII. he states that he wrote the work while leading the life of a religious student (probably at Benares) and while wholly engaged in the contemplation of the deity. He must have arrived at a certain age at that time, for throughout he gives us the benefit of his experience, and of his opinions, and these bear the stamp of age rather than youth; indeed the work could hardly have been written by a young man.

In a beautiful verse of the Vedas of the Christians it has been said of the peaceful dead, that they rest from their labours, and that their works do follow them. Yes indeed, the works of men of genius do follow them, and remain as a lasting treasure. And though there may be disputes and discussions about the immortality of the body or the soul, nobody can deny the immortality of genius which ever remains as a bright and guiding star to the struggling humanities of succeeding ages. This work, then, which has stood the test of centuries, has placed Vatsyayana among the immortals, and on This, and on Him no better elegy or eulogy can be written than the following lines:

"So long as lips shall kiss, and eyes shall see,
So long lives This, and This gives life to Thee."

Contents of the work

237

239

The Perfumed Garden
of
Cheikh Nefzaoui

Note to the 1866 Edition

The *Perfumed Garden* was translated into French before the year 1850, by a Staff Officer of the French army in Algeria. An autograph edition, printed in the italic character, was printed in 1876, but, as only twenty-five copies are said to have been made, the book is both rare and costly, while, from the peculiarity of its type, it is difficult and fatiguing to read. An admirable reprint has, however, been recently issued in Paris, with the translator's notes and remarks, revised and corrected by the light of the fuller knowledge of Algeria which has been acquired since the translation was made. From that last edition the present translation (an exact and literal one) has been made, and it is the first time that the work – one of the most remarkable of its kind – has appeared in the English language.

Notes of the translator
Respecting the Cheikh Nefzaoui

The name of the Cheikh has become known to posterity as the author of this work, which is the only one attributed to him.

In spite of the subject-matter of the book and the manifold errors found in it, and caused by the negligence and ignorance of the copyists, it is manifest that this treatise comes from the pen of a man of great erudition, who had a better knowledge in general of literature and medicine than is commonly found with Arabs.

According to the historical notice contained in the first leaves of the manuscript, and notwithstanding the apparent error respecting the name of the Bey who was reigning in Tunis, it may be presumed that this work was written in the beginning of the sixteenth century, about the year 925 of the Hegira.

As regards the birthplace of the author, it may be taken for granted, considering that the Arabs habitually joined the name of their birthplace to their own, that he was born at Nefzaoua, a town situated in the district of that name on the shore of the lake Sebkha Melrir, in the south of the kingdom of Tunis.

The Cheikh himself records that he lived in Tunis, and it is most probable the book was written in that city. According to tradition, a particular motive induced him to undertake a work entirely at variance with his simple tastes and retired habits.

His knowledge of law and literature, as well as of medicine, having been reported to the Bey of Tunis, this ruler wished to invest him with the office of cadi, although he was unwilling to occupy himself with public functions.

As he, however, desired not to give the Bey cause for offence, whereby he might have incurred danger, he merely requested a short delay, in order to be able to finish a work which he had in hand.

This having been granted, he set himself to compose the treatise which was then occupying his mind, and which, becoming known, drew so much attention upon the author, that it became henceforth impossible to confide to him functions of the nature of those of a cadi.

But this version, which is not supported by any authenticated proof, and which represents the Cheikh Nefzaoui as a man of light morals, does not seem to be admissible. One need only glance at the book to be convinced that its author was animated by the most praiseworthy intentions, and that, far from being in fault, he deserves gratitude for the services he has rendered to humanity. Contrary to the habits of the arabs, there exists no commentary on this book; the reason may, perhaps be found in the nature of the subject of which it treats, and which may have frightened, unnecessarily, the serious and the studious. I say unnecessarily, because this book, more than any other, ought to have commentaries; grave questions are treated in it, and open out a large field for work and meditation.

What can be more important, in fact, than the study of the principles upon which rest the happiness of man and woman, by reason of their mutual relations; relations which are themselves dependent upon character, health, temperament and the constitution, all of which it is the duty of philosophers to study. I have endeavoured to rectify this omission by notes, which, incomplete as I know them to be, will still, to a certain point, serve for guidance.

In doubtful and difficult cases, and where the ideas of the author did not seem to be clearly set out, I have not hesitated to look for enlightenment to the savants of sundry confessions, and by their kind assistance many difficulties, which I believed insurmountable, were conquered. I am glad to render them here my thanks.

Amongst the authors who have treated of similar subjects, there is not one that can be entirely compared with the Cheikh; for his book reminds you, at the same time, of Aretin, of the book *Conjugal Love*, and of Rabelais; the resemblance to this last is sometimes so striking that I could not resist the temptation to quote, in several places, analogous passages.

But what makes this treatise unique as a book of its kind, is the seriousness with which the most lascivious and obscene matters are presented. It is evident that the author is convinced of the importance of this subject, and that the desire to be of use to his fellow-men is the sole motive of his efforts.

With the view to give more weight to his recommendations, he does not hesitate to multiply his religious citations, and in many cases invokes even the authority of the Koran, the most sacred book of the Mussulmans.

It may be assumed that this book, without being exactly a compilation, is not entirely due to the genius of the Cheikh Nefzaoui, and that several parts may have been borrowed from Arabian and Indian writers. For instance, all the record of Moçailama and of Chedja is taken from the work of Mohammed ben Djerir el Taberi; the description of the different positions for coition, as well as the movements applicable to them, are borrowed from Indian works; finally, the book of *Birds and Flowers*, by Azeddine el Mocadecci, seems to have been consulted with respect to the interpretation of dreams. But an author certainly is to be commended for having surrounded himself with the lights of former savants, and it would be ingratitude not to acknowledge the benefit which his books have conferred upon people who were still in their infancy to the art of love.

It is only to be regretted that this work, so complete in many respects, is defective in so far as it makes no mention of a custom too common with the Arabs not to deserve particular attention. I speak of the taste so universal with the old Greeks and Romans, namely, the preference they give to a boy before a woman, or even to treat the latter as a boy.

There might have been given on this subject sound advice as well with regard to the pleasures mutually enjoyed by the women called *tribades*. The same reticence has been observed by the author with regard to *bestiality*. Nevertheless he does speak, in one story (i.e. *The History of Zohra*, in the twenty-first and concluding chapter of the work), of the mutual caresses of two women; and he relates an anecdote concerning a woman who provoked the caresses of an ass [which, as explained in the Introduction, has been eliminated from the present edition], thus revealing that he knew of such matters.

Lastly, the Cheikh does not mention the pleasures which the mouth or the hand of a pretty woman can give, nor the *cunnilinges*.

What may have been the motive for these omissions? The author's silence cannot be attributed to ignorance, for in the course of his work he has given proofs of an erudition too extended and various to permit a suspicion of his knowledge. Should we look for the cause of this gap to the contempt which the Mussulman in reality feels for woman, and owing to which he may think that it would be degrading to his dignity as a man to descend to caresses otherwise regulated than by the laws of nature? Or did the author perhaps, avoid the mention of similar matter out of fear that he might be suspected of sharing tastes which, many people look upon as depraved?

However this may be, the book contains much useful information and a large number of curious cases, and I have undertaken the translation because, as the Cheikh Nefzaoui says in his preamble: "I swear before God, certainly! the knowledge of this book is necessary. It will be only the shamefully ignorant, the enemy of all science, who does not read it, or who turns it into ridicule."

The perfumed Garden

Introduction

General remarks about coition

Praise be given to God, who has placed man's greatest pleasure in the natural parts of woman, and has destined the natural parts of man to afford the greatest enjoyment to woman.

He had not endowed the parts of woman with any pleasurable or satisfactory feeling until the same have been penetrated by the instrument of the male; and likewise the sexual organs of man know neither rest nor quietness until they have entered those of the female.

Hence the mutual operation. There takes place between the two actors wrestling, intertwinings, a kind of animated conflict. Owing to the contact of the lower parts of the two bellies, the enjoyment soon comes to pass. The man is at work as with a pestle, while the woman seconds him by lascivious movements; finally comes the ejaculation.

The kiss on the mouth, on the two cheeks, upon the neck, as well as the sucking of fresh lips, are gifts of God, destined to provoke erection at the favourable moment. God also was it who has embellished the chest of the woman with breasts, has furnished her with a double chin, and has given brilliant colours to her cheeks.

He has also gifted her with eyes that inspire love, and with eyelashes like polished blades.

He has furnished her with a rounded belly and a beautiful navel, and with majestic *buttocks*; and all these wonders are borne up by the thighs. It is between these that God has placed the arena of the combat; when this is provided with ample flesh, it resembles the head of a lion. It is called *vulva*. Oh! how many heroes!

God has furnished this object with a mouth, a tongue, two lips; it is like the impression of the hoof of the gazelle in the sands of the desert.

The whole is supported by two marvellous columns, testifying to the might and the wisdom of God; they are not too long nor too short; and they are graced with knees, calves, ankles, and heels, upon which rest precious rings.

Then the Almighty has plunged woman into a sea of splendours, of voluptuousness, and of delights, and covered her with precious *clothing*, with brilliant girdles and clothing provoking smiles.

So let us praise and exalt him who has created woman and her beauties, with her appetising body; who has given her hair, a beautiful figure, a bosom with breasts which are swelling, and amorous ways, which awaken desires.

The Master of the Universe has bestowed upon them the empire of seduction; all men, weak or strong, are subjected to the weakness for the love of woman. The state of humility in which are the hearts of those who love and are separated from the object of their love, makes their hearts burn with love's fire; they are oppressed with a feeling of servitude, contempt and misery; they suffer under the vicissitudes of their passion: and all this as a consequence of their burning desire of contact.

I, the servant of God, am thankful to him that no one can help falling in love with beautiful women, and that no one can escape the desire to possess them, neither by change, nor flight, nor separation.

I testify that there is only one God, and that he has no associate. I shall adhere to this precious testimony to the day of the last judgment.

I likewise testify as to our lord and master, Mohammed, the servant and ambassador of God, the greatest of the prophets (the benediction and pity of God be with him and with his family and disciples!) I keep prayers and benedictions for the day of retribution, that terrible moment.

The origin of this work

I have written this magnificent work after a small book called *The Torch of the World*, which treats of the mysteries of pro creation.

This latter work came to the knowledge of the Vizir of our master Abd-el-Aziz, the ruler of Tunis.

This illustrious Vizir was his poet, his companion, his friend and private secretary. He *gave good advice*, true, sagacious and wise the most learned man of his time, and well acquainted with all things. He called himself Mohammed ben Ouana ez Zonaoui, and traced his origin from Zonaoua. He had been brought up at Algiers, and in that town our master Abd-el-Aziz el Hafsi had made his acquaintance.

On the day when Algiers was taken, that ruler fled with him to Tunis (which land may God preserve in his power till the day of resurrection), and named him his Grand Vizir.

When the above mentioned book came into his hands, he sent for me, and pressed me to come and see him. I went forthwith to his house, and he received me most honorably.

Three days after he came to me, and showing me my book, said, "This is your work." Seeing me blush, he added, "You need not be ashamed; everything you have said in it is true; no one need be shocked at your words. Moreover, you are not the first who has treated this matter; and I swear by God that it is necessary to know this book. It is only the shameless bore and the enemy of all science who will not read it, or make fun of it. But there are other things which you will have to *rite* about yet." I asked him what these things were, and he answered, "I wish that you would add to the work a supplement, treating of the remedies of which you have said nothing, and adding all the relevant facts omitting nothing. You will describe in the same the motives of the act of procreation, as well as the matters that prevent it. You will mention the means for undoing stays, and the way to increase the size of the virile member, when too small, and to make it resplendent. You will further cite those means which remove the unpleasant smells from the armpits and the natural parts of women, and those which will contract those parts. You will further speak of pregnancy, so as to make your book perfect and wanting in nothing. And, finally, you will have done your work, if your book satisfy all wishes."

I replied to the Vizir: "Oh, my master, all you have said here ist not difficult to do, if it is the pleasure of God on high."

I forthwith went to work on the composition of this book, imploring the assistance of God (may he pour his blessing on his prophet, and may happiness and pity be with him).

I have called this work *The Perfumed Garden for the Soul's Recreation (Er Roud el Âater p'nezaha el Khater).*

And we pray to God, who directs everything for the best (and there is no other God than He, and there is nothing good that does not come from Him), to lend us His help, and lead us in good ways; for there is no power nor joy but in the high and mighty God.

I have divided this book into twenty-one chapters, in order to make it easier reading for the *taleb* (student) who wishes to learn, and to facilitate his search for what he wants. Each chapter relates to a particular subject, be it physical, or anecdotal, or treating of the wiles and deceits of women.

I

Concerning praiseworthy men

Learn, o vizir (God's blessing be upon you), that there are different sorts of men and women; that amongst these are those who are worthy of praise, and those who deserve reproach.

When a meritorious man finds himself near to women, his member grows, gets strong, vigorous and hard; he is not quick to ejaculate, and after the trembling caused by the emission of the sperm, he is soon stiff again.

Such a man is liked and appreciated by women; this is because the woman loves the man only for the sake of coition. His member should, therefore, be of ample dimensions and length. Such a man ought to be broad in the chest, and heavy in the buttocks; he should know how to regulate his emission, be easily aroused; his member should reach to the end of the canal of the female, and completely fill the same in all its parts. Such a one will be well beloved by women, for, as the poet says:

I have seen women trying to find in young men
The durable qualities which grace the man of full power,
The beauty, the enjoyment, the reserve, the strength,

257

The full-formed member providing a lengthened coition,
A heavy buttocks, a slowly coming emission,
A light chest, as it were floating upon them;
The spermal ejaculation slow to arrive, so as
To furnish a long drawn-out enjoyment.
His member soon to be prone again for erection,
To ply the plane again and again and again on their vulvas,
Such is the man whose devotion gives pleasure to women,
And who will ever stand high in their esteem.

Qualities which women are looking for in men

The tale goes, that on a certain day, Abd-el-Melik ben Merouane, went to see Leilla, his mistress, and put various questions to her. Amongst other things, he asked her what were the qualities which women looked for in men.
Leilla answered him: "Oh, my master, they must have cheeks like ours." "And hair like ours; finally they should be like to you, O prince of believers, for, surely, if a man is not strong and rich he will obtain nothing from women."

Various lengths of the virile member

The virile member, to please women, must have at most a length of the breadth of twelve fingers, or three handbreadths, and at least six fingers, or a hand and a half breadth.
There are men with members of twelve fingers, or three hand-breadths; others of ten fingers, or two and a half hands. And others measure eight fingers, or two hands. A man whose member is of less dimensions cannot please women.

The use of perfumes, by man as well as by woman, excites to the act of copulation. The woman, inhaling the perfumes employed by the man, becomes intoxicated; and the use of scents has often proved a strong help to man, and assisted him in getting possession of a woman.

On this subject it is told of Moçailama, the impostor, the son of Kaiss (whom God may curse!), that he pretended to have the gift of prophecy, and imitated the Prophet of God (blessings and salutations to him). For which reasons he and a great number of Arabs have incurred the wrath of the Almighty.

Moçailama, the son of Kaiss, the impostor, misconstrued likewise the Koran by his lies and deceit; and on the subject of a chapter of the Koran, which the angel Gabriel (Hail be to him) had revealed to the Prophet (the mercy of God and hail to him), people of bad faith had gone to see Moçailama, who had told them, "To me also has the angel Gabriel revealed a similar chapter."

He derided the chapter headed "The Elephant", saying, "In this chapter of the Elephant I see the elephant. What is the elephant? What does it mean? What is this animal? It has a tail and a long trunk. Surely it is a creation of our God, the magnificent."

The chapter of the Koran named the *Kouter* was also a subject of controversy. He said, "We have given you precious stones for yourself, and preference to any other man, but take care not to be proud of them."

Moçailama thus perverted various chapters in the Koran by his lies and his impostures.

He had been at his work when he heard the Prophet (the salutation and mercy of God be with him) spoken of. He heard that after he had placed his venerable hands upon a bald head, the hair had immediately grown; that when he spat into a pit, water came in abundantly, and that the dirty water turned at once clean and good for drinking; that when he spat into an eye that was blind or blurred, the sight was at once restored to it, and when he placed his hands upon the head of a child, saying, "Live for a century", the child lived to be a hundred years old. When the disciples of Moçailama saw these things or heard speak of them, they came to him and said, "Have you no knowledge for Mohammed and his doings?" He replied, "I shall do better than that."

Now, Moçailama was an enemy of God, and when he put his luckless hand on the head of someone who had not much hair, the man was at once quite bald; when he spat into a well with a scanty supply of water, sweet as it was, it was turned dirty by the will of God; if he spat into a ailing eye, that eye lost its sight at once, and when he laid his hand upon the head of an infant, saying, "Live a hundred years", the infant died within an hour.

See, brothers, what happens to those whose eyes remain closed to the light, and who are deprived of the assistance of the Almighty!

And these were the actions of the Beni-Temim, called *Chedjâ el Temimia,* who pretended to be a prophetess. She had heard of Moçailama, and he likewise of her.

This woman was powerful, for the Beni-Temim form a numerous tribe. She said, "Prophecy cannot belong to two persons. Either he is a prophet, and then I and my disciples will follow his laws, or I am a prophetess, and then he and his disciples will follow my laws."

This happened after the death of the Prophet (the salutation and mercy of God be with him).

Chedjâ then wrote to Moçailama a letter, in which she told him, "It is not proper that two persons should at one and the same time profess prophecy; it is for one only to be a prophet. We will meet, we and our disciples, and examine each other. We shall discuss about that which has come to us from God (the Koran), and we will follow the laws of him who shall be acknowledged as the true prophet."

She then closed her letter and gave it to a messenger, saying to him: "Go with this letter, to Yamama, and give it to Moçailama ben Kaiss. I shall follow you, with the army."

Next day the prophetess mounted her horse, with her cavalry and followed the trail of her envoy. When the latter arrived at Moçailama's place, he greeted him and gave him the letter.

Moçailama opened and read it, and understood its contents. He was dismayed, and began to discuss with the people of his *goum,* one after another, but he did not see anything in their advice or in their views that could rid him of his embarrassment.

While he was so perplexed, one of the superior men of his *goum* came forward and said to him: "Oh, Moçailama, calm your soul and cool your eyes. I will give you the advice of a father to his son."

Moçailama said to him: "Speak, and may your words be true."

And the other one said: "Tomorrow morning erect outside the city a tent of coloured brocades, provided with silk furniture of all sorts. Fill the tent afterwards with a variety of different perfumes, amber, musk, and all sorts of scents, as rose, orange flowers, jonquils, jessamine, hyacinth, carnation and other plants. This done, have placed there several and other plants. This done, have placed there several gold censers filled with green aloes, ambergris, *nedde* and so on. Then fix the hangings so that none of these perfumes can escape out of the tent. Then, when you find the vapour strong enough to impregnate water, sit down on your throne, and send for the prophetess to come and see you in the tent, where she will be alone with you. When you are thus together there, and she inhales the perfumes, she will delight in the same, all her bones will be gently relaxed, and finally she will be swooning. When you see her thus far gone, ask her to grant you her favours; she will not hesitate to offer them. Having once possessed her, you will be freed of the embarrassment caused to you by her and her *goum*."

Moçailama exclaimed: "You have spoken well. As God lives, your advice is good and well thought out." And he had everything arranged accordingly.

When he saw that the perfumed vapour was dense enough to impregnate the water in the tent he sat down upon his throne and sent for the prophetess. On her arrival he gave orders to admit her into the tent; she entered and remained alone with him. He engaged her in conversation.

While Moçailama spoke to her she lost all her presence of mind, and became embarrassed an confused.

When he saw her in that state he knew that she desired intercourse, and he said: "Come, rise and let me have possession of you; this place has been prepared for that purpose. If you like you may lie on your back, or you can place yourself on all fours, or kneel as in prayer, with your brow touching the ground, and your buttocks in the air, forming a tripod. Say which position you prefer, and you shall be satisfied."

The prophetess answered, "I want it done in all ways. Let the revelation of God descend upon me, O Prophet of the Almighty."

He at once hurled himself upon her, and enjoyed her as he liked. She then said to him, "When I am gone from here, ask my *goum* to give me to you in marriage". When she had left the tent and met her disciples, they said to her, "What is the result of the conference, O prophetess of God?" and she replied, "Moçailama has shown me what has been revealed to him, and I found it to be the truth, so obey him."

Then Moçailama asked her in marriage from the *goum,* which was granted to him. When the *goum* asked about the marriage-dowry of his future wife, he told them, "I excuse you from saying the prayer '*aceur*'" (which is said at three or four o'clock). Ever from that time the Beni-Temim do not pray at that hour; and when they are asked the reason, they answer, "It is on account of our prophetess; she only knows the way to the truth." And, in fact, they recognized no other prophet.

On this subject a poet has said:

For us a female prophet has arisen;
Her laws we follow; for the rest of mankind
The prophets that appeared were always men.

The death of Moçailama was foretold by the prophecy of Abou Beker (to whom God be good). He was, in fact, killed by Zeid ben Khettab. Other people say it was done by Ouhcha, one of his disciples. God only knows whether it was Ouhcha. He himself says on this point, "I have killed in my ignorance the best of men, Haman ben Abd el Mosaleb, and then I killed the worst of men, Moçailama. I hope that God will pardon one of these actions in consideration of the other."

The meaning of these words, "I have killed the best of men" is, that Ouhcha, before having yet known the prophet, had killed Hamza (to whom God be good), and having afterwards embraced Islamism, he killed Moçailama.

As regards Chedja et Temimia, she repented by God's grace, and took to the Islamitic faith; she married one of the Prophet's followers (God be good to her husband).

Thus finishes the story.

The man who deserves favours is, in the eyes of women, the one who is anxious to please them. He must be of good presence, excel in beauty those around him, be of good shape and well-formed proportions; true and sincere in his speech with women; he must likewise be generous and brave, not boastful, and pleasant in conversation. A slave to his promise, he must always keep his word, ever speak the truth, and do what he has said.

The man who boasts of his relations with women, of their acquaintance and good will to him, is a dastard. He will be spoken of in the next chapter.

There it a story that once there lived a king named Mamoum, who had a court fool of the name of Bahloul, who amused the princes and Vizirs.

One day this buffoon appeared before the King, who was amusing himself. The King bade him to sit down, and then asked him, turning away, "Why have you come, O son of a bad woman?"

Bahloul answered, "I have come to see what has come to our Lord, whom may God make victorious."

"And what has come to you?" replied the King, "and how are you getting on with your new and with your old wife?" For Bahloul, not content with one wife, had married a second one.

"I am not happy", he answered, "neither with the old one, nor with the new one; and moreover poverty over-powers me."

The King said, "Can you recite any verses on this subject?"

The buffoon having answered in the affirmative, Mamoum commanded him to recite those he knew, and Bahloul began as follows:

Poverty holds me in chains; misery torments me:

I am being scourged with all misfortunes;

Ill luck has cast me in trouble and peril,

And has drawn upon me the contempt of man.

God does not favour a poverty like mine;

That is reproachful in every one's eyes
Misfortune and misery for a long time
Have held me tightly; and no doubt of it
My dwelling house will soon not know me more.
Mamoum said to him, "Where are you going to?"
He replied, "To God and his Prophet, O prince of the believers."
"That is good!" said the King, "those who take refuge in God and his Prophet,
and then in us, will be made welcome. But can you now tell me some more verses
about your two wives, and about what comes to pass with them?"
"Certainly", said Bahloul.
"Then let us hear what you have to say!"
Bahloul then began his poem:
By reason of my ignorance I have married two wives –
And why do you complain, O husband of two wives?
I said to myself, I shall be like a lamb between them;
I shall take my pleasure upon the bosoms of my two sheep,
And I have become like a ram between two female jackals,
Days follow upon days, and nights upon nights,
And their yoke bears me down during both days and nights.
If I am kind to one, the other gets vexed.
And so I cannot escape from these two furies.
If you want to live well and with a free heart,
And with your hands unclenched, then do not marry.
If you must wed, then marry one wife only:
One alone is enough to satisfy two armies.
When Mamoum heard these words he began to laugh, till he nearly tumbled
over. Then, as a proof of his kindness, he gave to Bahloul his golden robe, a most
beautiful garment.
Bahloul went in high spirits towards the dwelling of the Grand Vizir. Just then
Hamdonna looked from the height of her palace in that direction, and saw him.
She said to her negress, "By the God of the temple of Mecca! There is Bahloul
dressed in a fine gold-worked robe! How can I manage to get possession of it?"

The negress said, "Oh, my mistress, you would not know how to get hold of that robe."

Hamdonna answered, "I have thought of a trick whereby to achieve my ends, and I shall get the robe from him."

"Bahloul is a sly man", replied the negress. "People think generally that they can make fun of him; but, for God, it is he who really makes fun of them. Give up the idea, mistress mine, and take care that you do not fall into the snare which you intend setting for him."

But Hamdonna said again, "It must be done!" She then sent her negress to Bahloul, to tell him that he should come to her.

He said, "By the blessing of God, to him who calls you, you shall answer", and went to Hamdonna.

Hamdonna welcomed him and said: "Oh, Bahloul, I believe you come to hear me sing." He replied: "Most certainly, oh, my mistress! You have a marvellous gift for singing."

"I also think that after having listened to my songs, you will be pleased to take some refreshments."

"Yes", said he.

Then she began to sing admirably, so as to make people who listened die with love.

After Bahloul had heard her sing, refreshments were served; he ate, and he drank. Then she said to him: "I do not know why, but I fancy you would gladly take off your robe, to make me a present of it." And Bahloul answered: "Oh, my mistress! I have sworn to give it to her to whom I have done as a man does to a woman."

"Do you know what that is, Bahloul?" said she.

"Do I know it?" replied he. "*I*, who am instructing God's creatures in that art? It is I who make them copulate in love, who initiate them in the delights a female can give, show them how one must caress a woman, and what will excite and satisfy her. Oh, my mistress, who should know the art of coition if it is not I?"

Hamdonna was the daughter of Mamoum, and the wife of the Grand Vizir. She was endowed with the most perfect beauty; of a superb figure and harmonious form. No one in her time surpassed her in grace and perfection. Heroes on seeing her became humble and submissive, and looked down to the ground for fear of temptation, so many charms and perfections had God lavished on her. Those who looked steadily at her were troubled in their mind, and oh! how many heroes imperilled themselves for her sake. For this very reason Bahloul had always avoided meeting her for fear of succumbing to the temptation; and, fearing for his peace of mind, had never, until then, been in her presence.

Bahloul began to converse with her. Now he looked at her and soon bent his eyes to the ground, fearful of not being able to control his passion. Hamdonna burned with desire to have the robe, and he would not give it up without being paid for it.

"What price do you demand", she asked. To which he replied, "Coition, O apple of my eye."

"You know what that is, O Bahloul?" said she.

"By God", he cried; "no man knows women better than I; they are the occupation of my life. No one has studied all their concerns more than I. I know what they are fond of; for learn, oh, lady mine, that men choose different occupations according to their genius and their bent. The one takes, the other gives; this one sells, the other buys. My only thought is of love and of the possession of beautiful women. I heal those that are lovesick, and bring a solace to their thirsting vaginas."

Hamdonna was surprised at his words and the sweetness of his language. "Could you recite me some verses on this subject?" she asked.

"Certainly", he answered.

"Very well, O Bahloul, let me hear what you have to say."

Bahloul recited as follows:

Men are divided according to their affairs and doings;

Some are always in spirits and joyful, others in tears.

There are those whose life is restless and full of misery,

While, on the contrary, others are steeped in good fortune,

Always in luck's happy way, and favoured in all things.

I alone a indifferent to all such matters.

What care I for Turkomans, Persians, and Arabs?
My whole ambition is in love and coition with women,
No doubt nor mistake about that!
If my member is without vulva, my state becomes frightful,
My heart then burns with a fire which cannot be quenched.
Look at my member erect! There it is — admire its beauty!
It calms the heat of love and quenches the hottest fires
By its movement in and out between your thighs.
Oh, my hope and my apple, oh, noble and generous lady,
If one time will not suffice to appease thy fire,
I shall do it again, so as to give satisfaction;
No one may reproach you, for all the world does the same.
But if you choose to deny me, then send me away!
Chase me away from thy presence without any fear or remorse!
Yet reflect, and speak and augment not my trouble,
But, in the name of God, forgive me and do not reproach me.
While I am here let thy words be kind and forgiving.
Let them not fall upon me like sword-blades, keen and cutting!
Let me come to you and do not repel me.
Let me come to you like one that brings drink to the thirsty;
Hasten and let my hungry eyes look at thy bosom.
Do not withhold from me love's joys, and do not be bashful,
Give yourself up to me — I shall never cause you trouble,
Even were you to fill me with sickness from head to foot.
I shall always remain as I am, and you as you are,
Knowing that I am the servant, and you are the mistress ever.
Then shall our love be veiled? It shall be hidden for all time,
For I keep it a secret and I shall be mute and muzzled.
It is by God's will that everything happen,
And he has filled me with love; but today my luck is ill.
While Hamdonna was listening she nearly swooned, and set herself to examine
the member of Bahloul, which stood erect like a column between his thighs.

269

Now she said to herself: "I shall give myself up to him", and now, "No I will not." During this uncertainty she felt a yearning for pleasure deep within her parts privy; and Eblis made flow from her natural parts a moisture, the fore-runner of pleasure. She then no longer combated her desire to have intercourse with him, and reassured herself by the thought: "If this Bahloul, after having had his pleasure with me, should divulge it no one will believe his words."

She requested him to remove his robe and to come into her room, but Bahloul replied: "I shall not undress till I have satisfied my desire, O apple of my eye." Then Hamdonna rose, trembling with excitement for what was to follow; she undid her girdle, and left the room, Bahloul following her and thinking: "Am I really awake or is this a dream?" He walked after her till she had entered her boudoir. Then she threw herself on a couch of silk, which was rounded on the top like a vault, lifted her clothes up over her thighs, trembling all over, and all the beauty which God had given her was in Bahloul's arms.

Bahloul examined the belly of Hamdonna, round like an elegant cupola, his eyes dwelt upon a navel which was like a pearl in a golden cup; and descending lower down there was a beautiful piece of nature's workmanship, and the whiteness and shape of her thighs surprised him.

Then he pressed Hamdonna in a passionate embrace, and soon saw the animation leave her face; she seemed almost unconscious. She had lost her head; and holding Bahloul's member in her hands, excited and aroused him more and more.

Bahloul said to her: "Why do I see you so troubled and beside yourself?" And she answered: "Leave me, O son of a debauched women! By God, I am like a mare in heat, and you continue to excite me still more with your words, and what words! They would set any woman on fire, if she was the purest creature in the word. You will insist in making me succumb by your talk and your verses."

Bahloul answered: "Am I then not like your husband?" "Yes", she said, "but a woman becomes excited on account of the man, as a mare on account of the horse, whether the man be the husband or not; with this difference, however, that the mare gets lusty only at certain periods of the year, and only then receives the stallion, while a woman can always be aroused by words of love. Both these dispositions have met within me, and, as my husband is absent, make haste, for he will soon be back."

Bahloul replied: "Oh, my mistress, my loins hurt me and prevent me mounting upon you. You take the man's position, and then take my robe and let me depart."

Then he laid himself down in the position the woman takes in receiving a man; and his member was standing up like a column.

Hamdonna threw herself upon Bahloul, took his member between her hands and began to look at it. She was astonished at its size, strength and firmness, and cried: "Here we have the ruin of all women and the cause of many troubles. O Bahloul! I never saw a more beautiful dart than yours!" Still she continued keeping hold of it, and rubbed its head against the lips of her vulva till the latter seemed to say: "O member, come into me."

Then Bahloul inserted his member into the vagina of the Sultan's daughter, and she, settling down upon his engine, allowed it to penetrate entirely into her furnace till nothing more could be seen of it, not the slightest trace, and she said: "How lascivious has God made woman, and how indefatigable after her pleasures." She then gave herself up to an up-and-down dance, moving her bottom like a riddle; to the right and left, and forward and backward; never was there such a dance as this.

The Sultan's daughter continued her ride upon Bahloul's member till the moment of enjoyment arrived, and the contraction of the vulva seemed to pump the member as though by suction; just as an infant sucks the teat of the mother. The climax of enjoyment came to both simultaneously, and each took the pleasure with avidity.

Then Hamdonna seized the member in order to withdraw it, and slowly, slowly she made it come out, saying: "This is the deed of a vigorous man." Then she dried it and her own private parts with a silken kerchief, and rose.

Bahloul also got up and prepared to depart, but she said, "And the robe?"

He answered, "Why, O mistress! You have been riding me, and still want a present?"

"But", said she, "did you not tell me that you could not mount me on account of the pains in your loins?"

"It matters but little", said Bahloul. "The first time it was your turn, the second will be mine, and the price for it will be the robe, and then I will go."

Hamdonna thought to herself, "As he began he may now go on; afterwards he will go away." So she laid herself down, but Bahloul said, "I shall not lie with you unless you undress entirely."

Then she undressed until she was quite naked, and Bahloul fell into an ecstasy on seeing the beauty and perfection of her form. He looked at her magnificent thighs and rebounding navel, at her belly vaulted like an arch, her plump breasts standing out like hyacinths. Her neck was like a gazelle's, the opening of her mouth like a ring, her lips fresh and red like a bloody sabre. Her teeth might have been taken for pearls and her cheeks for roses. Her eyes were black and well slit, and her eyebrows of ebony resembled the rounded flourish of the *letter written* by the hand of a skilful writer. Her forehead was like the full moon in the night.

Bahloul began to embrace her, to suck her lips and to kiss her bosom; he drew her fresh saliva and bit her thighs. So he went on till she was ready to swoon, and could scarcely stammer, and her eyes became veiled. Then he kissed her vulva, and she moved neither hand nor foot. He looked lovingly upon the secret parts of Hamdonna, beautiful enough to attract all eyes with their purple centre. Bahloul cried, 'Oh, the temptation of man!' and still he bit her and kissed her till her desire was roused to its full pitch. Her sighs came quicker, and grasping his member with her hand she made it disappear in her vagina.

Then it was he who moved hard, and she who responded eagerly, the overwhelming pleasure simultaneously calming their fervour.

Then Bahloul got off her, dried his pestle and her mortar, and prepared to retire. But Hamdonna said, "Where is the robe? You mock me, O Bahloul." He answered, "O my mistress, I shall only part with it for a consideration. You have had your dues and I mine. The first time was for you, the second time for me; now the third time shall be for the robe."

This said, he took it off, folded it, and put it in Hamdonna's hands, who, having risen, laid down again on the couch and said, "Do what you like!"

Forthwith Bahloul threw himself upon her, and with one push completely buried his member in her vagina; then he began to work as with a pestle, and she to move her bottom, until both again did flow over at the same time. Then he rose from her side, left his robe, and went. The negress said to Hamdonna, "O my mistress, is it not as I have told you? Bahloul is a bad man, and you could not get the better of him. They consider him as a subject for mockery, but, before God, he is making fun of them. Why would you not believe me?"

Hamdonna turned to her and said, "Do not tire me with your remarks. It came to pass what had to come to pass, and on the opening of each vulva is inscribed the name of the man who is to enter it, right or wrong, for love or for hatred. If Bahloul's name had not been inscribed on my vulva he would never have go into it, had he offered me the universe with all it contains."

As they were talking there came a knock at the door. The negress asked who was there, and in answer the voice of Bahloul said, "It is I." Hamdonna, in doubt as to what the buffoon wanted to do, got frightened. The negress asked Bahloul what he wanted, and received the reply, "Bring me a little water." She went out of the house with a cup full of water. Bahloul drank, and then let the cup slip out of his hands, and it was broken. The negress shut the door upon Bahloul, who sat down on the threshold.

The buffoon being beside to the door, the Vizir, Hamdonna's husband, arrived, who said to him, "Why do I see you here, O Bahloul?" And he answered, "O my lord, I was passing through the street when I was overcome by a great thirst. A negress came and brought me a cup of water. The cup slipped from my hands and got broken. Then our lady Hamdonna took my robe, which the Sultan our Master had given me as payment."

Then said the Vizir, "Let him have his robe." Hamdonna at this moment came out, and her husband asked her whether it was true that she had taken the robe in payment for the cup. Hamdonna then cried, beating her hands together, "What have you done, O Bahloul?" He answered, "I have talked to your husband the language of my folly; talk to him, you, the language of your wisdom." And she, enraptured with the cunning he had displayed, gave him back his robe, and he departed.

273

II

Concerning women who deserve to be praised

Know, O Vizir (and the mercy of God be with you!) that there are women of all sorts; that there are such as are worthy of praise, and such as deserve nothing but contempt.

In order that a woman may be relished by men, she must have a perfect waist, and must be plump and lusty. Her hair will be black, her forehead wide, she will have eyebrows of Ethiopian blackness, large black eyes, with the whites in them very limpid. With cheek of perfect oval, she will have an elegant nose and a graceful mouth; lips and tongue vermilion; her breath will be of pleasant odour, her throat long, her neck strong, her bust and her belly large; her breasts must be full and firm, her belly in good proportion, and her navel well-developed and marked; the lower part of the belly is to be large, the vulva projecting and fleshy, from the point where the hairs grow, to the buttocks; the channel must be narrow and not moist, soft to the touch, and emitting a strong heat and no bad smell; she must have thighs and buttocks, firm the hips large and full, a waist of fine shape, hands and feet of striking elegance, plump arms, and well-developed shoulders. If one looks at a woman with those qualities in front, one is fascinated; if from behind, one dies with pleasure. Looked at sitting, she is a rounded dome; lying, a soft bed: standing, the staff of a standard. When she is walking, her natural parts appear to protrude under her clothing. She speaks and laughs rarely, and never without reason. She never leaves the house, even to see neighbours of her acquaintance. She has no women friends, gives her confidence to nobody, and her husband is her sole reliance. She takes nothing from anyone, except from her husband and her parents. If she sees relatives, she does not meddle with their affairs. She is not treacherous, and has no faults to hide, nor any false excuses. She does not try to entice people. If her husband shows his intention of performing the conjugal rite, she is agreeble to his desires and occasionally even provokes them. She assists him always in his affairs, and is sparing in complaints and tears; she does not laugh or rejoice when she sees her husband moody or sorrowful, but shares his troubles, and wheedles him into good humour, till he is quite content again. She does not surrender herself to anybody but her husband, even if abstinence would kill her. She hides her secret parts, and does not allow them to be seen; she is always elegantly attired, of the utmost personal propriety, and takes care not to let her husband see what might be repugnant to him. She perfumes herself with scents, uses antimony for her toilet, and cleans her teeth with souak. Such a woman is cherished by all men.

The story of the negro Dorérame

The story goes, and God knows its truth, that there was once a powerful King who had a large kingdom, armies and allies. His name was Ali ben Direme. One night, not being able to sleep at all, he called his Vizir, the Chief of the Police, and the Commander of his Guards. They presented themselves before him without delay, and he ordered them to arm themeselves with their swords. They did so at once, and asked him, "What news is there?"

He told them: "Sleep will not come to me; I wish to walk through the town tonight, and I must have you ready at my hand during my round."

"To hear is to obey", they replied.

The King then left, saying: "In the name of God! and may the blessing of the Prophet be with us, and benediction and mercy be with him."

His retinue followed, and accompanied him everywhere from street to street. So they went on, until they heard a noise in one of the streets, and saw a man in the most violent passion stretched on the ground, face downwards, beating his breast with a stone and crying, "Ah there is no longer any justice here below! Is there nobody who will tell the King what is going on in his states?" And he repeated incessantly: "There is no longer any justice! she has disappeared and the whole world is in mourning."

The King said to his attendants, "Bring this man to me quietly, and be careful not to frighten him." They went to him, took him by the hand, and said to him, "Rise and have no fear — no harm will come to you."

To which the man made answer, "You tell me that I shall not come to harm, and have nothing to be afraid of, and still you do not bid me welcome! And you know that the welcome of a believer is a warrant of security and forgiveness. Then, if the believer does not welcome the believer there is certainly ground for fear." He then got up, and went with them towards the King.

The King stood still, hiding his face with his *kaïk*, as also did his attendants. The latter had their swords in their hands, and leant upon them.

When the man had come close to the King, he said, "Greetings be with you, O Man!" The King answered, "I return your greetings, O man!" Then the man, "Why say you 'O Man?'" The King, "And why did you say 'O man?'"

"It is because I do not know your name." "And likewise I do not know yours!" The King then asked him, "What do these words mean I have heard: 'Ah! there is no more justice here below! Nobody tells the King what is going on in his states!' Tell me what has happened to you." "I shall tell it only to that man who can avenge me and free me from oppression and shame, if it so please Almighty God!"

The King said to him, "May God place me at your disposal for your revenge and deliverance from oppression and shame?"

"What I shall now tell you", said the man, "is marvellous and surprising. I loved a woman, who loved me also, and we were united in love. These relations lasted a long while, until an old woman enticed my mistress and took her away to a house of misfortune, shame and debauchery. Then sleep left me; I have lost all my happiness, and I have fallen into the abyss of misfortune."

The King then said to him, "Which is that house of ill repute, and with whom is the woman?"

The man replied, "She is with a negro of the name of Dorérame, who has at his house women beautiful as the moon, the likes of whom the King has not in this place. He has a mistress who has a profound love for him, is entirely devoted to him, and who sends him all he wants in the way of silver, beverages and clothing."

Then the man stopped speaking. The King was much surprised at what he had heard, but the Vizir, who had not missed a word of this conversation, had certainly made out, from what the man had said, that the negro was no other than his own.

The King requested the man to show him the house.

"If I show it you, what will you do?" asked the man.

"You will see what I shall do", said the King. "You will not be able to do anything", replied the man, "for it is a place which must be respected and feared. If you want to enter it by force you will risk death, for its master is formidable because of his strength and courage."

"Show me the place", said the King, "and have no fear." The man answered, "So be it as God will!"

He then rose, and walked before them. They followed him to a wide street, where he stopped in front of a house with tall doors, the walls being on all sides high and inaccessible.

They examined the walls, looking for a place where they might be scaled, but with no result. To their surprise they found the house to be as tightly sealed as a breastplate.

The King, turning to the man, asked him, "What is your name?"

"Omar ben Isad", he replied.

The King said to him, "Omar, are you demented?"

"Yes, my brother", answered he, "if it so pleases God on high!" And turning to the King he added, "May God assist you tonight!"

Then the King, addressing his attendants, said, "Are you determined? Is there one amongst you who could scale these walls?"

"Impossible!" they all replied.

Then said the King, "I myself will scale this wall, so please God on high! but by means of a *method* for which I require your assistance, and if you lend me the same I shall scale the wall, if it pleases God on high."

They said, "What is there to be done?"

"Tell me", said the King, "who is the strongest amongst you." They replied, "The Chief of the Police, who is your *Chaouch*."

The King said, "And who next?"

"The Commander of the Guards."

"And after him, who?" asked the King.

"The Grand Vizir."

Omar listened with astonishment. He knew now that it was the King, and his joy was great.

The King said, "Who is there yet?"

Omar replied, "I, O my master."

The King said to him, "O Omar, you have found out who we are; but do not betray our disguise, and you will be absolved from blame."

"To hear is to obey", said Omar.

The King then said to the *Chaouch*, "Rest your hands against the wall so that your back projects." The *Chaouch* did so.

Then said the King to the commander of the guards, "Mount upon the back of the *Chaouch*." He did so, and stood with his feet on the other man's shoulders.

Then the King ordered the Vizir to mount, and he got on the shoulders of the commander of the guards, and put his hands against the wall.

Then said the King, "O Omar, mount upon the highest place!" And Omar, surprised by this *method*, cried, "May God lend you his help, O our master, and assist you in your just enterprise!" He then got on to the shoulders of the *Chaouch*, and from there upon the back of the Commander of the Guards, and then upon that of the Vizir, and, standing upon the shoulders of the latter, he took the same position as the others. There was now only the King left.

Then the King said, "In the name of God! and his blessing be with the prophet, upon whom be the mercy and salutation of God!" and, placing his hand upon the back of the *Chaouch*, he said, "Have a moment's patience; if I succeed you will be compensated!" He then did the same with the others, until he got upon Omar's back, to whom he also said, "O Omar, have a moment's patience with me, and I shall name you my private secretary. And, of all things, do not move!" Then, placing his feet upon Omar's shoulders, the King could with his hands grasp the terrace; and crying, "In the name of God! may he pour his blessings upon the Prophet, on whom be the mercy and salutation of God!", he made a *leap,* and stood upon the terrace.

Then he said to his attendants, "Descend now from each other's shoulders!" And they got down one after another, and they could not help admiring the ingenious idea of the King, as well as the strength of the *Chaouch* who carried four men at once.

The King then began to look for a place to descend but found *none.* He unrolled his turban, fixed one end with a single knot at the place where he was, and let himself down into the courtyard, which he explored until he found the door in the middle of the house fastened with an enormous lock. The solidity of this lock, and the obstacle it created, gave him a disagreeable surprise. He said to himself, "I am now in difficulty, but all comes from God; it was he who gave me the strength and the idea that brought me here; he will also provide the means for me to return to my companions."

He then set himself to examine the place where he found himself, and counted the chambers one after another. He found seventeen rooms, furnished in different styles, with tapestries and velvet hangings of various colours, from the first to the last.

Examining all round, he saw a place raised by seven steps, from which issued a great noise of voices. He went up to it, saying, "O God! favour my project, and let me come safe and sound out of here."

He mounted the first step, saying, "In the name of God the compassionate and merciful!" Then he began to look at the steps, which were of variously coloured marble – black, red, white, yellow, green and other shades.

Mounting the second step, he said, "He whom God helps is invincible!"

On the third step he said, "With the aid of God the victory is near."

And on the fourth, "I have asked victory of God, who is the most powerful helper."

Finally he mounted the fifth, sixth, and seventh steps, invoking the Prophet (with whom be the mercy and salvation of God).

He then arrived at the curtain hanging at the entrance; it was of red brocade. From there he examined the room, which was bathed in light, filled with many chandeliers, and candles burning in golden candlesticks. In the middle of this saloon played a jet of musk-water. A table-cloth extended from end to end, covered with various meats and fruits.

The saloon contained gilt furniture, the splendour of which dazzled the eye. In fact, everywhere, there were ornaments of all kinds.

On looking closer the King ascertained that round the table-cloth there were twelve maidens and seven women, all like moons; he was astonished at their beauty and grace. There were likewise with them seven negroes, and this sight filled him with surprise. His attention was above all attracted by a woman like the full moon, of perfect beauty, with black eyes, oval cheeks, and a lithe and graceful waist; she humbled the hearts of those who became enamoured of her.

Stupefied by her beauty, the King was as one stunned. He then said to himself, "How is there any getting out of this place? O my spirit, do not give way to love!"

And continuing his inspection of the room, he perceived in the hands of those who were present, glasses filled with wine. They were drinking and eating, and it was easy to see they were overcome with drink.

While the King was pondering how to escape his embarrassment, he heard one of the women saying to one of her companions, calling her by name, "Oh, so and so, rise and light a torch, so that we two can go to bed, for sleep is overpowering us. Come, light the torch, and let us retire to the other room."

They rose and lifted up the curtain to leave the room. The King hid himself to let them pass; then, perceiving that they had left their chamber to do something necessary and obligatory in human beings, he took advantage of their absence, entered their apartment, and hid himself in a cupboard.

Whilst he was in hiding the women returned and shut the doors. Their minds were obscured by the effect of wine; they pulled off all their clothes and began to caress each other mutually. The King said to himself, "Omar has told me the truth about this house of misfortune as an abyss of debauchery."

When the women had fallen asleep the King rose, extinguished the light, undressed, and laid down between the two. He had taken care during their conversation to impress their names on his memory. So he was able to say to one of them, "You, so and so, where have you put the door-keys?" speaking very low.

The woman answered, "Go to sleep, you whore, the keys are in their usual place."

The King said to himself, "There is no might and strength but in God the Almighty and Benevolent!" and was much troubled.

And again he asked the woman about the keys, saying, "Daylight is coming. I must open the doors. There is the sun. I am going to open the house."

And she answered, "The keys are in the usual place. Why do you bother me? Sleep, I say, till it is day."

And again the King said to himself, "There is no might and strength but in God the Almighty and Benevolent, and surely if it were not for the fear of God I should run my sword through her." Then he began again, "Oh, you, so and so!" She said, "What do you want?"

"I am uneasy", said the King, "about the keys; tell me where they are?"

And she answered, "Your hussy! Does your vulva itch for coition? Cannot you do without for a single night? Look! the Vizir's wife has withstood all the entreaties of the negro, and rejected him for six months! Go, the keys are in the negro's pocket. Do not say to him, 'Give me the keys', but say, 'Give me your member.' You know his name is Dorérame."

The King was now silent, for he knew what to do. He waited a short time till the woman was asleep; then he dressed himself in her clothes, and concealed his sword under them; his face he hid under a veil of red silk. Thus dressed he looked like other women. Then he opened the door, stole softly out, and placed himself behind the curtains of the saloon entrance. He saw only some people sitting there; the remainder were asleep.

The King made the following silent prayer, "O my soul, let me follow the right path, and let all those people among whom I find myself be stunned with drunkenness, so that they cannot know the King from his subjects, and God give me strength."

He then entered the saloon saying: "In the name of God!" and he tottered towards the bed of the negro as if drunk. The negroes and the women took him to be the woman whose clothes he had taken.

Dorérame had a great desire to have his pleasure with that woman, and when he saw her sit down by the bed he thought that she had broken her sleep to come to him, perhaps for love games. So he said, "Oh, you, so and so, undress and get into my bed, I shall soon be back."

The King said to himself, "There is no might and strength but in the High God, the Benevolent!" Then he searched for the keys in the clothes and pockets of the negro, but found nothing. He said, "God's will be done!" Then raising his eyes, he saw a high window; he reached up with his arm, and found gold embroidered garments there; he slipped his hands into the pockets, and, oh, surprise! he found the keys. He examined them and counted seven, corresponding to the number of the doors of the house, and in his joy, he exclaimed, "God, be praised and glorified!" Then he said, "I can only get out of here by a ruse." Then feigning sickness, and appearing as if he wanted to vomit violently, he held his hand before his mouth, and hurried to the centre of the courtyard. The negro said to him, "God bless you! oh, so and so! any other woman would have been sick into the bed!"

The King then went to the inner door of the house, and opened it; he closed it behind him, and so from one door to the other, till he came to the seventh, which opened into the street. Here he found his companions again, who had been extremely anxious, and who asked him what he had seen?

Then said the King:

"This is not the time to answer. Let us go into this house with the blessing of God and with his help."

They resolved to be upon their guard, there being in the house seven negroes, twelve maidens, and seven women, beautiful as moons.

The Vizir asked the King, "What garments are these?" And the King answered, "By silent; without them I should never have got the keys."

He then went to the room where were the two women, with whom he had been lying, took off the clothes in which he was dressed, and put on his own, taking good care of his sword. Going to the saloon, where the negroes and the women were, he and his companions positioned themselves behind the door-curtain. After having looked into the saloon, they said, "Amongst all these women there is none more beautiful than the one seated on the elevated cushion!" The King said, "I reserve her for myself, if she does not belong to someone else."

While they were examining the interior of the saloon, Dorérame descended from the bed, and after him one of those beautiful women. Then another negro got on the bed with another woman, and so on till the seventh. They rode them in this way, one after the other, excepting the beautiful woman mentioned above, and the maidens. Each of these women appeared to mount upon the bed with marked reluctance, and descended, after the coition was finished, with her head bent down. The negroes, however, were lusting after, and pressing one after the other, the beautiful woman. But she spurned them all, saying, "I shall never consent to it, and as to these virgins, I take them also under my protection." Dorérame then rose and went up to her, holding in his hands his member in full erection, stiff as a pillar. He hit her with it on the face and head, saying, "Six times this night I have pressed you to surrender to my desires, and you always refuse; but now I must have you, even this night."

When the woman saw the stubbornness of the negro and the state of drunkenness he was in, she tried to soften him by promises. "Sit down here by me", she said, "and tonight your desires shall be satisfied."

The negro sat down near her with his member still erect as a column. The King could scarcely master his surprise.

Then the woman began to sing the following verses, chanting them from the bottom of her heart:

I prefer a young man for coition, and him only;
He is full of courage – he is my sole ambition,
His member is strong to deflower the virgin,
And richly proportioned in all its dimensions;
It has a head like to a brazier.
Enormous, and none like it in creation;
Strong it is and hard, with the head rounded off.
It is always ready for action and does not die down;
It never sleeps, owing to the violence of its love.
It sighs to enter my vulva, and sheds tears on my belly;
It asks not for help, not being in want of any;
It has no need of an ally, and stands alone the greatest fatigues.
And nobody can be sure of what will result from its efforts.
Full of vigour and life, it bores into my vagina,
And it works about there in action constant and splendid.
First from the front to the back, and then from the right to the left;
Now it is crammed hard in by vigorous pressure,
Now it rubs its head on the orifice of my vagina.
And he strokes my back, my stomach, my sides,
Kisses my cheeks, and soon begins to suck at my lips.
He embraces me close, and makes me roll on the bed,
And between his arms I am like a corpse without life.
Every part of my body receives in turn his love-bites,
And he covers me with kisses of fire;
When he sees me excited he quickly comes to me,
Then he opens my thighs and kisses my belly,
And puts his tool in my hand to make it knock at my door.
Soon he is in the cave, and I feel pleasure approaching.
He shakes me and thrills me, and passionately we both are working,
And he says, "Receive my seed!" and I answer, "Oh give it beloved one!
It shall be welcome to me, you light of my eyes!

Oh, you soul of my soul, go on with fresh vigour,

For you must not yet withdraw it from me; leave it there,

And this day will then be free of all sorrow."

He has sworn to God to have me for seventy nights,

And what he wished for he did, in the way of kisses and embraces, during all those nights.

When she had finished, the King, in great surprise, said, "How lascivious has God made this woman." And turning to his companions, "There is no doubt that this woman has no husband, and has not been debauched, for, certainly that negro is in love with her, and she has nevertheless rejected him."

Omar ben Isad took the word, "This is true, O King! Her husband has been now away for nearly a year, and many men have endeavoured to debauch her, but she has resisted."

The King asked, "Who is her husband?" And his companions answered, "She is the wife of the son of your father's Vizir."

The King replied, "You speak true; I have indeed heard it said that the son of my father's Vizir had a wife without fault, endowed with beauty and perfection and of exquisite shape; not adulterous and innocent of debauchery."

"This is the same woman", said they.

The King said, "No matter how, but I must have her", and turning to Omar, he added, "Where, amongst these women, is your mistress?" Omar answered, "I do not see her, O King!" Upon which the King said, "Have patience, I will show her to you." Omar was quite surprised to find that the King knew so much. "And this then is the negro Dorérame?" asked the King.

"Yes, and he is a slave of mine", answered the Vizir. "By silent, this is not the time to speak", said the King.

While this conversation was going on, the negro Dorérame, still desirous of obtaining the favours of that lady, said to her, "I am tired of your lies, O Beder el Bedour" (full moon of the full moons), for so she called herself.

The King said, "He who called her so called by her true name, for she is the full moon of the full moons, afore God!"

However, the negro wanted to draw the woman away with him, and hit her in the face.

The King, mad with jealousy, and with his heart full of anger, said to the Vizir, "Look what your negro is doing! By God! he shall die the death of a villain, and I shall make an example of him, and a warning to those who would imitate him!"

At that moment the King heard the lady say to the negro, "You are betraying your master the Vizir with his wife, and now you betray her, in spite of your intimacy with her and the favours she grants to you. And surely she loves you passionately, and you are pursuing another woman!"

The King said to the Vizir, "Listen, and do not speak a word."

The lady then rose and returned to the place where she had been before, and began to recite:

Oh, men! listen to what I say on the subject of woman,
Her thirst for coition is written between her eyes.
Do not put trust in her vows, even were she the Sultan's daughter.
Woman's malice is boundless; not even the King of kings
Would suffice to subdue it, whate'er be his might.
Men, take heed and shun the love of woman!
Do not say, "Such a one is my well beloved";
Do not say, "She is my life's companion."
If I deceive you, then say my words are untruths.
As long as she is with you in bed, you have her love,
But a woman's love is not enduring, believe me.
Lying upon her breast, you are her love-treasure;
Whilst the coition goes on, you have her love, poor fool!
But, soon, she looks upon you as a fiend;
And this is a fact undoubted and certain.
The wife receives the slave in the bed of the master,
And the serving-men subdue upon her their lust.
Certain it is, such conduct is not to be praised and honoured.

But the virtue of women is frail and fickle,
And the man thus deceived is looked upon with contempt.
Therefore a man with a heart should not put trust in a woman.

At these words the Vizir began to cry, but the King bade him to be quiet. Then the negro recited the following verses in response to those of the lady:

We negroes have had our fill of women,
We fear not their tricks, however subtle they be.
Men confide in us with regard to what they cherish.
This is no lie, remember, but is the truth, as you know.
Oh, you women all! for sure you have not patience when the virile member you are wanting,
For in the same resides your life and death;
It is the end and all of your wishes, secret or open.
If your anger and wrath are aroused against your husbands,
They appease you simply by introducing their members.
Your religion resides in your vulva, and the manly member is your soul.
Such you will always find is the nature of woman.

With that, the negro threw himself upon the woman, who pushed him back. At this moment, the King felt his heart oppressed; he drew his sword, as did his companions, and they entered the room. The negroes and women saw nothing but brandished swords.
One of the negroes rose, and rushed upon the King and his companions, but the *Chaouch* severed with one blow his head from his body. The King cried, "God's blessing upon you! Your arm is not withered and your mother has not borne a weakling. You have struck down your enemies, and paradise shall be your dwelling and place of rest!"
Another negro got up and aimed a blow at the *Chaouch*, which broke the sword of the *Chaouch* in two. It had been a beautiful weapon, and the *Chaouch*, on seeing it ruined, broke out into the most violent rage; he seized the negro by the

arm, lifted him up, and threw him against the wall, breaking his bones. Then the King cried, "God is great. He has not dried up your hand. Oh, what a *Chaouch*! God grant you his blessing."

The negroes, when they saw this, were cowed and silent, and the King, master now of their lives, said, "The man that lifts his hand only, shall lose his head!" And he commanded that the remaining five negroes should have their hands tied behind their backs.

This having been done, he turned to Beder el Bedour and asked her, "Whose wife are you, and who is this negro?"

She then told him what he had heard already from Omar. And the King thanked her, saying, "May God give you his blessing." He then asked her, "How long can a woman patiently do without coition?" She seemed amazed, but the King said, "Speak, and do not be embarrassed."

She then answered, "A well-born lady of good family can remain for six months without; but a lowly woman of no breeding, who does not respect herself when she can lay her hand upon a man, will have him upon her; his stomach and his member will know her vagina."

Then said the King, pointing to one of the women, "Who is this one?" She answered, "This is the wife of the *Kadi*." "And this one?" "The wife of the second Vizir." "And this?" "The wife of the chief of the *Muftis*." "And that one?" "The Treasurer's." "And those two women that are in the other room?" She answered, "They have received the hospitality of the house, and one of them was brought here yesterday by an old woman; the negro has so far not got possession of her."

Then said Omar, "This is the one I spoke to you about, O my master." "And the other woman? To whom does she belong?" said the King.

"She is the wife of the *Amine* of the carpenters", she answered.

Then said the King, "And these girls, who are they?"

She answered, "This one is the daughter of the clerk of the treasury; this other one the daughter of the *Mohtesib*, the third is the daughter of the *Bouab*, the next one the daughter of the *Amine* of the *Moueddin;* that one the daughter of the standard-keeper. At the invitation of the King, she passed them thus all in review pointed them all out to the King.

291

The King then asked for the reason of so many women being brought together there.

Beder el Bedour replied, "O master of ours, the negro knows no other passions than for coition and good wine. He keeps making love night and day, and his member rests only when he himself is asleep."

The King asked further, "What does he live upon?'

She said, "Upon yolks of eggs fried in fat and swimming in honey, and upon white bread; he drinks nothing but old muscatel wine."

The King said, "Who has brought these women here, who, all of them, belong to officials of the State?"

She replied, "O master of ours, he has in his service an old woman who has had the run of the houses in the town; she chooses and brings to him any woman of superior beauty and perfection; but she serves him only against good payment in silver, dresses, etc., precious stones, rubies, and other objects of value."

"And whence does the negro get that silver?" asked the King. The lady remaining silent, he added, "Give me some information, please."

She signified with a sign from the corner of her eye that he had got it all from the wife of the Grand Vizir.

The King understood her, and continued, "O Beder el Bedour! I have faith and confidence in you, and your testimony will have in my eyes the value of that of the two *Adels*. Speak to me without reserve about yourself."

She answered him, "I have not been touched, and however long this might have lasted the negro would not have had his desire satisfied."

"Is this so?" asked the King.

She replied, "It is so!" She had understood what the King wanted to say, and the King had seized the meaning of her words.

"Has the negro respected *my* honour? Inform me about that", said the King.

She answered "He has respected your honour as far as your wives are concerned. He has not pushed his criminal deeds that far; but if God had spared his days there is no certainty that he would not have tried to soil what he should have respected."

The King having asked her then who those negroes were, she answered, "They are his companions. After he had quite indulged himself with the women he had had brought to him, he handed them over to them, as you have seen. If it were not for the protection of a woman where would that man be?"

Then spoke the King, "O Beder el Bedour, why did not your husband ask my help against this oppression? Why did you not complain?"

She replied, "O King of the time, O beloved Sultan, O master of numerous armies and allies! As regards my husband I was so far unable to inform him of my lot; as to myself I have nothing to say but what you know by the verses I sang just now. I have given advice to men about women from the first verse to the last."

The King said, "O Beder el Bedour! I like you, I have put the question to you in the name of the chosen Prophet (the benediction and mercy of God be with him!). Inform me of everything; you have nothing to fear; I grant you complete pardon. Has this negro not enjoyed you? For I presume that none of you were beyond his attempts and had her honour safe."

She replied, "O King of our time, in the name of your high rank and your power! Look! He, about whom you ask me, I would not have accepted him as a legitimate husband; how could I have consented to grant him the favour of an illicit love?"

The King said, "You appear to be sincere, but the verses I heard you sing have roused doubts in my soul."

She replied, "I had three motives for employing that language. Firstly, I was at that moment in heat, like a young mare; secondly, Eblis had excited my natural parts; and lastly, I wanted to quiet the negro and make him have patience, so that he should grant me some delay and leave me in peace until God would deliver me of him."

The King said, "Do you speak seriously?" She was silent. Then the King cried, "O Beder el Bedour, you alone shall be pardoned!" She understood that it was she only that the King would spare from the punishment of death. He then cautioned her that she must keep the secret, and said he wanted to leave now. Then all the women and virgins approached Beder el Bedour and implored her, saying, "Help us, for you have power over the King"; and they shed tears over her hands, and in despair threw themselves down.

Beder el Bedour then called the King back, as he was going, and said to him "O our master! you have not granted me any favour yet." "How", said he, "I have sent for a beautiful mule for you; you will mount her and come with us. As for these women, they must all of them die."

She then said, "O our master! I ask you and implore you to authorise me to make a stipulation which you will accept." The King made an oath that he would fulfil it. Then she said, "I ask as a gift the pardon of all these women and of all these maidens. Their deaths would moreover cause the most terrible consternation over the whole town."

The King said, "There is no might nor power but in God, the merciful!" He then ordered the negroes to be taken out and beheaded. The only exception he made was with the negro Dorérame, who was enormously stout and had a neck like a bull. They cut off his ears, nose, and lips; likewise his virile member, which they put into his mouth, and then hung him on a gallows.

Then the King ordered the seven doors of the house to be closed, and returned to his palace.

At sunrise he sent a mule to Beder el Bedour, in order to let her be brought to him. He made her dwell with him, and found her to be excelling all those who excel.

Then the King caused the wife of Omar ben Isad to be restored to him, and he made him his private secretary. After which he ordered the Vizir to repudiate his wife. He did not forget the *Chaouch* and the Commander of the Guards, to whom he made large presents, as he had promised, using for that purpose the negro's hoards. He sent the son of his father's Vizir to prison. He also caused the old go-between to be brought before him, and asked her, "Give me all the particulars about the conduct of the negro, and tell me whether it was well done to bring in that way women to men." She answered, "This is the trade of nearly all old women." He then had her executed, as well as all old women who followed that trade, and thus cut off in his State the tree of procurement at the root, and burnt the trunk.

He besides sent back to their families all the women and girls, and bade them repent in the name of God.

This story presents but a small part of the tricks and stratagems used by women against their husbands.

The moral of the tale is, that a man who falls in love with a woman imperils himself, and exposes himself to the greatest troubles.

III

About men who are to be held in contempt

Know, o my brother (to whom God be merciful), that a man who is misshapen, of coarse appearance, and whose member is short, thin and flabby, is contemptible in the eyes of women.

When such a man has intercourse with a woman, he does not do his business with vigour and in a manner to give her enjoyment. He lays himself down upon her without previous foreplay, he does not kiss her, nor twine himself round her; he does not bite her, nor suck her lips, nor tickle her.

He gets upon her before she has begun to long for pleasure, and then he introduces with infinite trouble a member soft and weak. Scarcely has he commenced when he is already done for; he makes one or two movements, and then sinks upon the woman's breast to emit his sperm; and that is the most he can do. This done he withdraws his organ, and makes all haste to get down again from her.

Such a man – as was said by a writer – is quick in ejaculation and slow as to erection; after the trembling, which follows the ejaculation of the seed, his chest is heavy and his sides ache.

Qualities like these are no recommendation with women. Despicable also is the man who is false in his words; who does not fulfil the promise he has made; who never speaks without telling lies, and who conceals from his wife all his doings, except the adulterous exploits which he commits.

Women cannot esteem such men, as they cannot give them any enjoyment.

It is said that a man of the name of Abbés, whose member was extremely small and slight, had a very corpulent wife, whom he could not manage to satisfy in coition, so that she soon began to complain to her female friends about it. This woman possessed a considerable fortune, whilst Abbés was very poor, and when he wanted anything, she was sure not to let him have what he wanted.

One day he went to see a wise man, and submitted his case to him.

The sage told him: "If you had a fine member you might have her fortune. Do you not know that women's religion is in their vulvas? But I will prescribe you a remedy which will do away with your troubles."

Abbés lost no time in making up the remedy according to the recipe of the wise man, and after he had used it his member grew to be long and thick. When his wife saw it in that state she was surprised; but it was still better when he made her experience enjoyment which she had not been accustomed to; he began in fact to work her with his tool in quite a remarkable manner, to such a point that she trembled and sighed and sobbed and cried out during the act.

As soon as the wife found in her husband such eminently good qualities she gave him her fortune, and placed her person and all she had at his disposal.

IV

About women who are to be held in contempt

Know, o Vizir (to whom God be merciful), that women differ in their natural dispositions: there are women who are worthy of all praise; and there are, on the other hand, women who only merit contempt.

The woman who merits the contempt of men is ugly and garrulous; her hair is wodly her forehead projecting, her eyes are small and dim, her nose is enormous, the lips lead-coloured, the mouth large, the cheeks wrinkled and she shows gaps in her teeth; her cheekbones shine purple, and she sports bristles on her chin; her head sits on a skinny neck, with over-developed tendons; her shoulders are contracted and her chest is narrow, with flabby dangling breasts, and her belly is like an empty leather-bottle, with the navel standing out like a heap of stones; her flanks are shaped like arches; the bones of her spinal column may be counted; there is no flesh upon her rump; her vulva is large and cold.

Finally, such a woman has large knees and feet, big hands and emaciated legs. A woman with such blemishes can give no pleasure to men in general, and least of all to him who is her husband or who enjoys her favours.

The man who aproaches a woman like that with his member in erection will find it presently soft and relaxed, as though he was only close to a beast of burden. May God keep us from a woman of that description!

Contemptible likewise is the woman who is constantly laughing out; for, as it was said by an author, "If you see a woman who is always laughing, fond of gaming and jesting, always running to her neighbours, meddling with matters that are no concern of hers, plaguing her husband with constant complaints, allying herself with other women against him, playing the grand lady, accepting gifts from everybody, know that that woman is a whore without shame."

And again to be despised is the woman of a sombre, frowning nature, and one who is prolific in gossip; the woman who is light-headed in her relations with men, or contentious, or fond of tittle-tattle and unable to keep her husband's secrets, or who is malicious. The woman of a malicious nature talks only to tell lies; if she makes a promise she does so only to break it, and if anybody confides in her, she betrays him; she is debauched, dishonest, unseemly, coarse and violent; she cannot give good advice; she is always occupied with the affairs of other people, and with such as bring harm, and is always on the watch for frivolous news; she is fond of rest, but not of work; she uses unbecoming words in addressing a Mussulman, even to her husband; invectives are always at the tip of her tongue; she breathes a bad odour which infects you, and sticks to you even after you have left her.

And not less contemptible is she who talks to no purpose, who is a hypocrite and does nothing good; she, who, when her husband asks her to fulfil the conjugal act, refuses to listen to his demand; the woman who does not assist her husband in his affairs; and finally, she who plagues him with unceasing complaints and tears.

A woman of that sort, seeing her husband irritated or in trouble does not share his affliction; on the contrary, she laughs and jests all the more, and does not try to drive away his ill-humour by endearments. She is more generous with her body to other men than to her husband; it is not for his sake that she adorns herself, and it is not to please him that she tries to look well. Far from that; with him she is very untidy, and does not mind letting him see things and habits about her person which must be repugnant to him. Lastly, she never uses either *Atsmed* nor *Souak*.

No happiness can be hoped for a man with such a wife. God keep us from such a one!

V

Relating to the act of copulation

Know, o Vizir (and God protect you!), that if you wish for coition, in joining the woman you should not have your stomach loaded with food and drink, only in that condition will your intercourse be wholesome and good. If your stomach is full, only harm can come of it to both of you; you will have threatening symptoms of apoplexy and gout, and the least evil that may result from it will be the inability of passing your urine, or weakness of sight.

Let your stomach then be free from excessive food and drink, and you need not apprehend any illness.

Before setting to work with your wife excite her with love-play, so that the copulation will finish to your mutual satisfaction.

Thus it will be well to play with her before you introduce your member and accomplish the intercourse. You will excite her by kissing her cheeks, sucking her lips and nibbling at her breasts. You will lavish kisses on her navel and thighs, and titillate the lower parts. Bite at her arms, and neglect no part of her body; cling close to her bosom, and show her your love and submission. Interlace your legs with hers, and press her in your arms, for, as the poet has said:

305

Under her neck my right hand has served her for a cushion,
And to draw her to me
I have sent out my left hand,
Which bore her up as a bed.

When you are close to a woman, and you see her eyes getting dim, and hear her, yearning for coition, heave deep sighs, then let your and her yearning be joined into one, and let your lubrication rise to the highest point; for this will be the moment most favourable to the game of love. The pleasure which the woman then feels will be extreme; as for yourself, you will cherish her all the more, and she will continue her affection for you, for it has been said:

If you see a woman heaving deep sighs, with her lips getting red and her eyes languishing, when her mouth half opens and her movements grow careless; when she appears to be disposed to go to sleep, walks hesitantly and is prone to yawn, know that this is the moment for coition; and if you there and then make your way into her you will procure for her an unquestionable treat. You yourself will find the mouth of her womb clasping your instrument, which is undoubtedly the crowning pleasure for both, for this before everything begets affection and love.

The following precepts, coming from a profound connoisseur in love affairs, are well known:

Woman is like a fruit, which will not yield its sweetness until you rub it between your hands. Look at the basil plant; if you do not rub it warm with your fingers it will not emit any scent. Do you not know that the amber, unless it be handled and warmed, keeps hidden within its pores the aroma contained in it. It is the same with woman. If you do not animate her with your love-play mixed with kissing, nibbling and touching, you will not obtain from her what you are wishing; you will feel no enjoyment when you share her bed, and you will waken in her heart neither inclination nor affection, nor love for you; all her qualities will remain hidden.

It is reported that a man, having asked a woman what means were the most likely to create affection in the female heart, with respect to the pleasures of coition, received the following answer:

O you who question me, those things which develop the taste for coition are the love-play and touches which precede it, and then the close embrace at the moment of ejaculation!

Believe me, the kisses, nibblings, suction of the lips, the close embrace, the visits of the mouth to the nipples of the bosom, and the sipping of the fresh saliva, these are the things to render affection lasting.

In acting thus, the two orgasms take place simultaneously, and enjoyment comes to the man and woman at the same moment. Then the man feels the womb grasping his member, which gives to each of them the most exquisite pleasure.

This it is which gives birth to love, and if matters have not been managed this way the woman has not had her full share of pleasure, and the delights of the womb are wanting. Know that the woman will not feel her desires satisfied, and will not love her rider unless he is able to act up to her womb; but when the womb is made to enter into action she will feel the most violent love for her cavalier, even if he be unsightly in appearance.

Then do all you can to provoke a simultaneous discharge of the two spermal fluids; herein lies the secret of love.

One of the scholars who have occupied themselves with this subject has related the confidences which one of them made to him like this:

O you men, one and all, who are soliciting the love of woman and her affection, and who wish that sentiment in her heart to be of an enduring nature, play with her before coition; prepare her for enjoyment, and neglect nothing to attain that end. Explore her with the utmost attention, and, entirely occupied with her, let nothing else engage your thoughts. Do not let the moment propitious for pleasure pass away; that moment will be when you see her eyes humid, half open. Then go to work, but, remember, not till your kisses and toyings have taken effect.

After you have got the woman into a proper state of excitement, O men! put your member into her, and, if you then observe the proper movements, she will experience a pleasure which will satisfy all her desires.

Lie on her breast, rain kisses on her cheeks, do not let your member quit her vagina. Push for the mouth of her womb. This will crown your labour.

If, by God's favour, you have found this delight, take good care not to withdraw your member, but let it remain there, and absorb an endless pleasure! Listen to the sighs and heavy breathing of the woman. They witness the intensity of the bliss you have given her.

And after the enjoyment is over, and your amorous struggle has come to an end, be careful not to get up at once, but withdraw your member cautiously. Remain close to the woman, and lie down on the right side of the bed that witnessed your enjoyment. You will find this pleasant, and you will not be like a fellow who mounts the woman like of a mule, without any regard to refinement, and who, after the emission, hastens to get his member out and to rise. Avoid such manners, for they rob the woman of all her lasting delight.

In short, the true lover of coition will not fail to observe all that I have recommended; for, from the observance of my recommendations will result the pleasure of the woman, and these rules comprise everything essential in that respect.

God has made everything for the best!

VI

Concerning everything that is favourable to the act of coition

Know, o Vizir (God be good to you!), if you would have pleasant coition, which ought to give an equal share of happiness to the two participants and be satisfactory to both, you must first of all play with the woman, excite her with kisses, by nibbling and sucking her lips, by caressing her neck and cheeks. Turn her over in the bed, now on her back, now on her stomach, till you see by her eyes that the time for pleasure is near, as I have mentioned in the preceding chapter, and certainly I have not been sparing with my observations.

Then when you observe the lips of a woman trembing and getting red, and her eyes languishing, and her sighs becoming quicker, know that she is eager for coition; then get between her thighs, so that your member can enter into her vagina. If you follow my advice, you will enjoy a pleasant embrace, which will give you the greatest satisfaction, and leave with you a delicious remembrance. Someone has said:

If you desire coition, place the woman on the ground, cling closely to her bosom, with her lips close to yours; then clasp her to you, suck her breath, bite her; kiss her breasts, her stomach, her hips, press her close in your arms, so as to make her faint with pleasure; when you see her so far gone, then push your member into her. If you have done as I said, the enjoyment will come to both of you simultaneously. This it is which makes the pleasure of the woman so sweet. But if you neglect my advice the woman will not be satisfied and you will not have given her any pleasure.

The coition being finished, do not get up at once, but come down softly on her right side, and if she has conceived, she will bear a male child, if it please God on high!

Wise men and scholars (may God grant to all his forgiveness!) have said:

If anyone placing his hand upon the vulva of a woman that is with child pronounces the following words: "In the name of God! may he grant salutation and mercy to his Prophet (salutation and mercy be with him). Oh! my God! I pray to thee in the name of the Prophet to let a boy issue from this conception", it will come to pass by the will of God, and in consideration for our lord Mohammed (the salutation and grace of God be with him), the woman will be delivered of a boy.

Do not drink rain-water directly after copulation, because this liquid weakens the kidneys.

If you want to repeat the coition, perfume yourself with sweet scents, then join the woman, and you will arrive at a happy result.

Do not let the woman perform the act of coition mounted upon you, for fear that in that position some drops of her seminal fluid might enter the canal of your member and cause a severe urethritis.

Do not work hard directly after coition as this might affect your health adversely, but go to rest for some time.

Do not wash your member directly after having withdrawn it from the vagina of the woman, until the irritation has gone down somewhat; then wash it and its opening carefully. Otherwise, do not wash your member frequently. Do not leave the vulva directly after the emission, as this may cause sores.

The ways of doing it to women are numerous and variable. And now is the time to make known to you the different positions which are usual.

God, the magnificent, has said:

"Women are your field. Go upon your field as you like." According to your wish you can choose the position you like best, provided, of course, that coition takes place in the spot destined for it, that is, in the vulva.

Manner the first – Make the woman lie upon her back, with her thighs raised, then, getting between her legs, introduce your member into her. Pressing your toes to the ground, you can move within her in a convenient, measured way. This is a good position for a man with a long verge.

Manner the second – If your member is a short one, let the woman lie on her back, lift her legs into the air, so that her right leg be near her right ear, and the left one near her left ear, and in this position, with her buttocks lifted up, her vulva will project forward. Then put in your member.

Manner the third – Let the woman stretch herself upon the ground, and place yourself between her thighs; then putting one of her legs upon your shoulder, and the other under your arm, near the armpit, get into her.

Manner the fourth – Let her lie down, and put her legs on your shoulders; in this position your member will just face her vulva, which must not touch the ground. And then introduce your member.

Manner the fifth – Let her lie down on her side, then lie yourself down by her on your side, and getting between her thighs, put your member into her vagina. But sidelong coition predisposes for rheumatic pains and sciatica.

Manner the sixth – Make her get down on her knees and elbows, as if kneeling in prayer. In this position the vulva is projected backwards; you then attack her from that side, and put your member into her.

Manner the seventh – Place the woman on her side, and squat between her thighs, with one of her legs on your shoulder and the other between your thighs, while she remains lying on her side. Then you enter her vagina, and make her move by drawing her towards your chest by means of your hands, with which you hold her embraced.

Manner the eighth – Let her stretch herself upon the ground, on her back, with her legs crossed; then mount her like a cavalier on horseback, being on your knees, while her legs are placed under her thighs, and put your member into her vagina.

Manner the ninth – Place the woman so that she leans with her front, or, if you prefer it, her back upon a moderate elevation, with her feet set upon the ground. She thus offers her vulva to the introduction of your member.

Manner the tenth – Place the woman near to a low divan, the back of which she can take hold of with her hands; then, getting under her, lift her legs to the height of your navel, and let her clasp you with her legs on each side of your body; in this position plant your member into her, seizing with your hands the back of the divan. When you begin the action your movements must respond to those of the woman.

Manner the eleventh – Let her lie upon her back on the ground with a cushion under her posterior; then getting between her legs, and letting her place the sole of her right foot against the sole of her left foot, introduce your member.

There are other positions besides the above named in use among the peoples of India. It is well for you to know that the inhabitants of those parts have multiplied the different ways to enjoy women, and they have advanced farther than we in the knowledge and investigation of coitus.

Amongst those manners are the following, called:

1. *El asemeud,* the stopper.
2. *El modefedâ,* frog fashion.
3. *El mokefâ,* with the toes cramped.
4. *El mokeurmeutt,* with legs in the air.
5. *El setouri,* he-goat fashion.
6. *El loulabi,* the screw of Archimedes.
7. *El kelouci,* the summersault.
8. *Hachou en nekanok,* the tail of the ostrich.
9. *Lebeuss el djoureb,* fitting on of the sock.

10. *Kechef el astine,* reciprocal sight of the posteriors.

11. *Nezâ el kouss,* the rainbow arch.

12. *Nesedj el kheuzz,* alternative piercing.

13. *Dok el arz,* pounding on the spot.

14. *Nik el kohoul,* coition from the back.

15. *El keurchi,* belly to belly.

16. *El kebachi,* ram-fashion.

17. *Dok el outed,* driving the peg home.

18. *Sebek el heub,* love's fusion.

19. *Tred ech chate,* sheep-fashion.

20. *Kalen el miche,* interchange in coition.

21. *Rekeud el aïr,* the race of the member.

22. *El modakheli,* the fitter-in.

23. *El khouariki,* the one who stops in the house.

24. *Nik el haddadi,* the smith's coition.

25. *El moheundi,* the seducer.

First manner – *El asemeud* (the stopper). Place the woman on her back, with a cushion under her buttocks, then get between her legs, resting the points of your feet against the ground; bend her two thighs against her chest as far as you can; place your hands under her arms so as to embrace her or cramp her shoulders. Then introduce your member, and at the moment of ejaculation draw her towards you. This position is painful for the woman, for her thighs being bent upwards and her buttocks raised by the cushion, the walls of her vagina tighten, and the uterus tending forward there is not much room for movement, and scarcely space enough for the intruder; consequently the latter enters with difficulty and strikes against the uterus. This position should therefore not be adopted, unless the man's member is short or soft.

Second manner – *El modefedâ* (frog fashion). Place the woman on her back, and arrange her thighs so that they touch the heels, which are thus coming close to the buttocks; then down you sit happily facing the vulva, in which you insert your member; you then place her knees under your arm-pits; and taking firm hold of the upper part of her arms, you draw her towards you at the climax.

Third manner – *El mokefâ* (with the toes cramped). Place the woman on her back, and squat on your knees, between her thighs, gripping the ground with your toes; raise her knees as high as your sides, in order that she may cross her legs over your back, and then pass her arms round your neck.

Fourth manner – *El mokeurmeutt* (with legs in the air). The woman lying on her back, you put her thighs together and raise her legs up until the soles of her feet look at the ceiling; then folding her within your thighs you insert your member, holding her legs up with your hands.

Fifth manner – *El setouri* (he-goat fashion). The woman being crouched on her side, you let her stretch out the leg on which she is resting, and squat down between her thighs with your calves bent under you. Then you lift her uppermost leg so that it rests on your back, and introduce your member. During the action you take hold of her shoulders, or, if you prefer it, by the arms.

Sixth manner – *El loulabi* (the screw of Archimedes). The man being stretched on his back the woman sits on his member, facing him; she then places her hands upon the bed so that she can keep her stomach from touching the man's, and moves up and downwards, and if the man is supple he assists her from below. If in this position she wants to kiss him, she need only stretch her arms along the bed.

Seventh manner – *El kelouci* (the summersault). The woman must wear a pair of pantaloons, which she lets drop upon her heels; then she stoops, placing her head between her feet, so that her neck is in the opening of her pantaloons. At that moment, the man, seizing her legs, turns her upon her back, making her perform a summersault; then with his legs curved under him he brings his member right against her vulva, and, slipping it between her legs, inserts it. It is alleged that there are women who, while lying on their back, can place their feet behind their head without the help of pantaloons or hands.

Eighth manner – *Hachou en nekanok* (the tail of the ostrich). The woman lying on her back along the bed, the man kneels in front of her, lifting up her legs until her head and shoulders only are resting on the bed; his member having penetrated into her vagina, he seizes and sets into motion the buttocks of the woman who, on her part, twines her legs around his neck.

Ninth manner – *Lebeuss el djoureb* (fitting on of the sock). The woman lies on her back. You sit down between her legs and place your member between the lips of her vulva, which you fit over it with your thumb and first finger; then you move so as to procure for your member, as far as it is in contact with the woman, a lively rubbing, which action you continue until her vulva gets moistened with the liquid emitted from your member. When she is thus well prepared for enjoyment by the alternate coming and going of your weapon in her scabbard, put it into her in full length.

Tenth manner – *Kechef el astine* (reciprocal sight of the posteriors). The man lying stretched out on his back, the woman sits down upon his member with her back to the man's face, who presses her sides between his thighs and legs, whilst she places her hands upon the bed as a support for her movements, and lowering her head, her eyes are turned towards the buttocks of the man.

Eleventh manner – *Nezâ el kouss* (the rainbow arch). The woman is lying on her side; the man also on his side, with his face towards her back, pushes in between her legs and introduces his member, with his hands lying on the upper part of her back. As to the woman, she then gets hold of the man's feet, which she lifts up as far as she can, drawing him close to her; thus she forms with the body of the man an arch, of which she is the rise.

Twelfth manner – *Nôsedj el kheuzz* (the alternate movement of piercing). The man in sitting position places the soles of his feet together, and lowering his thighs, draws his feet nearer to his member; the woman sits down upon his feet, which he takes care to keep firm together. In this position the two thighs of the woman are pressed against the man's flanks, and she puts her arms round his neck. Then the man clasps the woman's ankles, and drawing his feet nearer to his body, brings the woman, who is sitting on them, within range of his member, which then enters her vagina. By moving his feet he sends her back and brings her forward again, without ever withdrawing his member entirely.

The woman makes herself as light as possible, and assists as well as she can in this come-and-go movement; her cooperation is, in fact, indispensable for it. If the man apprehends that his member may come out entirely, he takes her round the waist.

Thirteenth manner – *Dok el arz* (pounding on the spot). The man sits down with his legs stretched out; the woman then places herself astride on his thighs, crossing her legs behind the back of the man, and places her vulva opposite his member, which she guides into her vagina; she then places her arms round his neck, and he embraces her sides and waist, and helps her to rise and descend upon his member. She must assist in his work.

Fourteenth manner – *Nik el kohoul* (coitus from the back). The woman lies down on her stomach and raises her buttocks by help of a cushion; the man approaches from behind, stretches himself on her back and inserts his tool, while the woman twines her arms round the man's elbows. This is the easiest of all methods.

Fifteenth manner – *El keurchi* (belly to belly). The man and the woman are standing upright, face to face; she opens her thighs; the man then brings his feet forward between those of the woman, who also advances hers a little. In this position the man must have one of his feet somewhat in advance of the other. Each of the two has the arms round the other's hips; the man introduces his member, and the two move thus intertwinded in a manner called *neza' el dela*, which I shall explain later, if it please God the Almighty. (See first manner).

Sixteenth manner – *El kebachi* (ram-fashion). The woman is on her knees, with her forearms on the ground; the man approaches from behind, kneels down, and lets his member penetrate into her vagina, which she presses out as much as possible; he will do well in placing his hands on the woman's shoulders.

Seventeenth manner – *Dok el outed* (driving the peg home). The woman enfolds with her legs the waist of the man, who is standing, with her arms passed round his neck, steadying herself by leaning against the wall. Whilst she is thus suspended the man inserts his pin into her vulva.

Eighteenth manner – *Sebek el heub* (love's fusion). While the woman is lying on her right side, extend yourself on your left side; your left leg remains extended, and you raise your right one till it is up to her flank, when you lay her upper leg upon your side. Thus her uppermost leg serves the woman as a support for her back. After having introduced your member you move as you please, and she responds to your action as she pleases.

316

Nineteenth manner – *Tred ech chate* (coitus of the sheep). The woman is on her hands and knees; the man, behind her, lifts her thighs till her vulva is on a level with his member, which he then inserts. In this position she ought to place her head between her arms.

Twentieth manner – *Kaleb el miche* (interchange in coition). The man lies on his back. The woman, gliding in between his legs, places herself upon him with her toe-nails against the ground; she lifts up the man's thighs, turning them against his own body, so that his virile member faces her vulva, into which she guides it; she then places her hands upon the bed by the sides of the man. It is, however, indispensable that the woman's feet rest upon a cushion to enable her to keep her vulva in line with his member.

In this position the roles are reversed, the woman fulfilling that of the man, and vice-versa.

There is a variation to this manner. The man stretches himself out upon his back, while the woman kneels with her legs under her, but between his legs. The rest conforms exactly to what has been said above.

Twenty-first manner – *Rekeud el aïr* (the race of the member). The man, on his back, supports himself with a cushion under his shoulders, but his posterior must retain contact with the bed. Thus placed, he draws up his thighs until his knees are on a level with his face; then the woman sits down, impaling herself on his member; she must not lie down, but keep seated as if on horseback, the saddle being represented by the knees and the stomach of the man. In that position she can, by the play of her knees, work up and down and down and up. She can also place her knees on the bed, in which case the man accentuates the movement by plying his thighs, whilst she holds with her left hand on to his right shoulder.

Twenty-second manner – *El modakheli* (the fitterin). The woman is seated on her coccyx, with only the points of her buttocks touching the ground; the man takes the same position, her vulva facing his member. Then the woman puts her right thigh over the left thigh of the man, whilst he on his part puts his right thigh over her left one.

The woman, seizing with her hands her partner's arms, gets his member into her vulva; and each of them leaning alternately a little back, and holding each other by the upper part of the arms, they initiate a swaying movement, moving softly and keeping their movements in exact rhythm by the assistance of their heels, which are resting on the ground.

Twenty-third manner – *El khouariki* (the one who stops at home). The woman being couched on her back, the man lies down upon her, with cushions held in his hands.

After his member is in, the woman raises her buttocks as high as she can off the bed, the man following her up with his member well inside; then the woman lowers herself again upon the bed, giving some short shocks, and although they do not embrace, the man must stick like glue to her. This movement they continue, but the man must make himself light and must not be heavy, and the bed must be soft; otherwise the exercise cannot be kept up without a break.

Twenty-fourth manner – *Nik el haddadi* (the coition of the blacksmith). The woman lies on her back with a cushion under her buttocks, and her knees raised as far as possible towards her chest, so that her vulva stands out as a target; she then guides her partner's member in.

The man executes for some time the usual action of coition, then draws his tool out of the vulva, and glides it for a moment between the thighs of the woman, as the smith withdraws the glowing iron from the furnace in order to plunge it into cold water. This manner is called *sferdgeli,* position of the quince.

Twenty-fifth manner – *El moheundi* (the seducer). The woman lying on her back, the man sits between her legs, with his rump on his feet; then he raises and separates the woman's thighs, placing her legs under his arms, or over his shoulders; he then takes her round the waist, or seizes her shoulders.

The preceding descriptions furnish a large number of procedures, that cannot easily be all put to the test; but with such a variety to choose from, the man who finds one of them difficult to practise, can easily find plenty of others more to his convenience.

I have not made mention of positions which it appeared to me impossible to realize, and if there be anybody who thinks that those which I have described are not exhaustive, he has only to look for new ones.

It cannot be denied that the Indians have surmounted the greatest difficulties in respect to coition. As a grand exploit, origination with them, the following may be cited:

The woman being stretched out on her back, the man sits down on her chest, with his back turned to her face, his knees turned forward and his nails gripping the ground; he then raises her hips, arching her back until he has brought her vulva face to face with his member, which he then inserts, and thus achieves his purpose.

This position, as you perceive, is very fatiguing and very difficult to attain. I even believe that the only realization of it consists in words and designs. With regard to the other methods described above, they can only be practised if both man and woman are free from physical defects, and of similar build; for instance, one or the other of them must not be humpbacked, or very little, or very tall, or too obese. And I repeat, that both must be in perfect health.

I shall now treat of coition between two persons of different build. I shall particularise the positions that will suit them in treating each of them individually. I shall first discuss of the coition of a lean man and a corpulent woman, and the different postures they may assume for the act, assuming the woman to be lying down, and being turned successively over on her four sides.

If the man wants to work her sideways he takes the thigh of the woman which is uppermost, and raises it as high as possible on his flank, so that it rests over his waist; he uses her undermost arm as a pillow for the support of his head, and he takes care to place a thick cushion beneath his undermost hip, so as to elevate his member to the necessary height, which is indispensable on account of the thickness of the woman's thighs.

But if the woman has an enormous abdomen, projecting by reason of its obesity over her thighs and flanks, it will be best to lay her on her back, and to lift up her thighs towards her belly; the man kneels between them, having hold of her waist with his hands, and drawing her towards him; and if he cannot manage her because of the obesity of her belly and thighs, he must with his two arms encircle her buttocks, but it is thus impossible for him to work her conveniently, owing to the lack of movement of her thighs, which are impeded by her belly. He may, however, support them with his hands, but let him take care not to place them over his own thighs, as, owing to their weight, he would not have the power nor the opportunity to move. As the poet has said:

If you have to explore her, lift up her buttocks,
In order to work like the rope thrown to a drowning man.
You will then seem between her thighs
Like a rower seated at the end of the boat.

The man can likewise couch the woman on her side, with the undermost leg in front; then he sits down on the thigh of that leg, his member being opposite her vulva, and lets her raise the upper leg, which she must bend at the knee. Then, with his hands seizing her legs and thighs, he introduces his member, with his body lying between her legs, his knees bent, and the points of his feet against the ground, so that he can raise his posterior, and prevent her thighs from impeding the entrance. In this position they can enter into action.

If the woman's belly is enlarged by reason of her being with child, the man lets her lie down on one side; then placing one of her thighs over the other, he raises them both towards the stomach, without their touching the latter; he then lies down behind her on the same side, and can thus fit his member in. In this way he can thrust his tool in entirely, particularly by raising his foot, which is under the woman's leg, to the height of her thigh. The same may be done with a barren woman; but it is particularly to be recommended for the woman who is *pregnant*, as the above position offers the advantage of procuring her the pleasure she desires, without exposing her to any danger.

In the case of the man being obese, with a very pronounced roundness of stomach, and the woman being thin, the best course to follow is to let the woman take the active part. To this end, the man lies down on his back with his thighs close together, and the woman lowers herself upon his member, astride of him; she rests her hands upon the bed, and he seizes her arms with his hands. If she knows how to move, she can thus, in turn, rise and sink upon his member; if she is not adroit enough for that movement, the man lends a movement to her

320

buttocks by the play of one of his thighs behind them. But if the man assumes this position, it may sometimes become prejudicial to him, inasmuch as some of the female sperm may penetrate into his urethra, and serious illness may result. It may also happen – and that is just as bad – that the man's sperm cannot pass out, and returns into the urethra.

If the man prefers that the woman should lie on her back, he places himself, with his legs folded under him, between her legs, which she parts only moderately. Thus, his buttocks are between the woman's legs, with his heels touching them. In performing this way he will, however, feel fatigue, owing to the position of his stomach resting upon the woman's, and the inconvenience resulting therefrom; and, besides, he will not be able to get his whole member in the vulva. It will be similar when both lie on their sides, as mentioned above in the case of pregnant women.

When both man and woman are fat, and wish to unite in coition, they cannot contrive to do it without trouble, particularly when both have prominent stomachs. In these circumstances the best way to go about it is for the woman to be on her knees with her hands on the ground, so that her posterior is elevated; then the man separates her legs, leaving the points of the feet close together and the heels parted; he then attacks her from behind, kneeling and holding up his stomach with his hand, and so introduces his member. Resting his stomach upon her buttocks during the act he holds the thighs or the waist of the woman with his hands. If her posterior is too low for his stomach to rest upon, he must place a cushion under her knees to remedy this.

I know of no other position so favourable as this for the coition of a fat man with a fat woman.

If, in fact, the man gets between the legs of a woman on her back under the above named circumstances, his stomach, touching the woman's thighs, will not allow him to make free use of his tool. He cannot even see her vulva, or only in part; it may be almost said that it will be impossible for him to accomplish the act. On the other hand, if the man makes the woman lie upon her side, and then places himself, with his legs bent behind her, pressing his stomach upon the upper part of her posterior, she must draw her legs and thighs up to her stomach,

323

in order to lay bare her vagina and allow the introduction of his member; but if she cannot sufficiently bend her knees, the man can neither see her vulva, nor explore it.

If, however, the stomach of each person is not exaggeratedly large, they can manage very well all positions. Only they must not be too long in coming to the climax, as they will soon feel fatigued and lose their breath.

In the case of a very big man and a very little woman, the difficulty to be solved is how to contrive that their sexual organs and their mouths can meet at the same time. To gain this end the woman had best lie on her back; the man places himself on his side near her, passes one of his hands under her neck, and with the other raises her thighs till he can put his member against her vulva from behind, the woman remaining still on her back. In this position he holds her up with his hands by the neck and the thighs. He can then enter her body, while the woman on her part puts her arms round his neck, and approaches her lips to his. If the man wishes the woman to lie on her side, he gets between her legs, and, placing her thighs so that they are in contact with his sides, one above and one under, he glides in between them till his member is facing her vulva from behind; he then presses his thighs against her buttocks, which he seizes with one hand in order to make them move; the other hand he has round her neck. If the man then likes, he can get his thighs over those of the woman, and press her towards him; this will make it easier for him to move.

As regards the copulation of a very small man and a tall woman, the two performers cannot kiss each other while in action unless they take one of the three following positions, and even then they will become fatigued.

First position – The woman lies on her back, with a thick cushion under her buttocks, and a similar one under her head; she then draws up her thighs as far as possible towards her chest. The man lies down upon her, introduces his member, and takes hold of her shoulders, drawing himself up towards them. The woman winds her arms and legs round his back, whilst he holds on to her shoulders, or, if he can, to her neck.

Second position – Man and woman lie both on their side, face to face; the woman slips her undermost thigh under the man's flank, drawing it at the same time higher up; she does the like with her other thigh over his; then she arches her stomach out, while his member is penetrating into her. Both should have hold of her other's neck, and the woman, crossing her legs over his back, should draw the man towards her.

Third position – The man lies on his back, with his legs stretched out; the woman sits on his member, and, stretching herself down over him, draws up her knees to the height of her stomach; then, laying her hands over his shoulders, she draws herself up, and presses her lips to his.

All these postures are more or less fatiguing for both; people can, however, choose any other position they like; but they must be able to kiss each other during the act. I will now speak to you of those who are little, due to of being humpbacked. Of these there are several kinds.

First, there is the man who is crookbacked, but whose spine and neck are straight. For him it is most convenient to unite with a little woman, but only from behind. Placing himself behind her posterior, he thus introduces his member into her vulva. But if the woman is in a stooping position, on her hands and feet, he will do still better. If the woman be afflicted with a hump and the man is straight, the same position is suitable.

If both of them are crookbacked they can take what position they like for coition. They cannot, however, embrace; and if they lie on their side, face to face, there will be left an empty space between them. And if one or the other lies down on the back, a cushion must be placed under the head and the shoulder, to hold them up, and fill the place which is left vacant.

In the case of a man whose malformation affects only his neck, so as to press his chin towards his chest, but who is otherwise straight, he can take any position he likes for performing the act, and give himself up to any embraces and caresses, always excepting kisses on the mouth. If the woman is lying on her back, he will appear in action as if he were butting at her like a ram. If the woman has her neck deformed in similar manner, their coition will resemble the mutual attack of two horned beasts with their heads. The most convenient position for them will be that the woman should stoop down, and he attack her from behind. The man whose hump appears on his back in the shape of only the half of a jar is not so much disfigured as the one of whom the poet has said:

Lying on his back he is a dish;
Turn him over, and you have a dish-cover.

In his case coition can take place as with any other man who is small in stature and straight; he cannot, however, easily lie on his back.

If a little woman is lying on her back, with a humpbacked man upon her belly, he will look like the cover over a vase. If, on the contrary, the woman is large-sized, he will have the appearance of a carpenter's plane in action. I have made the following verses on this subject:

The humpback is vaulted like an arch;
And seeing him you cry, "Glory be to God!"
You ask him how he manages in coitus?
"It is the retribution for my sins", he says.
The woman under him is like a board of deal;
The humpback, who explores her, does the planing.

I have also said in verse:
The humpback's spinal cord is tied in knots,
The Angels tire with writing all his sins;
In trying for a wife of proper shape;
And for her favours, she repulses him,
And says, "Who bears the wrongs we shall commit?"
And he, "I bear them well upon my hump!"
And then she mocks him saying, "Oh, you plane
Destined for making shavings! take a deal board!"

If the woman has a hump as well as the man, they may take any of the various positions for coition, always observing that if one of them lies on the back, the hump must be surrounded with cushions, as with a turban, thus having a nest to lie in, which guards its top, which is very tender. In this way they can embrace closely.

If the man is humped both on back and chest he must renounce the embrace and the clinging, but can otherwise take any position he likes for coition. Yet generally speaking, the action must always be troublesome for himself and the woman. I have written on this subject:

The humpback engaged in the act of coition
Is like a vase provided with two handles.
If he is burning for a woman, she will tell him,
"Your hump is in the way; you cannot do it;
Your member would find a place to rummage in,
But on your chest the hump, where would it be?"

If both the woman and the man have double humps, the best position they can assume for coitus is the following: "Whilst the woman is lying on her side, the man introduces his member after the fashion described previously in respect to pregnant women. Thus the two humps do not encounter one another. Both are lying on their sides, and the man attacks from behind. Should the woman be on her back, her hump must be supported by a cushion, whilst the man kneels between her legs, she holding up her posterior. Thus placed, their two humps are not near each other, and all inconvenience is avoided.

The same is the case if the woman stoops down with her head, with her rump in the air, after the manner of *El kouri*, which position will suit both of them, if they have the chest malformed, but not the back. One of them then performs the action of come-and-go. But the most curious and amusing description which I have ever met in this respect, is contained in these verses:

Their two extremities are close together,
And nature made a laughing stock of them;
Foreshortened he appears as if cut off;
He looks like someone bending to escape a blow,
Or like a man who has received a blow
And shrivels down so as to miss a second.

327

If a man's spine is curved about the hips and his back is straight, so that he looks as though he was in prayer, half prostrated, coition for him is very difficult; owing to the reciprocal positions of his thighs and his stomach, he cannot possibly insert his member entirely, as it lies so far back between his thighs. The best for him to do is to stand up. The woman stoops down before him with her hands to the ground and her posterior in the air; he can thus introduce his member as a pivot for the woman to move upon, for, be it observed, he cannot easily move himself. It is the manner *El kouri*, with the difference, that it is the woman who moves.

A man may be attacked by the illness called *ikaad*, or *zomana* (paralysis), which compels him to be constantly seated. If this affliction only affects his knees and legs, his thighs and spinal column remaining sound, he can use all the different positions for coition, except those where he would have to stand up. In the case of his buttocks being affected, even if he is otherwise perfectly well, it is the woman who will have to make all the movements.

Know that the most enjoyable coitus does not always exist in the manners described here; I only give them, so as to render this work as complete as possible. Sometimes most enjoyable coition takes place between lovers, who, not quite perfect in their proportions, find their own means for their mutual gratification. It is said that there are women of great experience who, lying with a man, elevate one of their feet vertically in the air, and upon that foot a lamp is set full of oil, and with the wick burning. While the man is ramming them, they keep the lamp steady and burning, and the oil is not spilled. Their coition is in no way impeded by this exhibition, but it must require great previous practice on the part of both.

Assuredly the Indian writers have in their works described a great many ways of making love, but the majority of them do not give enjoyment, and give more pain than pleasure. That which is to be looked for in coition, the crowning point of it, is the enjoyment, the embrace, the kisses. This is the distinction between the coitus of men and that of animals. No one is indifferent to the enjoyment which proceeds from the difference between the sexes, and the man finds his greatest joy in it.

If the desire of love in man is roused to its highest pitch, all the pleasure of coition becomes easy for him, and he satisfies his yearning in any way.

It is well for the lover of coition to put all these ways to the test, so as to ascertain which is the position that gives the greatest pleasure to both combatants. Then he will know which to choose for the meeting, and in satisfying his desires retain the woman's affection.

Many people have tried all the positions I have described, but none has been as much approved of as the *Dok el arz*.

A story is told on this subject of a man who had a wife of incomparable beauty, graceful and accomplished. He used to explore her in the ordinary manner, never having recourse to any other. The woman experienced none of the pleasure which ought to accompany the act, and way consequently generally very moody after the coition was over.

The man complained about this to an old dame, who told him, "Try different ways in uniting yourself to her, until you find the one which best satisfies her. Then work her in this fashion only, and her affection for you will know no limit."

He then tried upon his wife various manners of coition, and when he came to the one called *Dok el arz* he saw her overcome by violent raptures of love, and at the climax pleasure he felt her womb grasp his member energetically; and she said to him, biting his lips. "This is the real way of making love!"

These demonstrations proved to the lover, in fact, that his mistress felt in that position the most lively pleasure, and he always afterwords worked with her in that way. Thus he attained his end, and caused the woman to love him to the point of madness.

Therefore try different manners; for every woman likes one in preference to all other for her pleasure. The majority of them have, however, a predilection for the *Dok el arz*, as, during it belly is pressed to belly, mouth glued to mouth, and the action of the womb is rarely absent.

I have now only to mention the various movements practised during coitus, and shall describe some of them.

First movement – Neza el dela (the bucket in the well). The man and woman join in close embrace after the introduction. Then he gives a push, and withdraws a little; the woman follows him with a push, and also retires. So they continue their alternate movement, keeping proper time. Placing foot against foot, and hand against hand, they keep up the motion of a bucket in a well.

Second movement – El netahi (the mutual shock). After the introduction, they each draw back, but without dislodging the member completely. Then they both push tightly together, and thus go on keeping time.

Third movemend – El motadani (the approach). The man moves as usual, and then stops. Then the woman, with the member in her receptacle, begins to move like the man, and then stops. And they continue this way until the ejaculation comes.

Fourth movement – Khiate el heub (Love's tailor). The man, with his member being only partially inserted in the vulva, keeps up a sort of quick friction with the part that is in, and then suddenly plunges his whole member in up to its root. This is the movement of the needle in the hands of the tailor, of which the man and woman must take notice.

Such a movement only suits those men and women who can at will delay the climax. With those who are otherwise constituted it would act too quickly.

Fifth movement – Souak el feurdj (the toothpick in the vulva). The man introduces his member between the walls of the vulva, and then drives it up and down, and right and left. Only a man with a very vigorous member can execute this movement.

Sixth movement – Tâchik el heub (the boxing up of love). The man introduces his member entirely into the vagina, so closely that his hairs are completely mixed up with the woman's. In that position he must now move forcibly, without withdrawing his tool in the least.

This is the best of all the movements, and is particularly well adapted to the position *Dok el arz*. Women prefer it to any other kind, as it procures them the extreme pleasure of seizing the member with their womb; and satisfies their lust most completely.

Those women called *tribades* always use this movement in their mutual caresses. And it provokes prompt ejaculation both with man and woman.

Without kissing, no kind of position or movement procures the fullest pleasure; and those positions in which the kiss is not practicable are not entirely satisfactory, considering that the kiss is one of the most powerful stimulants to the work of love.

I have said in verse:

The languishing eye
Puts in connection soul with soul,
And the tender kiss
Takes the message from member to vulva.

The kiss is assumed to be an integral part of coition. The best kiss is the one impressed on humid lips combined with the suction of the lips and tongue, which particularly provokes the flow of sweet and fresh saliva. It is for the man to bring this about by slightly and softly nibbling his partner's tongue, when her saliva will flow sweet and exquisite, more pleasant than pure honey, and which will not mix with the saliva of her mouth. This action will give the man a trembling sensation, which will run all through his body, and is more intoxicating than wine drunk to excess.

A poet has said:

In kissing her, I have drunk from her mouth
Like a camel that drinks from the oasis;
Her embrace and the freshness of her mouth
Give me a languor that goes to my marrow.

The kiss should be melodious; it originates with the tongue touching the palate, lubricated by saliva. It is produced by the movement of the tongue in the mouth and by the displacement of the saliva, provoked by the suction.

The kiss given to the superficial outer part of the lips, and making a noise comparable to the one by which you call your cat, gives no pleasure. It is well enough thus applied to children and hands.

The kiss I have described above is the one for coitus and is full of voluptuousness.

A vulgar proverb says:
A humid kiss
Is better than a hurried coitus.

I have composed on this subject the following lines:
You kiss my hand – my mouth should be the place!
O woman, thou who art my idol!
It was a fond kiss you gave me, but it is lost,
The hand cannot appreciate the nature of a kiss.

The three words, *Kobla, letsem,* and *bouss* are used indifferently to indicate the kiss on the hand or on the mouth. The word *ferame* means specially the kiss on the mouth.
An Arab poet has said:

The heart of love can find no remedy
In witch's sorcery nor amulets,
Nor in the fond embrace without a kiss,
Nor in a kiss without coitus.

And the author of the work, "The Jewels of the Bride and the Rejoicing of Souls", has added to the above, as complement and commentary, the two following verses:
Nor in converse, however unrestrained,
But in the placing of legs on legs (coition).

Remember that all caresses and all sorts of kisses, as described, are of no account without the introduction of the member. Therefore abstain from them, if you do not want action; they only fan a fire to no purpose. The passion which is excited resembles in fact a fire which is being lighted; and just as water only can extinguish the latter, so only the emission of the sperm can calm the lust and satisfy the desire.

The woman gains no more than the man from caresses without coition. It is said that Dahama bent Mesedjel appeared before the Governor of the province of Yamama, with her father and her husband, El Adjadje, alleging that the latter was impotent, and did not copulate with her nor come near her.

Her father, who assisted her in her case, was reproached for interfering with her grievance by the people of Yamama, who said to him, "Are you not ashamed to help your daughter in bringing a claim for coition?"

To which he answered, "It is my wish that she should have children; if she loses them it will be by God's will; if she brings them up they will be useful to her." Dahama formulated her claim thus in coming before the Governor: "There stands my husband, and until now he has never touched me." The Governor objected, saying, "No doubt this is because you have been unwilling?" "On the contrary", she replied, "it is for him that I open my thighs and lie down on my back." Then cried the husband, "O Emir, she lies; in order to possess her I have to fight with her." The Emir pronounced the following judgment: "I give you", he said, "a year's time to prove her allegation to be false." He decided thus out of regard for the man. El Adjadje then went away reciting those verses:

Dahama and her father Mesedjel thought
The Emir would decide upon my impotence.
Is not the stallion sometimes lazy-minded?
And yet he is so large and vigorous.

Returned to his house he began to kiss and caress his wife; but his efforts went no farther, he remained incapable of giving proof of his virility. Dahama said to him, "Keep your caresses and embraces; they do not satisfy love. What I desire is a solid and stiff member, the sperm of which will flow into my womb." And she recited to him the following verses:

Before God! it is in vain to try with kisses
To entertain me, and with your embracings!
To still my torments I must feel a member,
Ejaculating sperm into my uterus.

333

El Adjadje, in despair, conducted her forthwirth back to her family, and, to hide his shame, repudiated her that very night.

A poet said on that occasion:

What are caresses to an ardent woman,
Or costly vestments and fine jewellery,
If the man's organs do not meet her own,
And she is yearning for the virile member?

Know then that the majority of women do not find full satisfaction in kisses and embraces without coition. For them satisfaction resides only in the member, and they like the man who enters them, even if he is ugly and misshapen. A story also goes on this subject that Moussa ben Mesâb betook himself one day to a woman in the town who had a female slave, an excellent singer, whom he wanted to buy from her. This woman was resplendently beautiful, and independent of her charming appearance, she had a large fortune. He saw at the same time in the house a young man of bad shape and ungainly appearance, who went to and from giving orders.

Moussa asked who the man was, she told him, "This is my husband, and for him I would give my life!" "This is a hard slavery", he said, "to which you are reduced, and I am sorry for you. We belong to God, and shall return to him! but what a misfortune it is that such incomparable beauty and such delightful forms as I see in you should be for such a man!"

She made answer, "O son of my mother, if he could do to you from behind what he does for me in front, you would sell your lately acquired fortune as well as your patrimony. He would appear to you beautiful, and his plain looks would be changed into beauty."

"May God preserve him to you!" said Moussa.

It is also said that the poet Farazdak met one day a woman on whom he cast a glance burning with love, and who for that reason thus addressed him: "What makes you look at me in this fashion? Had I a thousand vulvas, there would be nothing to hope for you!" "And why?" said the poet. "Because your appearance is not attractive", she said, "and what you keep hidden will be no better." He replied,

"If you would put me to the proof, you would find that my interior qualities are of a nature to make you forget my auter appearance." He then uncovered himself, and let her see a member the size of the arm of a young girl. At that sight she felt herself burning ardently with amorous desire. He saw this, and asked her to let him caress her. Then she uncovered herself and showed him her mount of Venus, vaulted like a dome.

He then performed the act with her, and recited these verses:

I have plied in her my member, big as a virgin's arm;
A member with a round head, and prompt to attack;
Measuring in length a span and a half,
And, oh! I felt as though I had put it in a brazier.

He who seeks the pleasure a woman can give must satisfy her amorous desire for ardent caresses, as described. He will see her swooning with lust, her vulva will get moist, her womb will stretch forward, and the two sperms will come together.

Of matters which are injurious in the act of copulation

Know, o Vizir (to whom God be good!), that the ills caused by coition are numerous. I will mention to you some of them, which to know is essential, in order to be able to avoid them.

Let me tell you in the first place that coition, if performed standing; affects the knee-joints and brings about nervous shiverings; and if performed sideways will predispose your system towards gout and sciatica, which resides chiefly in the hip joint.

Do not mount upon a woman fasting or immediately before eating a meal, or else you will have pains in your back, you will lose your vigour, and your eyesight will get weaker.

If you do it with the woman astride you, your spinal cord will suffer and your heart will be affected; and if in that position the smallest drop of the usual secretions of the vagina enters your urethral canal, a painful stricture may occur.

Do not leave your member in the vulva after ejaculation, as this might cause gravel, or softening of the vertebral column, or the rupture of blood vessels, or lastly, inflammation of the lungs.

Too much exercise after coition is also detrimental.

Avoid washing your member after the copulation, as this may cause sores. As to coition with old women, it acts like a fatal poison, and it has been said, "Do not have intercourse with old women, be they as rich as Karoun." And it has further been said, "Beware of mounting old women; even if they overwhelm you with favours." And again, "The coitus of old women is a venomous meal."

Know that the man who works a woman younger than he is himself acquires new vigour; if she is of the same age as he is he will derive no advantage from it; and, finally, if it is a woman older than himself she will take all his strength out of him for herself. The following verses treat this subject:

Be on your guard and shun coition with old women;

In her bosom she bears the poison of the *arakime*.

A proverb says also, "Do not serve an old woman, even if she offered to feed you with semolina and almond bread."

The excessive practice of coition injures the health on account of the expenditure of too much sperm. For as butter made of cream represents the quintessence of the milk, and if you take the cream off, the milk loses its qualities, even so does the sperm form the quintessence of nutrition, and its loss is debilitating. On the other hand, the condition of the body, and consequently the quality of the sperm depends directly upon the food you take. If, therefore, a man will passionately give himself up to the enjoyment of coition, without undergoing too great fatigue, he must live upon strengthening food, exciting sweetmeats aromatic plants, meat, honey, eggs, and other similar foods. He who follows such a régime is protected against the following accidents, to which excessive coition may lead.

Firstly, the loss of generative power.

Secondly, the deterioration of his sight; for although he may not become blind, he will at least have to suffer from eye diseases if he does not follow my advice.

Thirdly, the loss of his physical strength; he may become like the man who wants to fly but cannot, who pursuing somebody cannot catch him, or who carrying a burden, or working, soon gets tired and prostrated.

He who does not want to feel the necessity for coition uses camphor. Half of a

mitskal of this substance, steeped in water, makes the man who drinks of it insensible to the pleasures of copulation. Many women use this remedy when in fits of jealousy against rivals, or when they need rest after great excesses. Then they try to procure camphor that has been left after a burial, and shrink from no expense of money to get such from the old women who have the charge of the corpses. They also make use of the flower of henna, which is called *faria*; they steep the same in water, until it turns yellow, and thus supply themselves with a beverage which has almost the same effect as camphor.

I have treated of these remedies in the present chapter, although this is not their proper place; but I thought that this information, as here given, may be of use to many persons.

There are certain things which will become injurious if constantly indulged in and which in the end affect the health. Such are: too much sleep, long voyages at unfavourable times, which, particularly in cold countries, may weaken the body and cause disease of the spine. The same effects may arise from the habitual handling of those materials which cause cold and humidity, like plaster, etc. For people who have difficulty in passing water coitus is harmful.

The habit of consuming acid food is debilitating.

To keep one's member in the vulva of a woman after ejaculation has taken place, be it for a long or a short time, enfeebles that organ and makes it less fit for coition.

If you are lying with a woman, make love several times if you feel inclined, but take care not to overdo it, for it is true that "He who plays the game of love for his own sake, and to satisfy his desires, feels the most intense and durable pleasure; but he who does it to satisfy the lust of another person will languish, lose all his desire, and finish by becoming impotent for coition."

The sense of these words is, that a man when he feels disposed for it can give himself up to the exercise of coitus with more or less ardour according to his desires, and at the time which best suits him, without any fear of future impotence, if his enjoyment is provoked and regulated only by his feeling the desire to lie with a woman.

But he who makes love for the sake of somebody else, that is to say only to satis-fy the passion of his mistress, and tries all he can to attain that impossibility, that man will act against his own interest and imperil his health to please another person.

As injurious may be considered coition in the bath or immediately after leaving the bath; after having been bled or purged or such like. Coitus after a heavy bout of drinking is likewise to be avoided. To indulge coitus with a woman during menstruation is as detrimental to the man as to the woman herself, as at that time her blood is impure and her womb cold, and if the least drop of blood should get in the man's urinary canal numerous ailments may occur. As to the woman, she feels no pleasure during and at such time holds coitus in aversion. As regards copulation in the bath, some say that there is no pleasure to be derived from it, if, as is believed, the degree of enjoyment is dependent upon the warmth of the vulva; for in the bath the vulva cannot be otherwise than cold, and consequently unfit for giving pleasure. And it is besides not to be forgotten that the water penetrating into the sexual parts of man or woman may lead to grave consequences.

Coitus after a full meal may cause rupture of the intestines. It is also to be avoided after undergoing great fatigue, or at a time of very hot or very cold weather.

Amongst the accidents which may attend the act of coition in hot countries may be mentioned sudden blindness without any previous symptoms. The repetition of the coitus without washing the parts ought to be shunned, as it may enfeeble the virile power.

The man must also abstain from copulation with his wife if he is in a state of legal impurity, for if she should become pregnant by such coition the child could not be sound.

After ejaculation do not remain close to the woman, as the disposition for re-commencing will suffer by doing so.

Care is to be taken not to carry heavy loads on one's back or to over-exert the mind, if one does not want the coitus to be impeded. It is also not good constant-ly to wear clothing made of silk, as they impair all the energy for copulation.

Silken cloths worn by women also harm the capacity for erection of the virile member.

Fasting, if prolonged, calms sexual desire; but in the beginning it excites the same.

Abstain from greasy liquids, as in the course of time they diminish the strength necessary for coition.

The effect of snuff, whether plain or scented, is similar.

It is bad to wash the sexual parts with cold water directly after copulation; in general, washing with cold water calms down the desire, while warm water strengthens it.

Conversation with a young woman excites in a man the erection and passion commensurate with the youthfulness of the woman.

An Arab addressed the following recommendation to his daughter at the time when he led her to her husband: "Perfume yourself with water!" meaning that she should frequently wash her body with water in preference to perfumes; the latter, moreover, not being suitable for everyone.

It is also reported that a woman having said to her husband, "You are then a nobody, as you never perfume yourself!" he answered, "Oh, you slut! it is for the woman to emit a sweet odour."

The abuse of coition is followed by loss of the taste for its pleasures; and to remedy this loss the sufferer must anoint his member with a mixture of the blood of a he-goat with honey. This will achieve for him a marvellous effect in making love.

It is said that reading the Koran also predisposes for copulation.

Remember that a prudent man will beware of abusing the enjoyment of coition. The sperm is the water of life; if you use it economically you will always be ready for love's pleasures; it is the light of your eye; do not be lavish with it at all times and whenever you have a fancy for enjoyment, for if you are not sparing with it you will expose yourself to many ills. Wise medical men say, "A robust constitution is indispensable for copulation, and he who is endowed with it may give himself up to the pleasure without danger; but it is otherwise with the weakly man; he runs into danger by indulging freely with women."

The sage, Es Sakli, has thus determined the limits to be observed by man as to the indulgence of the pleasures of coition: Man, be he phlegmatic or sanguine, should not make love more than twice or thrice a month; cholic or hypochondriac men only once or twice a month. It is nevertheless a well established fact that nowadays men of any of these four temperaments are insatiable as to coition, and give themselves up to it day and night, not caring that they expose themselves to numerous ills, both internal and external.

Women are more favoured than men in indulging their passion for coition. It is in fact their speciality; and for them it is all pleasure; while men run many risks in abandoning themselves without reserve to the pleasures of love.

Having thus treated of the dangers which may occur from the coitus, I have considered it useful to bring to your knowledge the following verses, which contain hygienic advice in their respect. These verses have been composed by the order of Haroun er Rachid by the most celebrated physicians of his time, whom he had asked to inform him of the remedies for successfully combating the ills caused by coition.

Eat slowly, if your food shall do you good,
And take good care, that it be well digested.
Beware of things which want hard mastication;
They are bad nourishment, so keep from them.
Drink not directly after finishing your meal,
Or else you go half way to meet an illness.
Keep not within you what is of excess,
And if you were in most susceptible circles,
Attend to this well before seeking your bed,
For rest this is the first necessity.
From medicines and drugs keep well away,
And do not use them unless very ill.
Use all precautions proper, for they keep
Your body sound, and are the best support.
Don't be too eager for round-breasted women;
Excess of pleasure soon will make you feeble,

And in coition you may find a sickness;
And then you find too late that in coition
Our spring of life runs into woman's vulva.
And before all beware of aged women,
For their embraces will to you be poison.
Each second day a bath should wash you clean;
Remember these precepts and follow them.
Those were the rules given by the sages to the master of benevolence and goodness, to the generous of the generous.
All sages and physicians agree in saying that the ills which afflict man originate in the abuse of coition. The man therefore who wishes to preserve his health, and particularly his sight, and who wants to lead a pleasant life, will indulge with moderation in love's pleasures, aware that the greatest evils may spring therefrom.

VIII

The various names given to the sexual parts of man

Know, o Vizir (to whom God be good!), that man's member has different names, such as:

El de keur, the virile member.
El kamera, the penis.
El aïr, the member for generation.
El hamama, the pigeon.
El teunnana, the tinkler.
El heurmak, the indomitable.
El ahlil, the liberator.
El zeub, the verge.
El hammache, the exciter.
El nâasse, the sleeper.
El zodamme, the crowbar.
El khiade, the tailor.
Mochefi el relil, the extinguisher of passion.

El khorrate, the turnabout.
El deukkak, the striker.
El âouame, the swimmer.
El dekhal, the housebreaker.
El âour, the one-eyed.
El fortass, the bald.
Abou aïne, the one with an eye.
El atsar, the pusher.
El dommar, the strong-headed.
Abou rokba, the one with a neck.
Abou quetaïa, the hairy one.
El besiss, the impudent one.
El mostahi, the shame-faced one.
El bekkaï, the weeping one.
El hezzaz, the rummager.
El lezzaz, the unionist.
Abou lâaba, the expectorant.
El fattache, the searcher.
El hakkak, the rubber.
El mourekhi, the flabby one.
El motelâ, the ransacker.
El mokcheuf, the discoverer.

As regards the names of *kamera* and *dekeur,* their meaning is plain. *Dekeur* is a word which signifies the male of all creatures, and is also used in the sense of "mention" and "memory". When a man has an accident with his member, when it has been amputated, or has become weak, and he can, in consequence, no longer fulfil his conjugal duties, they say of him: "the member of such a one is dead"; which means: the remembrance of him will be lost, and his generation is cut off at the root. When he dies they will say. "His member has been cut off", meaning "His memory is departed from the world."

The *dekeur* plays also an important part in dreams. The man who dreams that his member has been cut off is certain not to live long after that dream, for, as said above, it presages the loss of his memory and the extinction of his race. I shall treat this subject more particularly in the interpretation of dreams.

The teeth (*senane*) represent years (*senine*); if therefore a man sees in a dream a fine set of teeth, this is for him the sign of a long life.

If he sees his nail (*defeur*) reversed or upside down, this is an indication that the victory (*defeur*) which he has gained over his enemies will change sides; and from a victor, he will become the vanquished; inversely, if he sees the nail of his enemy turned the wrong way, he can conclude that the victory which had been with his enemy will soon return to him.

The sight of a lily (*sonsana*) is the prognostication of a misfortune which will last a year (*son*, misfortune; *sena*, year).

The appearance of ostriches (*nâmate*) in dreams is of bad omen, because their name being formed of *nâa* and *mate*, signifies "news of death", namely, peril. To dream of a shield (*henafa*) means the happening of all sorts of misfortune, for this word, by a change of letters, gives *koul afa*, "all bad luck".

The sight of a fresh rose (*ouarde*) announces the arrival (*ouroud*) of a pleasure to make the heart tremble with joy; whilst a faded rose indicates deceitful news. It is the same with baldness of the temples, and similar things.

The jessamine (*yasmine*) is formed of *yas*, signifying deception, or the happening of a thing contrary to your wish, and *mine*, which means untruth. The man, then, who sees a jessamine in his dream is to conclude that the deception, *yas*, in the name *yasmine*, is an untruth, and will thus be assured of the success of his enterprise. However, the prognostications furnished by the jessamine have not the same character of certainty as those given by the rose. It differs, in fact, greatly from this latter flower, inasmuch as the slightest breath of wind will upset it.

The sight of a saucepan (*beurma*) announces the conclusion (*anuberame*) of affairs in which one is engaged. Abou Djahel (God's curse be upon him!) has added that this conclusion would take place during the night.

A jar (*khabia*) is the sign of wickedness (*khebets*) in every kind of affair, unless it is one that has fallen into a pit or a river and got broken, so as to let escape all the calamities contained in it.

The sawing of wood (*nechara*) means good news (*bechara*).

The inkstand (*douaïa*) indicates the remedy (*doua*), namely, the cure of a malady, unless it be burnt, broken or lost, when it means the contrary.

The turban (*âmama*) if seen to fall over the face and cover the eyes an omen of blindness (*âina*), from which God preserve us!

The finding again in good condition of a gem that has been lost or forgotten is a sign of success.

If one dreams that he gets out of a window (*taga*) he may know that he will come with advantage out of all transactions he may have, whether important or not. But if the window seen in the dream is narrow so that he had some trouble to get out of it, this will be to him a sign that in order to be successful he will have to make efforts in proportion to the difficulty experienced by him in getting out. The bitter orange signifies that from the place where it was seen malicious statements will come.

Trees (*achedjar*) mean discussions (*mechadjera*).

The carrot (*asefnaria*) indicates misfortune (*asef*) and sorrow.

The turnip (*cufte*) means for the man that has seen it a matter that is past and gone (*ameur fate*), so that there is no going back to it. The matter is weighty if it appeared large, of no importance if seen small; in short, important in proportion to the size of the turnip that has been seen.

A musket seen without its being fired means a conspiracy, and of no importance. But if it seen going off it is a sign that the moment has arrived for the realisation of the plot.

The sight of fire is of bad omen.

If the pitcher (*brik*) of a man who has turned to God breaks, this is a sign that his repentance is in vain, but if the glass out of which he drinks wine breaks, this means that he returns to God.

If you have dreamed of feasts and sumptuous banquets, be sure that quite contrary things will come to pass.

If you have seen somebody bidding good-bye to people on their going away you may be certain that it will be the latter who will shortly wish him a good journey; for the poet says:

If you have seen your friend saying good-bye, rejoice;
Let your soul be content as to him who is far away,
For you may look forward to his speedy return,
And the heart of him who said adieu will come back to you.

The coriander (*keusbeur*) signifies that the vulva (*keuss*) is in proper condition. On this subject there is a story that the Sultan Haroun er Rachid having with him several persons of rank with whom he was familiar, rose and left them to go to one of his wives, whom he wanted to enjoy. He found her suffering from menstruation, and returned to his companions to sit down with them, resigned to his disappointment.

Now it so happened that a moment afterwards the woman found herself free from her discharge. When she had assured herself of this, she washed herself and sent to the Sultan, by one of her negresses, a plate of coriander.

Haroun er Rachid was seated amongst his friends when the negress brought the plate to him. He took it and examined it, but did not understand the meaning of its being sent to him by his wife. At last he handed it to one of his poets, who, having looked at it attentively, recited to him the following verses:

She has sent you coriander (*keusbeur*),
White as sugar;
I have placed it in my palm,
And concentrated all my thoughts upon it,
In order to find out its meaning;
And I have seized it. O my master, what she wants to say,
Is "My vulva is restored to health" (*keussi beuri*).

Er Rachid was surprised at the wit shown by the woman, and at the poets's perception. Thus that which was to remain a mystery remained hidden, and that which was to be known was divulged.

A drawn sword is a sign of war, and the victory will remain with him who holds its hilt.

A bridle means servitude and oppression. A long beard points to good fortune and prosperity; but it is said that it is a sign of death if it reaches down to the ground.

Others pretend that the intelligence of each man is in an inverse proportion to the length of his beard; that is to say, a big beard denotes a small mind. A story goes in this respect, that a man who had a long beard saw one day a book with the following sentence inscribed on its back: "He whose chin is adorned with a large beard is as foolish as his beard is long." Afraid of being taken for a fool by his acquaintances, he thought of getting rid of what there was too much of, and to this end, it being night-time, he grasped a handful of his beard close to the chin, and set the remainder on fire by the light of the lamp. The flame ran rapidly up the beard and reached his hand, which he had to withdraw quickly on account of the heat. Thus his beard was burnt off entirely. Then he wrote on the back of the book, under the above mentioned sentence, "These words are entirely true. I, who am now writing this, have proved their truth." Being himself convinced that the weakness of the intellect is proportioned to the length of the beard.

On the same subject it is related that Haroun er Rachid, being in a kiosk, saw a man with a long beard. He ordered the man to be brought before him, and when he was there he asked him, "What is your name?" "Abou Arouba", replied the man.

"What is your profession?"

"I am a master in argument."

Haroun then gave him the following case to solve. A man buys a he-goat, who, in excreting his excrements, hits the buyer's eye with part of it and injures the same. "Who has to pay for damages?" "The seller", promptly says Abou Arouba. "And why?" asked the Kalif. "Because he has sold the animal without warning the buyer that it has a catapult in its anus", answered the man. At these words the Kalif began to laugh immoderately, and recited the following verses:

When the beard of the young man
Has grown down to his navel,

The shortness of his intellect is, in my eyes,
Proportioned to the length his beard has grown.

It is declared by many authors that amongst proper names there are such as bring luck, and others that bring ill luck, according to their meaning.

The names Ahmed, Mohammed, Hamdonna, Hamdoun, indicate in encouters and in dreams the lucky result arrived at in a transaction. Ali, Alia, indicate the height and elevation of rank. Naserouna, Naseur, Mansour, Naseur Allah signify triumph over enemies. Salem, Salema, Selim, Selimane indicate success in all affairs; also safety for him who is in danger. Fetah Allah, Fetah indicate victory, like all the other names which in their meaning speak of lucky things. The names Râd, Râda signify thunder, tumult, and comprise everything in connection with this meaning. Abou el Feurdj and Ferendj indicate joy; Ranem and Renime success, Khalf Allah and Khaleuf compensation for a loss, and benediction. The sense of Abder Rassi, Hafid and Mahfond is favourable. The names including the words *latif* (benevolent), *mourits* (helpful), *hanine* (compassionate), *aziz* (beloved), carry with them, in conformity with the sense of these words, the ideas of benevolence, *lateuf* (charity), *iratsa* (compassion), *hanana*, and *aiz* (favour). As an example of words of an unfavourable omen I will cite *el ouar, el ouara*, which imply the idea of difficulties. To support the truth of the preceding observations I will refer to this saying of the Prophet (the salutation and benevolence of God to him!). "Compare the names appearing in your dreams with their meaning, so that you may draw therefrom your conclusions."

I must confess that this was not the place for treating of this subject, but one word leads on to more. I now return to the object of this chapter, viz: the different names of the sexual parts of man.

The name of *el aïr* is derived from *el kir* (the smith's bellows). In fact if you turn in the latter word the k, *kef*, so that it faces the opposite way, you will find the word reads *el aïr*. The member is so called on account of its alternate swelling and subsiding again. If swollen up it stands erect, and if not it sinks down flaccid. It is calles *el hamama* (the pigeon), because after having been swelled out it resembles at the moment when it returns to rest a pigeon sitting on her eggs.

El teunnana (the tinkler) – So called because every time it enters or comes out of the vulva in coition it makes a noise.

El heurmak (the indomitable) – It has received this name because when in a state of erection it begins to move its head, searching for the entrance to the vulva till it has found it, and it then walks in quite insolently, without asking leave.

El ahlil (the liberator) - Thus called because in penetrating into the vulva of a woman thrice repudiated it gives her the liberty to return to her first husband.

El zeub (the verge) – From the word *deub*, which means creeping. This name was given to the member because when it gets between a woman's thighs and feels a plump vulva it begins to creep upon the thighs and the Mount of Venus, then approaches the entrance of the vulva, and keeps creeping in until it is in possession and is comfortably lodged, and having it all its own way penetrates into the middle of the vulva, there to ejaculate.

El hammache (the exciter) – It has received this name because it irritates the vulva by its frequent entries and exits.

El nâasse (the sleeper) – From its deceitful appearance. When it gets into erection, it lengthens out and stiffens itself to such an extent that one might think it would never get soft again. But when it has left the vulva, after having satisfied its passion, it goes to sleep. There are members that fall asleep while inside the vulva but the majority of them come out still firm; but at that moment they get drowsy, and little by little they go to sleep.

El zoddame (the crowbar) – It is called so because when it meets the vulva and the same will not let it pass in directly, it forces the entrance with is head, breaking and tearing everything, like a wild beast in heat.

El khiate (the tailor) – It takes this name from the fact that it does not enter the vulva until it has manoeuvred about the entrance, like a needle in the hand of a tailor, creeping and rubbing against it until it is sufficiently roused, after which it enters.

Mochefi el relil (the extinguisher of passion) – This name is given to a member which is large, strong, and slow to ejaculate; such a member satisfies most completely the amorous wishes of a woman; for, after having wrought her up to the highest pitch, it allays her excitement better than any other. And, in the same way, it calms the ardour of the man. When it wants to get into the vulva, and arriving at the entrance, finds it closed, it laments, begs and promises: "Oh! my love! let me come in, I will not stay long." And when it has been admitted, it breaks its word, and makes a long stay, and does not take its leave till it has satisfied its ardour by the ejaculation of the sperm, coming and going, tilting high and low, and moving right and left. The vulva protests, "How about your word, you deceiver?" she says; "you said you would only stop in for a moment." And the member answers, "Oh, certainly! I shall not retire till I have encountered your womb; but after having found it, I will promise to withdraw at once." At these words, the vulva takes pity on him, and advances her womb, which clasps and kisses its head, as if saluting it. The member then retires with is passion cooled down.

El khorrate (the turnabout) - This name was given to it because on arriving at the vulva it pretends to come on important business, knocks at the door, turns about everywhere, without shame or bashfulness, investigating every corner to the right and left, forward and backward, and then all at once darts right to the bottom of the vagina for the ejaculation.

El deukkak (the striker) – Thus called because on arriving at the entrance of the vulva it gives a slight knock. If the vulva opens the door, it enters; if there is no response, it begins to knock again, and does not cease until it is admitted. The parasite who wants to get into the house of a rich man to be present at a feast does the same: he knocks at the door; and if it is opened, he walks in; but if there is no response to his knock, he repeats it again and again until the door is opened. And similarly the *deukkak* with the door of the vulva.
By "knocking at the door" is meant the friction of the member against the entrance of the vulva until the latter becomes moist. The appearance of this moisture is the phenomenon alluded to by the expression "opening the door."

El âouame (the swimmer) – Because when it enters the vulva it does not remain in one favourite place, but, on the contrary, turns to the right, to the left, goes forward, draws back, and then moves like swimming in the middle amongst its own sperm and the fluid coming from the vulva, as if in fear of drowning and trying to save itself.

El dekhal (the housebreaker) – Merits that name because on coming to the door of the vulva this one asks, "What do you want?" "I want to come in!" "Impossible! I cannot take you in on account of your size.' Then the member insists that the other one should only receive its head, promising not to come in entirely; it then approaches, rubs its head twice or thrice between the vulva's lips, till they get humid and thus lubriacated, then introduces first its head, and after, with one push, plunges in up to the testicles.

El aâouar (the one-eyed) – Because it has but one eye, which is not like other eyes, and does not see clearly.

El fortass (the bald one) - Because there is no hair on its head, which makes it look bald.

Abou aïne (he with one eye) – It has received this name because its one eye presents the peculiarity of being without pupil and eyelashes.

El âtsar (the stumbler) – It is called so because if it wants to penetrate in the vulva, as it does not see the door, it beats about above and below, and thus continues to stumble as over stones in the road, until the lips of the vulva get humid, when it manages to get inside. The vulva then says, "What has happened to you that made you stumble about so?" The member answers, "O my love, it was a stone lying in the road."

El dommar (the odd-headed) – Because its head is different from all other heads.

Abou rokba (the one with a neck) – That is the being with a short neck, a well developed throat, and thick at the end, a bald head, and who, moreover, has coarse and bristly hair from the navel to the pubis.

Abou guetaïa (the hairy one; who has a forest of hair) – This name is given to it when the hair is abundant about it.

El besiss (the impudent) – It has received this name because from the moment that it gets stiff and long it does not care for anybody, lifts impudently the clothing of its master by raising its head fiercely, and makes him ashamed while itself feels no shame. It acts in the same unabashed way with women, turning up their clothes and laying bare their thighs. Its master may blush at this conduct, but as to itself its stiffness and determination to plunge into a vulva only increase.

El mostahi (the shame-faced) – This sort of member which is met with sometimes, is capable of feeling ashamed and timid when facing a vulva which it does not know, and it is only after a little time that it gets bolder and stiffens. Sometimes it is even so much troubled that it remains incapable for the coitus, which happens in particular when a stranger is present, in which case it becomes quite unable to move.

El bekkai (the weeper) – So called on account of the many tears it sheds; as soon as it gets an erection, it weeps; when it sees a pretty face, it weeps; handling a woman, it weeps. It goes even so far as to weep tears sacred to memory.

El hezzaz (the rummager) – It is named thus because as soon as it penetrates into the vulva it begins to rummage about vigorously, until it has appeased its passion.

El lezzaz (the unionist) – Received that name because as soon as it is in the vulva it pushes and works till fur meets fur, and even makes efforts to force the testicles into it.

Abou làaba (the expectorant) – Has received this name because when coming near a vulva, or when it sees one, or even when merely thinking of it, or when its master touches a woman or plays with her or kisses her, its saliva begins to move and it has tears in its eye; this saliva is particularly abundant when it has been for some time out of work, and it will even wet then his master's clothing. This member is very common, and there are but few people who do not have it. The liquid it sheds is cited by lawyers under the name of *medi*. Its production is the result of toyings and of lascivious thoughts. With some people it is so abundant as to fill the vulva, so that they may erroneously believe that it comes from the woman.

El fattache (the searcher) – From its habit, when in the vulva, of turning in every direction as if in search of something; and that something is the womb. It will know no rest until it has found it.

El hakkak (the rubber) – It has got his name because it will not enter the vagina until it has rubbed its head against the entrance and the lower part of the belly. It is frequently mistaken for the next one.

El mourekhi (the flabby one) – The one who can never get in because it is too soft, and which is therefore content to rub its head against the entrance to the vulva until it ejaculates. It gives no pleasure to woman, but only inflames her passion without being able to satisfy it, and makes her cross and irritable.

El motelâ (the ransacker) – So named because it penetrates into the unusual places, makes itself well acquainted with the state of vulvas, and can distinguish their qualities and faults.

El mokcheuf (the discoverer) – Has been called this because in getting up and raising its head, it raises the clothes which hide it, and uncovers its master's nakedness, and because it is also not afraid to lay bare the vulvas which it does not yet know, and to lift up the clothes which cover them without shame. It is not susceptible to any sense of bashfulness, cares for nothing and respects nothing. Nothing which concerns the coitus is strange to it; it has a profound knowledge of the state of humidity, freshness, dryness, rightness or warmth of vulvas, which it explores assiduously. There are, in fact, certain vulvas of an exquisite exterior, plump and fine outside, while their inside leaves much to wish for, and they give no pleasure, owing to their being not warm, but very humid, and having other similar faults. It is for this reason that the *mokcheuf* tries to find out about things concerning the coitus, and has received this name.

These are the principal names that have been given to the virile member according to its qualities. Those who think that the number of these names is not exhaustive can look for more; but I think I have given a list of names long enough to satisfy my readers.

IX

Various names given to the sexual organs of women

El feurdj, the slit.
El keuss, the vulva.
El kelmoune, the voluptuous.
El ass, the primitive.
El zerzour, the starling.
El cheukk, the chink.
Abou tertour, the one with a crest.
Abou khochime, the one with a little nose.
El gueunfond, the hedgehog.
El sakouti, the silent one.
El deukkak, the crusher.
El tseguil, the importunate.
El taleb, the yearning one.
El hacene, the beautiful.
El neuffakh, the one that swells.
Abou djebaha, the one with a projection.

El ouasâ, the vast one.

El dride, the large one.

Abou beldoum, the glutton.

El mokâour, the bottomless.

Abou cheufrine, the two lipped.

Abou âungra, the humpbacked.

El rorbal, the sieve.

El hezzaz, the restless.

El lezzaz, the unionist.

El moudd, the accommodating.

El moudine, the assistant.

El meusboul, the long one.

El molki, the duellist.

El harrab, the fugitive.

El sabeur, the resigned.

El moseuffah, the barred one.

El mezour, the deep one.

El âddad, the biter.

El menssass, the sucker.

El zeunbur, the wasp.

El harr, the hot one.

El ladid, the delicious one.

As regards the vulva called *el feurdj*, the slit, it has this name because it opens and shuts again when ardently yearning for coitus, like the one of a mare in heat at the approach of the stallion. This word, however, is applied indiscriminately to the natural parts of men and women, for God the Supreme has used this expression in the Koran, Chap. XXXIII. v. 35, "*El hafidine feurodjahoum ou el hafidate.*" The proper meaning of *feurdj* is slit, opening, passage; people say "I have found a *feurdj* in the mountains", *viz.*, a passage; there is then a *soukoune* upon the *ra* and a *fatcha* upon the *djine,* and in this sense it means also the natural parts of woman. But if the *ra* is marked with a *fatcha* is signifies deliverance from misfortunes.

The person who dreams of having seen the vulva, *feurdj*, of a woman will know that "if he is in trouble God will free him of it; if he is in a perplexity he will soon get out of it; and lastly if he is in poverty he will soon become wealthy, because *feurdj*, by transposing the vowels, will mean the deliverance from evil. By analogy, if he wants a thing he will get it; if he has debts, they will be paid."

It is considered more lucky to dream of the vulva as open. But if the one seen belongs to a young virgin it indicates that the door of consolation will remain closed, and the thing which is desired is not obtainable. It is a proved fact that the man who sees in his dream the vulva of a virgin that has never been touched will certainly be involved in difficulties, and will not be lucky in his affairs. But if the vulva is open so that he can look well into it, or even if it is hidden but he is free to enter it, he will bring the most difficult tasks to a successful end after having first failed in them, and this after a short delay, by the help of a person whom he never thought of.

He who has seen in his dream a man making love to a young girl, and when the same is getting off her managed to see at that moment her vulva, will bring his business to a happy end, after having first failed to do so, by the help of the man he has seen. If it is himself who made love to the girl and he has seen her vulva, he will succeed by his own efforts to realize the most difficult problems, and be successful in every respect. Generally speaking, to see the vulva in dreams is a good sign; so it is of good omen to dream of coition, and he who sees himself in the act, and finishing with the ejaculation, will meet success in all his affairs. But it is not the same with the man who merely begins coition and does not finish it. He, on the contrary, will be unlucky in every enterprise.

It is supposed that the man who dreams of making love to a woman will afterwards obtain from her what he wants.

The man who dreams of copulating with women with whom to have sexual intercourse is forbidden by religion, as for instance his mother, sister, etc. (*maharine*), must consider this as a presage that he will go to sacred places (*moharreme*); and, perhaps, even journey to the holy house of God, and look there upon the grave of the Prophet.

As regards the virile member, it has been previously mentioned that to dream of accident occurring to that organ means the loss of all remembrance and the extinction of the race.

The sight of a pair of pantaloons (*seronal*) indicates the appointment to a place (*oulaïa*), by reason of the analogy of the letters composing the word *seronal* with those forming by transposition the two words *sir*, go, and *ouali*, named: "go to the post of which you are named." It is related that a man who had dreamed that the Emir had given him a pair of pantaloons became Cadi. Dreaming of pantaloons is also a sign of protection for the natural parts, and foretells success in business.

The almond (*louze*), a word composed of the same letters as *zal*, to cease, seen in a dream by a man in trouble means that he will be liberated from it; to a man who is ill, that he will be cured; in short that all misfortunes will end. Somebody having dreamed that he was eating almonds, asked a wise man the meaning of it; he received the answer, that by reason of the analogy of the letters in *louze* and *zal*, the ills that assailed him would disappear; and the event justified the explanation.

The sight of a molar tooth (*deurss*) in a dream indicates enmity. The man, therefore, who has seen his tooth drop out may be sure that his enemy is dead. This arises from the word *deurss*, signifying both an enemy and a molar, and one can say at the same time, "It is my tooth and it is my enemy."

The window (*taga*) and the shoe *(medassa)* reminds you of women. The vulva resembles in fact, when invaded by the member, a window with a man putting his head in to look about, or a shoe that is being put on. Consequently, he who sees himself in his dream getting in at a window, or putting on a shoe, has the certainty of getting possession of a young woman or a virgin, if the window is newly built, or the shoe new and in good condition; but that woman will be old according to the state of the window or shoe.

The loss of a shoe foretells to a man the loss of his wife.

To dream of something folded together, and which gets open, predicts that a secret will be divulged and made public. The same remaining folded up indicates, on the other hand, that the secret will be kept.

If you dream of reading a letter you will know that you will have news, which will be, according to the nature of the contents of the letter, good or bad.

The man who dreams of passages in the Koran or the Traditions, *Hadits*, will from the subjects treated therein draw his conclusions. For instance the passage, "He will grant you the help of God and immediate victory", will signify to him victory and triumph. "Certainly he (God) has the decision in his hands." "Heaven will open and offer its numerous entrances." And other similar passages indicate success.

A passage treating of punishments indicates punishment; from those treating of benefits a lucky event may be concluded. Such is the passage in the Koran, which says: "He who forgives sins is terrible in his inflictions."

Dreams about poetry and songs contain their explanation in the contents of the subject of the dream.

He who dreams of horses, mules, or asses may hope for good, for the Prophet (God's salutation and goodness be with him!) has said, "Men's fortunes are attached to the forelocks of their horses till the day of resurrection!" and it is written in the Koran, "God the Highest has thus willed it that they serve you as mounts and for pomp."

The correctness of these signs is not subject to any doubt.

He who dreams of seeing himself mounted upon an ass as a courier, and arriving at his destination, will be lucky in all things; but he who tumbles off the ass on his way is advised that he will be subject to accidents and misfortunes.

The fall of the turban from the head predicts ignominy, the turban being the Arabs' crown.

If you see yourself in a dream with naked feet it means a loss; and the bare head has the same significance.

By transposing the letters other analogies may be arrived at.

These explanations are not here in their place; but I have been induced to give them in this chapter on account of the use to which they may be put. Persons who would wish to know more on this subject have only to consult the book of Ben Sirine. I now return to the names given to the sexual parts of woman.

El keuss (the vulva) – This word serves as the name of a young woman's vulva in particular. Such a vulva is very plump and round in every direction, with long lips, grand slit, the edges well divided and symmetrical and rounded; it is soft, seductive, perfect throughout. It is the most pleasant and no doubt the best of all the different sorts. May God grant us the possession of such a vulva! Amen. It is warm, tight, and dry; so much so that one might expect to see fire burst from it. Its form is graceful, its odour pleasant; the whiteness of its outside sets off its carmine-red middle. There is no imperfection about it.

El relmoune (the voluptuous) – The name given to the vulva of a young virgin.

El ass (the primitive) – This is a name applicable to every kind of vulva.

El zerzour (the starling) – The vulva of a very young girl, or, as others claim falsely, of a brunette.

El cheukk (the chink) – The vulva of a bony, lean woman. It is like a chink in a wall, with not a vestige of flesh. May God keep us from it!

Abou tertour (the crested one) – It is the name given to a vulva with a red comb, like that of a cock, which rises at the moment of enjoyment.

Abou khochime (the snubnose) – Is a vulva with thin lips and a small tongue.

El gueunfond (the hedgehog) – The vulva of the old, decrepit woman, dried up with age and with bristly hair.

El sakouti (the silent one) – This name has been given to the vulva that is noiseless. The member may enter it a hundred times a day but it will not say a word, and will be content to look on without a murmur.

El deukkak (the crusher) – So called from its crushing movements upon the member. It generally begins to push the member, directly it enters, to the right and to the left, and to grip it with the womb, and would, if it could, absorb also the two testicles.

El tseguil (the importunate) – This is the vulva which is never tired of taking in the member. The latter might spend a hundred nights with it, and enter a hundred times every night, still that vulva would not be satisfied – nay, it would want still more, and would not allow the member to come out again at all, if it was possible. With such a vulva the roles are exchanged; the vulva is the pursuer, the member the pursued. Luckily it is a rarity, and only found in a small number of women, who are wild with passion, all on fire, aglow.

El taleb (the yearning one) – This vagina is met with in a few women only. With some it is natural; with others it becomes what it is by long abstinence. It is burning for a member, and, having got one in its embrace, it refuses to part with it until its fire is completely extinguished.

El hacene (the beautiful) – This is the vulva which is white, plump, in form vaulted like a dome, firm, and without any deformity. You cannot take your eyes off it, and to look at it changes a feeble erection into a strong one.

El neuffakh (the swelling one) – So called because a soft member coming near it, and rubbing its head against it a few times, at once swells and stands upright. To the woman who has such a one it gives excessive pleasure, for, at the moment of the climax, it opens and shuts convulsively, like the vulva of a mare.

Abou djebaha (one with a projection) – Some women have this sort of vulva, which is very large, with a pubis prominent like a projecting, fleshy forehead.

El ouasa (the vast one) – A vulva surrounded by a very large pubis. Women of that build are said to be of large vagina, because, although on the approach of the member it appears firm and impenetrable to such a degree that not even a *meroud* seems likely to be passed in, as soon as it feels the friction of the gland against its centre it opens wide at once.

El aride (the large one) – This is the vulva which is a wide as it is long; that is to say, fully developed all round, from side to side, and from the pubis to the perineum. It is the most beautiful to look upon. As the poet said:

It has the splendid whiteness of a forehead,
In its dimensions it is like the moon,
The fire that radiates from it is like the sun's,
And seems to burn the member which approaches;
Unless first moistened with saliva the member cannot enter,
The odour it emits is full of charms.

It is also said that this name applies to the vagina of women who are plump and fat. When such a one crosses her thighs one over the other the vulva stands out like the head of a calf. If she lays it bare it resembles a *saâ* for corn placed between her thighs; and, if she walks, it is apparent under her clothes by its wavy movement at each step. May God, in his goodness and generosity, let us enjoy such a vagina! It is of all the most pleasing, the most celebrated, the most wished for.

Abou belâoum (the glutton) – The vulva with a vast capacity for swallowing. If such a vulva has not been able to get coitus for some time it fairly engulfs the member that then comes near it, without leaving any trace of it outside, like as a man who is famished flings himself upon food that is offered to him, and would swallow them without chewing.

El mokâour (the bottomless) – This is the vagina of indefinite length, having, in consequence, the womb lying very far back. It requires a member of the largest dimensions; any other could not succeed in rousing its amorous sensibilities.

Abou cheufrine (the two lipped) – This name is given to the amply developed vagina of an excessively stout woman. Also to the vagina the lips of which having become flaccid, owing to weakness, are long and hanging.

Abou âungra (the humpbacked) – This vulva has the mount of Venus prominent and hard, standing out like the hump on the back of the camel, and reaching down between the thighs like the head of a calf. May God let us enjoy such a vulva! Amen!

El rorbal (the sieve) – This vulva on receiving a member seems to sift it all over, below, right and left, fore and aft, until the moment of pleasure arrives.

El hezzaz (the restless) – When this vagina has received the member it begins to move violently and without interruption until the member touches the womb and then knows no rest till it has hurried on the enjoyment and finished its work.

El lezzaz (the unionist) – The vagina which, having taken in the member, clings to it and pushes itself forward upon it so closely that, if the thing were possible, it would enfold the two testicles.

El moudd (the accommodating) – This name is applied to the vagina of a woman who has felt for a long time an ardent wish for coition. In ecstasy with the member it sees, it is glad to second its movements of coming and going; it offers its womb to the member by pressing it forward within reach, which is, after all, the best gift it can offer. Whatever place inside of it the member wants to explore, this vulva will make him welcome to, gracefully granting its wish; there is no corner it will not help the member to reach.

El mouâïne (the assistant) – This vulva is thus named because it assists the member to go in and out, to go up and down, in short, in all its movements, in such a way that if it desires to do a thing, to enter or to retire, to move about, etc., the vulva eagerly helps it, and answers to its appeal. By this aid the ejaculation is facilitated, and the enjoyment heightened.

El meusboul (the long one) – This name applies only to some vulvas; everyone knows that vulvas are far from being all of the same form and appearance. This vulva extends from the pubis to the anus. It lengthens out when the woman is lying down or standing, and contracts when she is sitting, differing in this respect from the vulva of a round shape. It looks like a splendid cucumber lying between the thighs. With some women it shows projecting under light clothing, or when they are bending back.

El molki (the duellist) – This is the vulva which, on the introduction of a member, performs the movement of coming and going, pushes itself upon it for fear of its retiring before the pleasure arrives. There is no enjoyment for it but the shock given to its womb by the member, and it is for this that it projects its womb to grip and suck the member's gland when the ejaculation takes place. Certain vulvas, wild with desire and lust, be it natural or an consequence of long abstention, throw themselves upon the approaching member, opening the mouth like a famished infant to whom the mother offers the breast. In the same way this vulva advances and retires upon the member to bring it face to face with the womb, as if in fear that, unaided, it could not find the same.

The vulva and the member resemble thus two skilful duellists, each time that one of them rushes its antagonist, the latter presents its shield to parry the blow and repulse the assault. The member represents the sword, and the womb the shield. The one who first ejaculates the sperm is vanquished; while the one who is slowest is the victor; and, assuredly, it is a fine fight! I should like thus to fight without stopping to the day of my death.

As the poet says:

I have let them see the effect of a subtle shadow,
Spinning like an ever busy spider.
They said to me, "How long will you go on?"
I answered them, "I will work till I am dead."

El harrab (the fugitive) – The vagina which, being very tight and short, is hurt by the penetration of a very large and stiff member; it tries to escape to the right and left. It is thus, people say, with the vagina of most virgins, which, not yet having made the acquaintance of the member and fearful of its approach, tries to get out of its way, when it glides in between the thighs and wants to be admitted.
El sabeur (the resigned) – This is the vulva which, having admitted the member, submits patiently to all its whims, and movements. It is also said that this vulva is strong enough to suffer resignedly the most violent and prolonged coitions. If it were assaulted a hundred times it would not be vexed or annoyed; and instead of being reproachful, it would give thanks to God. It will show the same patience if it has to do with several members who visit it successively.
This kind of vagina is found in women of a passionate temperament. If they only knew how to do it, they would not allow the man to dismount, nor his member to retire for a single moment.

El mousseuffah (the barred one) – This kind of vagina is not often met with. The defect which distinguishes it is sometimes natural, sometimes it is the result of an unskilfully performed operation of circumcision upon the woman. It can happen that the operator makes a false move with his instrument and injures the two lips, or even only one of them. In healing there forms a thick scar, which bars the passage, and in order to make the vagina accessible to the member, a surgical operation and the use of the scalpel will have to be resorted to.
El merour (the deep one) – The vagina which always has the mouth open, and the bottom of which is beyond sight. The longest members only can reach it.
El âddad (the biter) – The vulva which, when the member has go into it and is burning with passion, opens and shuts again upon the same fiercely. It is chiefly when the ejaculaton is coming that the man feels the head of his member bitten by the mouth of the womb. And certainly there is an attractive power in the

same when it clings, yearning for sperm, to the gland, and draws it in as far as it can. If God in his power has decreed that the woman shall become pregnant the sperm gets concentrated in the womb, where it is gradually given life; but if, on the contrary, God does not permit the conception, the womb expels the seed, which then runs over the vagina.

El meusass (the sucker) – This is a vagina which in its amorous passion in consequence of voluptuous loveplay, or of long abstinence, begins to suck the member which has entered it so forcibly as to deprive it of all its sperm, dealing with it as a child drawing on the breast of the mother.

The poets have described it in the following verses:

She – the woman – shows in turning up her robe
An object – the vulva – developed full and round,
In semblance like a cup turned upside down.
In placing thereupon your hand, you seem to feel
A well formed bosom, springy, firm, and full.
In boring in your lance it gets well bitten,
And drawn in by a suction, as the breast is by a child.
And after having finished, if you wish to re-commence,
You'll find it flaming hot as any furnace.

Another poet (may God grant all his wishes in Paradise!) has composed on the same theme the following lines:

Like to a man extended on his chest, she – the vulva – fills the hand
Which has to be well stretched to cover it.
The place it occupies is standing forth
Like an unopened bud of the blossom of a palm tree.
Assuredly the smoothness of its skin
Is like the beardless cheek of adolescence;
Its channel is but narrow,
The entrance to it is not easy,

And he who essays to get in
Feels as though he was butting against a coat of mail.
And at the introduction it emits a sound
Like to the tearing of a woven stuff.
The member having filled its cavity,
Receives the lively welcome of a bite,
Such as the nipple of the nurse receives
When placed between the nursling's lips for suction.
Its lips are burning,
Like a fire that is lighted,
And how sweet it is, this fire!
How delicious for me.

El zeunbour (the wasp) – This kind of vulva is known by the strength and roughness of its fur. When the member approaches and tries to enter it gets stung by the hairs as if by a wasp.

El harr (the hot one) – This is one of the most praiseworthy vulvas. Warmth is in fact very much esteemed in a vulva, and it may be said that the intensity of the enjoyment afforded by it is in proportion to the heat it develops.
Poets have praised it in the following verses:

The vulva possesses an intrinsic heat;
Shut in a solid heart (interior) and pent up breast (matrix).
Its fire communicates itself to him that enters it;
It equals in intensity the fire of love.
She is as tight as a well-fitting shoe,
Smaller than the circle of the apple of the eye.

El ladid (the delicious) – It has the reputation of affording an unprecedented pleasure, comparable only to the one felt by the beasts and birds of prey, and for which they fight bloody battles. And if such effects are produced upon animals, what must they be for man? And so it is that all wars spring from the search of

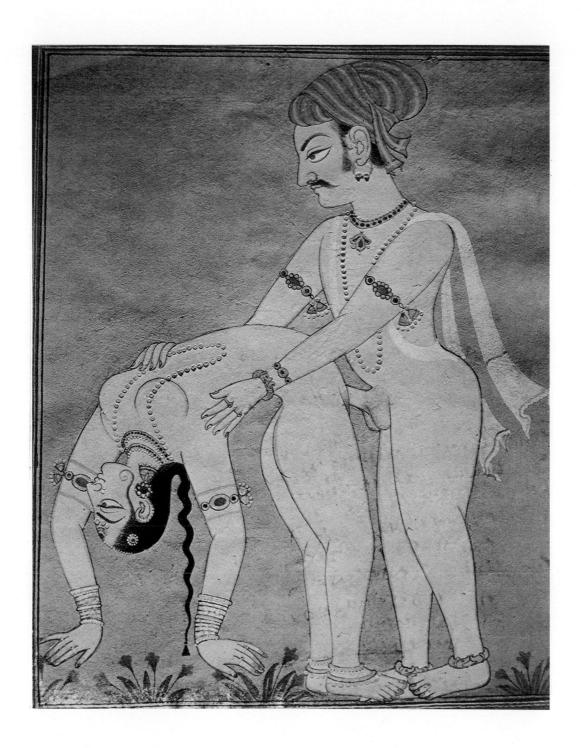

the voluptuous pleasure which the vagina gives, and which is the highest fortune of this world; it is a part of the delights of paradise awarded to us by God as a foretaste of what is waiting for us, namely, delights a thousand times superior, and above which only the sight of the Benevolent (God) is to be placed. More names might certainly be found applicable to the sexual organs of woman, but the number of those mentioned above appears to me ample. The principal object of this work is to collect together all the remarkable and attractive matters concerning in it, and the man to whom erection offers difficulties may be able to look into it for a remedy against his weakness. Wise physicians have written that people whose members have lost their strength, and are afflicted with impotence, should assiduously read books treating of coition, and study carefully the different kind of lovemaking, in order to recover their former vigour. A certain means of provoking erection is to look at animals in the act of coition. As it is not always everywhere possible to see animals whilst in the act of copulation, books on the subject of coition are indispensable. In every country, large or small, both the rich and poor have a taste for this sort of book, which may be compared to the stone of philosophy transforming common metals into gold. It is related (and God penetrates the most obscure matters, and is most wise!) that once upon a time, before the reign of the great Kalif Haroun er Rachid, there lived a buffoon, who was the amusement of women, old people and children. His name was Djoâidi. Many women granted him their favours freely, and he was much liked and well received by all. By princes, viziers and caïds he was likewise very well treated; in general all the world pampered him; at that time, indeed, any man that was a buffoon enjoyed the greatest respect, for which reason the poet has said:

Oh, Time! Of all the dwellers here below
You only elevate buffoons or fools,
Or him whose mother was a prostitute,
Or him whose anus as an inkstand serves,
Or him who from his youth has ben a pander;
Who has no other work but to bring the two sexes together.

Djoâidi related the following story:

I was in love with a woman who was all grace and perfection, beautiful of shape, and gifted with all imaginable charms. Her cheeks were like roses, her forehead lily white, her lips like coral; she had teeth like pearls, and breasts like pomegranates. Her mouth opened round like a ring; her tongue seemed to be incrusted with precious gems; her eyes, black and finely slit, had the languor of slumber, and her voice the sweetness of sugar. With her form pleasantly filled out, her flesh was mellow like fresh butter, and pure as the diamond.

As to her vulva, it was white, prominent, round as an arch; the centre of it was red, and breathed fire, without a trace of humidity; for, sweet to the touch, it was quite dry. When she walked it showed in relief like a dome or an inverted cup. In reclining it was visible between her thighs, looking like a kid couched on a hillock.

This woman was my neighbour. All the others played and laughed with me, jested with me, and met my suggestions with great pleasure. I revelled in their kisses, their close embraces and nibblings, and in sucking their lips, breasts, and necks. I had coition with all of them, except my neighbour, and it was exactly her I wanted to possess in preference to all the rest; but instead of being kind to me, she avoided me rather. When I contrived to take her aside to play with her and try to rouse her gaiety, and spoke to her of my desires, she recited to me the following verses, the sense of which was a mystery to me:

Among the mountain tops I saw a tent placed firmly,
Apparent to all eyes high up in mid-air.
But, oh! the pole that held it up was gone.
And like a vase without a handle it remained,
With all its cords undone, its centre sinking in,
Forming a hollow like that of a kettle.

Every time I told her of my passion she answered me with these verses, which to me were void of meaning, and to which I could make no reply, which, however, only excited my love all the more. I therefore inquired of all those I knew – amongst wise men, philosophers, and scholars – the meaning, but not one of them could solve the riddle for me, so as to satisfy my desire and appease my passion.

Nevertheless I continued my investigations, when at last I heard of a scholar named Abou Nouass, who lived in a far-off country, and who, I was told, was the only man capable of solving the enigma. I went to him, told him of the conversations I had with the woman, and recited to him the above-mentioned verses. Abou Nouass said to me, "This woman loves you to the exclusion of every other man. She is very corpulent and plump." I answered, "It is exactly as you say. You have described her as if she were before you, excepting what you say in respect of her love for me, for, until now, she has never given me any proof of it."

"She has no husband."

"This is so", I said.

Then he added, "I have reason to believe that your member is of small dimensions, and such a member cannot give her pleasure not satisfy her passion; for what she wants is a lover with a member like that of an ass. Perhaps it may not be so. Tell me the truth about this!" When I had reassured him on that point, affirming that my member, which began to rise at the expression of his doubtings, was full-sized, he told me that in that case all difficulties would disappear, and explained to me the sense of the verses as follows:

The *tent*, firmly planted, represents the vulva of grand dimension and placed well forward, the *mountains*, between which it rises, are the thighs. The *stake* which supported its centre and has been torn up, means that she has no husband, comparing the stake or pole that supports the tent to the virile member holding up the lips of the vulva. *She is like a vase without a handle;* this means if the pail is without a handle to hang it up by it is good for nothing, the pail representing the vulva, and the handle the member. *The cords are undone and its centre is sinking in;* that is to say, as the tent without a supporting pole caves in at the centre, inferior in this respect to the vault which remains upright without

379

support, so can the woman who has no husband not enjoy complete happiness. From the words, *It forms a hollow like that of a kettle,* you may judge how lascivious God has made that woman in her comparisons; she likens her vulva to a kettle, which serves to prepare the *tserid.* Listen; if the *tserid is* placed in the kettle, to turn out well it must be stirred by means of a *medeleuk* long and solid, whilst the kettle is steadied by the feet and hands. Only in that way can it be properly prepared. It cannot be done with a small spoon; the cook would burn her hands, owing to the shortness of the handle, and the dish would not be well prepared. This is the symbol of this woman's nature, O Djoâidi. If your member has not the dimensons of a respectable *medeleuk,* fit for the good preparation of the *tserid,* it will not give her satisfaction, and, moreover, if you do not hold her close to your chest, enfolding her with your hands and feet, it is useless to solicit her favours; finally if you let her consume herself by her own passion; like the bottom of the kettle which gets burnt if the *medeleuk* is not stirred upon it, you will not gratify her desire by the result.

You see now what prevented her from acceding to your wishes; she was afraid that you would not be able to quench her flame after having fanned it.

"But what is the name of this woman, O Djoâidi?"

"Fadehat el Djemal", (the sunrise of beauty), I replied.

"Return to her", said the sage, "and take her these verses, and your affair will come to a happy conclusion, please God! You will then come back to me, and inform me of what will have come to pass between you two."

I gave my promise, and Abou Nouass recited to me the following lines:

Have patience now, O Fadehat el Djemal,
I understand your words, and all shall see how I obey them.
O you! beloved and cherished by whoever
Can revel in your charms and glory in them!
O apple of my eye! You thought I was embarrassed
About the answer which I had to give you.
Yes, certainly! It was the love I bore you
Made me look foolish in the eyes of all you know.

380

They thought I was possessed of a demon;
Called me a Merry Andrew and buffoon.
For God! What of buffoonery I've got,
Should it be that
No other member is like mine? Here! see it, measure it!
What woman tastes it falls in love with me,
In violent love. It is a well known fact
That you from far may see it like a column.
If is erects itself it lifts my robe and shames me.
Now take it kindly, put it in your tent,
Which is between the well known mountains placed.
It will be quite at home there, you will find it
Not softening while inside, but sticking like a nail;
Take it to form a handle to your vase.
Come and examine it, and notice well
How vigorous it is and long in its erection!
If you but want a proper *medeleuk*,
A *medeleuk* to use between your thighs,
Take this to stir the centre of your kettle.
It will do good to you, O mistress mine!
Your kettle be it plated will be satisfied!

Having learnt these verses by heart, I took my leave of Abou Nouass and returned to Fadehat el Djemal. She was, as usual, alone. I gave a slight knock at her door; she came out at once, beautiful as the rising sun, and coming up to me, she said, "Oh! enemy of God, what business has brought you here to me at this time?"

I answered her, "O my mistress! a business of great importance."

"Explain yourself, and I will see whether I can help you", she said.

"I shall not speak to you about it until the door is locked", I answered.

"Your boldness today is very great", she said.

And I, "True, O my mistress! boldness is one of my qualities."

She then addressed me thus, "O enemy of yourself! O you most miserable of your race! If I were to lock the door, and you have nothing with which to satisfy my desires, what should I do with you? face of a Jew!"

"You will let me share your couch, and grant me your favours."

She began to laugh; and after we had entered the house, she told a slave to lock the house door. As usual, I asked her to respond to my proposals; she then recited to me again the above mentioned verses. When she had finished I began to recite to her those which Abou Nouass had taught me.

As I proceeded I saw her more and more moved, I observed her giving way, to yawn, to stretch herself, to sigh. I knew now I should arrive at the desired result. When I had finished my member was in such a state of erection that it became like a pillar, still lengthening. When Fadehat el Djemal saw it in that condition she hurled herself upon it, took it into her hands, and drew it towards her thighs. I then said, "O apple of my eyes! this may not be done here, let us go into your chamber."

She replied, "Leave me alone, O son of a debauched woman! Before God! I am losing my senses in seeing your member getting longer and longer, and lifting your robe. Oh, what a member! I never saw a finer one! Let it penetrate into this delicious, plump vulva, which maddens all who heard it described; for the sake of which so many died of love; and of which your superiors and masters themselves could not get possession."

I repeated, "I shall not do it anywhere else than in your chamber."

She answered, "If you do not enter this minute this tender vulva I shall die."

As I still insisted upon going to her room, she cried, "No, it is quite impossible; I cannot wait so long!"

I saw in fact her lips tremble, her eyes filling with tears. A general tremor ran over her, she changed colour, and laid herself down upon her back, baring her thighs, the whiteness of which made her flesh appear like crystal tinged with carmine.

Then I examined her vulva — a white cupola with a purple centre, soft and charming. It opened like that of a mare on the approach of a stallion.

At that moment she seized my member and kissed it, saying, "By the religion of my father! it must penetrate into my vulva!" and drawing nearer to me she pulled it towards her vagina.

I now hesitated no longer to assist her with my member, and placed it against the entrance to her vulva. As soon as the head of my member touched the lips, the whole body o Fadehat el Djemal trembled with excitement. Sighing and sobbing, she held me pressed to her bosom.

Again I profited by this moment to admire the beauties of her vulva. It was magnificent, its purple centre setting off its whiteness all the more. It was round, and without any imperfection; projecting like a splendidly curved dome over her belly. In one word, it was a masterpiece of creation as fine as could be seen. The blessing of God, the best creator, upon it.

And the woman who possessed this wonder had in her time no superior.

Seeing her then in such ecstasy, trembling like a bird, the throat of which is being cut, I pushed my dart into her. But thinking she might not be able to take in the whole of my member, I had entered cautiously, but she moved her buttocks furiously, saying to me, "This is not enough for my contentment." Making a strong push, I lodged my member completely in her, which made her utter a painful cry, but the moment after she moved with greater fury than before. She cried, "Do not miss the corners, neither high nor low, but above all things do not neglect the centre! The centre!" she repeated. "If you feel it coming, let it go into my so as to extinguish my passion." Then we moved alternately in and out, which was delicious. Our legs were interlaced, our muscles unbent, and so we went on with kisses and claspings until the climax came upon us simultaneously. We then paused to rest after this mutual conflict.

I wanted to withdraw my member, but she would not consent to this and begged of me not to take it out. I acceded to her wish, but a moment later she took it out herself, dried it, and replaced it in her vulva. We renewed our game, kissing, pressing, and moving in rhythm. After a short time, we rose and entered her chamber, without having this time accomplished the enjoyment. She gave me now a piece of an aromatic root, which she recommended me to keep in my mouth, assuring me that as long as I had it there my member would remain erect. Then she asked me to lie down, which I did. She mounted upon me, and taking my member into her hands, she made it enter entirely into her vagina. I was astonished at the vigour of her vulva and at the heat emitted from it. The opening of her womb in particular excited my admiration. I never had any experience like it; it closely clasped my member and pinched the gland.

With the exception of Fadehat el Djemal no woman had until then taken in my member to its full length. She was able to do so, I believe, owing to her being very plump and corpulent, and her vulva being large and deep.

Fadehat el Djemal, astride upon me, began to rise and descend; she kept crying out, wept, went slower, then accelerated her movements again, ceased to move altogether; when part of my member became visible she looked at it, then took it out altogether to examine it closely, then plunged it in again until it had disappeared completely. So she continued until the enjoyment overcame her again. At last, having dismounted from me, she now laid herself down, and asked me to get on to her. I did so, and she introduced my member entirely into her vulva.

We thus continued our caresses, changing our positions in turns, until night came on. I thought it proper to show a wish to go now, but she would not agree to this, and I had to give her my word that I would remain. I said to myself, "This woman will not let me go at any price, but when daylight comes God will advise me." I remained with her, and all night long we kept caressing each other, and took but little rest.

I counted that during that day and night, I accomplished twenty-seven times the act of coition, and I became afraid that I should nevermore be able to leave the house of that woman.

Having at last made good my escape, I went to visit Abou Nouass again, and informed him of all that happened. He was surprised and stupefied, and his first words were, "O Djoâidi, you can have neither authority nor power over such a woman, and she would make you do penance for all the pleasure you have had with other women!"

384

However, Fadehat el Djemal proposed to me to become her legitimate husband, in order to put a stop to the unpleasant rumours that were circulating about her conduct. I, on the other hand, was only on the look out for adultery. Asking the advice of Abou Nouass about it, he told me, "If you marry Fadehat el Djemal you will ruin your health, and God will withdraw his protection from you, and the worst of all will be that she will be unfaithful you, for she is insatiable with respect to the coitus, and would fill you with shame." And I answered him, "Such is the nature of women; they are insatiable as far as their vulvas are concerned, and so long as their lust is satisfied they do not care whether it be with a buffoon, a negro, a valet, or even with a man that is despised and condemned by society." On this occasion Abou Nouass depicted the character of women in the following verses:

Women are demons, and were born as such;
No one can trust them, as is known to all;
If they love a man, it is only out of caprice;
And he to whom they are most cruel loves them most.
Beings full of treachery and trickery, I declare
The man that loves you truly is a lost man;
He who believes me not can prove my word
By letting woman's love get hold of him for years!
If in your own generous mood you have given them
Your all and everything for years and years,
They will say afterwards, "I swear by God! my eyes
Have never seen a thing he gave me!"
After you have impoverished yourself for their sake,
Their cry from day to day will be for ever "Give!
Give man, Get up and buy and borrow."
If they cannot profit by you they'll turn against you;
They will tell lies about you and slander you.
They do not recoil to use a slave in the master's absence,
If once their passions are aroused, and they play tricks;

385

Assuredly, if once their vulva is in heat,
They only think of getting in some member in erection.
Preserve us, God! from woman's trickery;
And of old women in particular. So be it.

X

Concerning the Organs of Procreation of Animals

Know, o Vizir (God's blessing be with you!), that the sexual organs of the various male animals are not analogous to the different natures of the viril members which I have mentioned.

The members of animals are classed according to the species to which they belong, and these species are four in number.

1). The members of animals with hoofs, as the horse, mule, ass, which are of large size.

El rermoul, the colossus.

El kass, the serpent rolled up.

El fellag, the splitter.

El zellate, the club.

El heurmak, the indomitable.

El meunefoukh, the swollen.

Abou dommar, the one with a head.

Abou beurnita, the one with a hat.

El keurkite, the pointed staff.

El keuntra, the bridge.
El rezama, the mallet.
Abou sella, the fighter.
2). The members of animals which have the kind of feet called *akhfaf*, as, for instance, the camel.
El mâloum, the well-known.
El tonil, the long one.
El cherita, the riband.
El mostakime, the firm one.
El heurkal, the swinging one.
El mokheubbi, the hidden one.
El châaf, the tuft.
Tsequil el ifaha, the slow-coach.
3). The members of animals with split hoofs, like the ox, the sheep, etc.
El aceub, the nerve.
El heurbadj, the rod.
El sonte, the whip.
Requig er ras, the small head.
El tonil, the long one.
For the ram.
El aïçoub, the nervous.
And lastly, the members of animals with claws, as the lion, fox, dog, and other animals of this species.
El kedib, the verge.
El kibouss, the great gland.
El metemerole, the one that will lengthen.

It is believed that of all the animals of God's creation the lion is the most expert in respect to coition. If he meets the lioness he examines her before copulation. He will know if she has already been covered by a male. When she comes to him he smells at her, and if she has allowed herself to be covered by a boar he knows it immediately by the odour that animal has left upon her. He then smells her urine, and if the examination proves unfavourable, he gets into a rage, and begins to lash with his tail right and left. Woe to the animal that comes at that time near him; it is certain to be torn to pieces. He then returns to the lioness, who, seeing that he knows all, trembles with terror. He smells again at her, utters a roar which makes the mountains shake, and, falling upon her, tears her back with his claws. He even will go so far as to kill her, and then soil her body with his urine.

It is said that the lion is the most jealous and most intelligent of all animals. It is also declared that he is generous, and spares him who gets round him by fair words.

A man who on meeting a lion uncovers his sexual parts causes him to take to flight.

Whoever pronounces before a lion the name of Daniel (Hail be to him!), also sends him flying, because the prophet (Hail be to him!) has commanded the lion to do this on hearing his name. Therefore, when this name is pronounced, the lion departs without doing any harm. Several cases which prove his fact are cited.

XI

On the Deceits and Treacheries of Woman

Know, o Vizir (to whom God be good!) that the plottings of women are numerous and ingenious. Their tricks will deceive Satan himself, for God, the Highest has said (Koran, Chapter XII., verse 28), that the deceptive faculties of women are great, and he has likewise said (Koran, Chapter VI., verse 38), that the plottings of Satan are weak. Comparing the word of God as to the ruses of Satan and woman, contained in those two verses, it is easy to see how great these latter ones are.

Story of a Deceived Husband being Convicted Himself of Infidelity

It is related that a man fell in love with a woman of great beauty, and possessing all perfections imaginable. He had made many advances to her, which were repulsed; then he had endeavoured to seduce her by rich presents, which were likewise declined. He lamented, complained, and was extravagant with his money in order to conquer her, but to no purpose, and he grew lean as a ghost.

This lasted for some time, when he made the acquaintance of an old woman, whom he took into his confidence, complaining bitterly about it. She said to him, "I shall help you, please God."

Forthwith she made her way to the house of the woman, in order to get an interview with her; but on arriving there the neighbours told her that she could not get in, because the house was guarded by a ferocious bitch, which did not allow anyone to come in or to depart, and in her hatred always flew at the faces of people.

Hearing this, the old woman rejoiced, and said to herself, "I shall succeed, please God." She then went home, and filled a basket with bits of meat. Thus provided, she returned to the woman's house, and went in.

The bitch, on seeing her, rose to spring at her; but she produced the basket with its contents, and showed it her. As soon as the brute saw the food, is showed its satisfaction by the movements of its tail and nostrils. The old woman putting down the basket before it, spoke to it as follows, "Eat, O my sister. Your absence has been painful to me; I did not know what had become of you, and I have been looking for you a long time. Appease your hunger!"

While the animal was eating, and she stroked its back, the mistress of the house came to see who was there, and was not a little surprised to see the bitch, which would never allow anybody to come near her, so friendly with a strange person. She said, "O old woman, how is it that you know our dog?" The old woman gave no reply, but continued to caress the animal, and utter lamentations.

Then said the mistress of the house to her, "My heart aches to see you thus. Tell me the cause of your sorrow."

"This bitch", said the woman, "was formerly a woman, and my best friend. One fine day she was invited with me to a wedding; she put on her best clothes, and adorned herself with her finest jewelry. We then went together. On our way we were accosted by a man, who at her sight was seized with the most passionate love; but she would not listen to him. Then he offered brilliant presents, which she also declined. This man, meeting her some days later, said to her, 'Surrender yourself to my passion, or else I shall appeal to God to change you into a bitch.' She answered, 'Aappeal as much as you like.' The man then called the curse of

heaven upon that woman, and she was changed into a bitch, as you see here." At these words the mistress of the house began to cry and lament, saying, "O, my mother! I am afraid that I shall meet the same fate as this bitch." "Why, what have you done?" said the old woman. The other answered, "There is a man who has loved me since a long time, and I have refused to accede to his desires, nor did I listen to him, though the saliva was dried up in his mouth by his supplications; and in spite of the large expenses he had gone to in order to gain my favour I have always answered him that I should not consent, and now, O my mother, I am afraid that he might call to God to curse me."

"Tell me how to know this man", said the old woman, "for fear that you might become like this animal."

"But how will you be able to find him, and whom could I send to him?"

The old woman answered, "Me, daughter of mine! I shall render you this service, and find him."

"Make haste, O my mother, and see him before he appeals to God against me."

"I shall find him still this day", answered the old woman, "and please God, you shall meet him tomorrow."

With this, the old woman took her leave, went on the same day to the man who had made her his confidant, and told him of the meeting arranged for next day. So the next day the mistress of the house went to the old woman, for they had agreed that the rendezvous should take place there. When she arrived at the house she waited for some time, but the lover did not come. No doubt he had been prevented from making his appearance by some matter of importance. The old woman, reflecting upon this mischance, thought to herself, "There is no might nor power but in God, the Great." But she could not imagine what might have kept him away. Looking at the woman, she saw that she was agitated, and it was apparent that she wanted coition ardently. She got more and more restless, and presently asked, "Why does he not come?" The old woman made answer, "O my daughter, some serious affair must have interfered, probably necessitating a journey. But I shall help you under these circumstances." She then put on her *melahfa*, and went to look for the young man. But it was to no purpose, as she could not find out anything about him.

Still continuing her search, the old woman was thinking, "This woman is at this moment eagerly desiring a man. Why not try today another young man, who might calm her ardour? Tomorrow I shall find the right one." As she was thus walking and thinking she met a young man of very pleasing exterior. She saw at once that he was a fit lover, and likely to help her out of her trouble and she spoke to him: "O my son, if I were to introduce you to a lady, beautiful, graceful and perfect, would you make love to her?" "If your words are truth, I would give you this golden dinar!" said he. The old woman, quite enchanted, took the money, and conducted him to her house.

Now, it so happened that this young man was the husband of the lady, which the old woman did not know till she had brought him. And the way she found it out was this: She went first into the house and said to the lady, "I have not been able to find the slightest trace of your lover; but, failing him, I have brought you somebody to quench your passion for today. We will save the other for tomorrow. God has inspired me to do so."

The lady then went to the window to take a look at him whom the old woman wanted to bring to her, and catching sight of him, she recognized her husband, just on the point of entering the house. She did not hesitate, but hastily donning her *melahfa*, she went straight to meet him, and striking him in the face, she exclaimed, "O! enemy of God and of yourself, what are you doing here? You surely came with the intention to commit adultery. I have been suspecting you for a long time, and waited here every day, while I was sending out the old woman to coax you to come in. This day I have found you out, and denial is of no use. And you always told me that you were not a rake! I shall demand a divorce this very day, now I know your conduct!"

The husband, believing that his wife spoke the truth, remained silent and abashed.

Learn from this the deceitfulness of woman, and what she is capable of.

A story is told of a certain woman who was desperately in love with one of her neighbours, whose virtue and piety were well known. She declared to him her passion; but, finding all her advances constantly repulsed, in spite of all her wiles, she resolved to have her satisfaction nevertheless, and this is the way she went to achieve her purpose:

One evening she informed her negress that she intended to set a snare for that man, and the negress, by her order, left the street door open; then, in the middle of the night, she called the negress and gave her the following instructions: "Go and knock with this stone at our street door as hard as you can, without taking any notice of the cries which I shall utter, or the noise I make; as soon as you hear the neighbour opening his door, come back and knock the same way at the inner door. Take care that he does not see you, and come in at once if you observe somebody coming." The negress executed this order immediately.

Now, the neighbour was by nature a compassionate man, always disposed to assist people in distress, and his help was never asked in vain. On hearing the noise of the blows struck at the door and the cries of his neighbour, he asked his wife what this might mean, and she replied, "It is our neighbour so and so, who is attacked in her house by thieves." He went in great haste to her aid; but scarcely had he entered the house when the negress closed the door upon him. The woman seized him, and uttered loud screams. He protested, but the mistress of the house put, without any more ado, this condition before him. "If you do not consent to do with me so and so, I shall tell that you have come in here to rape me, and hence all this noise." "The will of God be done!" said the man, "nobody can go against Him, nor escape from His might." He then tried various tricks in order to escape, but in vain, for the mistress of the house recommenced to scream and make a row, which brought a good many people to the spot. He saw that his reputation would be compromised if he continued his resistance, and surrendered, saying, "Save me, and I am ready to satisfy you!" "Go into this chamber and close the door behind you", said the lady of the house, "if you want to leave this house with honour, and do not attempt escape unless you wish those people to know that you are the cause of all this commotion." When he saw how determined she was to have her way, he did as she had told him. She, on her part, went out to the neighbours thad had come to help her, and giving them some kind of explanation, dismissed them. They went away condoling with her. Left alone, she shut the doors and returned to her unwilling lover. She kept him in isolation for a whole week, and only set him free after she had completely drained him.

Learn from this the deceitfulness of women, and what they are capable of.

A Theft of Love

The following story is told of two women who inhabited the same house. The husband of one of them had a member long, thick and hard; while the husband of the other had, on the contrary, that organ little, insignificant and soft. The first one rose always pleasant and smiling; the other one got up in the morning in tears and vexation.

One day the two women were together, and spoke of their husbands.

The first one said, "I live in the greatest happiness. My bed is a couch of bliss. When my husband and I are together in it it is the witness of our supreme pleasure; of our kisses and embraces, of our joys and amorous sighs. When my husband's member is in my vulva it stops it up completely; it stretches itself out until it touches the bottom of my vagina, and it does not take its leave until it has visited every corner — threshold, vestibule, ceiling and centre. When the climax arrives it takes its position in the very centre of the vagina, which it floods with tears. It is in this way we quench our fire and appease our passion."

The second answered, "I live in the greatest grief; our bed is a bed of misery, and our coition is a union of fatigue and trouble, of hate and curse. When my husband's member enters my vulva there is a space left open, and it is so short it cannot touch the bottom. When it is in erection it is twisted all ways, and cannot procure any pleasure. Feeble and meagre, it can scarcely ejaculate a drop, and its service cannot afford pleasure to any woman."

Such was the almost daily conversation which the two women had together. It happened, however, that the woman who had so much cause for complaint thought in her heart how delightful it would be to commit adultery with the other one's husband. She thought to herself, "It must be brought about, if it be only for once." Then she watched her opportunity until her husband had to be absent for a night from the house.

In the evening she made preparation to get her project carried out, and perfumed herself with sweet scents and essences. When the night was advanced to about a third of its length, she noiselessly entered the chamber in which the other woman and her husband were sleeping, and groped her way to their couch. Finding that there was a free space between them, she slipped in. There was little room, but each of the spouses thought it was the pressure of the other, and gave way a little; and so she contrived to glide between them. She then quietly waited until the other woman was in a profound sleep, and then, approaching the husband, she brought her flesh in contact with his. He awoke, and smelling the perfumed odours which she exhaled, he was in erection at once. He drew her towards him, but she said, in a low voice, "Let me go to sleep!" He answered, "Be quiet, and let me do! The children will not hear anything!" She then pressed close up to him, so as to get him father away from his wife, and said, "Do as you like, but do not awaken the children, who are close by." She took these precautions for fear that his wife should wake up.

The man, however, roused by the odour of the perfumes, drew her ardently towards himself. She was plump and mellow, and her vulva projecting. He mounted upon her and said, "Take it (the member) in your hand, as usual!" She took it, and was astonished at its size and magnificence, then introduced it into her vulva.

The man, however, observed that his member had been taken in entirely, which he had never been able to do with his wife. The woman, on her part, found that she had never received such satisfaction from her husband.

The man was quite surprised. He worked his will upon her a second and third time but his astonishment only increased. At last he got off her, and stretched himself along her side.

As soon as the woman found that he was asleep, she slipped out, left the chamber, and returned to her own.

In the morning, the husband, on rising, said to his wife, "Your embraces have never seemed so sweet to me as last night, and I never breathed such sweet perfumes as those you exhaled." "What embraces and what perfumes are you speaking of?" asked the wife. "I have not a drop of perfume in the house." She called him a storyteller, and assured him that he must have been dreaming. He then began to consider whether he might not have deceived himself, and agreed with his wife that he must actually have dreamed it all.

Appreciate, after this, the deceitfulness of woman, and what they are capable of.

Story of the Woman with Two Husbands

It is related that a man, after having lived for some time in a country to which he had gone, became desirous of getting married. He addressed himself to an old woman who had experience in such matters, asking her whether she could find him a wife, and who replied, "I can find you a girl gifted with great beauty, and perfect in shape and comeliness. She will surely suit you, for, besides having these qualities, she is virtuous and pure. Only mark, her business occupies her all the day, but during the night she will be yours completely. It is for this reason she keeps herself reserved, as she apprehends that a husband might not agree to this."

The man replied, This girl need not be afraid. I, too, am not at liberty during the day, and I only want her for the night.

He then asked her in marriage. The old woman brought her to him, and he liked her. From that time they lived together, observing the conditions under which they had come together.

This man had an intimate friend whom he introduced to the old woman who had arranged his marriage according to the conditions mentioned, and this friend had requested the man to ask her to do him the same service. They went to the old woman and solicited her assistance in the matter. "This is a very easy matter", she said. "I know a girl of great beauty, who will dispel your heaviest troubles. Only the business she is carrying on keeps her at work all night, but she will be with your friend all day long." "This shall be no hindrance", replied the friend. She then brought the young girl to him. He was well pleased with her, and married her on the conditions agreed upon.

But before long the two friends found out that the two wives which the old hag had procured for them were only one woman.

Appreciate, after this, the deceitfulness of women, and what they are capable of.

Story of Bahia

It is related that a married woman of the name of Bahia (splendid beauty) had a lover whose relations to her were soon a mystery to no one, for which reason she had to leave him. Her absence affected him to such a degree that he fell ill, because he could not see her.

One day he went to see one of his friends, and said to him, "Oh, my brother! an uncontrollable desire has seized me, and I can wait no more. Could you accompany me on a visit I am going to pay to Bahia, the well-beloved of my heart?" The friend declared himself willing.

The next day they mounted their horses; and after a journey of two days, they arrived near the place where Bahia dwelt. There they stopped. The lover said to his friend, "Go and see the people that live about here, and ask for their hospitality, but take good care not to divulge our intentions, and try in particular to find the servant-girl of Bahia, to whom you can say that I am here, and whom you will charge with the message to her mistress that I would like to see her." He then described the servant-maid to him.

The friend went, met the servant, and told her all that was necessary. She went at once to Bahia, and repeated to her what she had been told.

Bahia sent to the friend the message, "Inform him who set you that the meeting will take place tonight, near such and such a tree, at such and such an hour." Returning to the lover, the friend communicated to him the decision of Bahia about the rendezvous.

At the hour that had been fixed, the two friends were near to the tree. They had not to wait long for Bahia. As soon as her lover saw her coming he rushed to meet her, kissed her, pressed her to his heart, and they began to embrace and caress each other.

The lover said to her, "O Bahia, is there no way to enable us to pass the night together without rousing the suspicions of your husband?" She answered, "Oh, before God! if it will give you pleasure, the means to achieve this are not lacking." "Hasten", said her lover, "to let me know how it may be done." She then asked him, "Your friend here, is he devoted to you, and intelligent?" He answered, "Yes." She then rose, took off her garments, and handed them to the friend, who gave her his, in which she then dressed herself; then she made the friend put on her clothes. The lover said, surprised, "What are you going to do?" "Be silent", she answered, and addressing herself to the friend, she gave him the following explanations: "Go to my house and lie down in my bed. After a third part of the night is passed, my husband will come to you and ask you for the pot into which they milk the camels. You will then take up the vase, but you must keep it in your hands until he takes it from you. This is our usual way. Then he will go and return with the pot filled with milk, and say to you, 'Here is the pot!' But you must not take it from him until he has repeated these words. Then take it out of his hands, or let him put it on the ground himself. After that, you will not see anything more of him till the morning. After he pot has been put on the ground, and my husband is gone, drink the third part of the milk, and replace the pot on the ground."

The friend went, observed all these recommendations, and when the husband returned with the pot full of milk he did not take it out of his hands until he had said twice, 'Here is the pot!' Unfortunately he withdrew his hands when the husband was going to set it down, the latter thinking the pot was being held, let it go, and the vase fell upon the ground and was broken. The husband, in the belief that he was speaking to his wife, exclaimed, "What have you been thinking of?" and beat him with it till it broke; then took another, and continued to batter him stroke on stroke enough to break his back. The mother and sister of Bahia came running to the spot to tear her from his hands. He had fainted. Luckily they succeeded in getting her husband away.

The mother of Bahia soon came back, and talked to him so long that he was fairly sick of her talk; but he could do nothing but be silent and weep. At last she finished, saying, "Have confidence in God, and obey your husband. As for your lover, he cannot come now to see and console you, but I will send your sister to keep you company." And so she went away.

She did send, indeed, the sister of Bahia, who began to console her and curse him who had beaten her. He felt his heart warming towards her, for he had seen that she was of resplendent beauty, endowed with all perfections, and like the full moon in the night. He placed his hand over her mouth, so as to prevent her from speaking, and said to her, "O, lady! I am not what you think. Your sister Bahia is at present with her lover, and I have run into danger to do her a service. Will you not take me under your protection? if you denounce me, your sister will be filled with shame; as for me, I have done my part, but may the evil fall back upon you!" The young girl then began to tremble like a leaf, in thinking of the consequences of her sister's doings, and then beginning to laugh, surrendered herself to the friend who proved himself so true. They passed the remainder of the night in bliss, kisses, embraces, and mutual enjoyment. He founds her the best of the best. In her arms he forgot the beating he had received, and they did not cease to play, toy, and make love till daybreak.

He then returned to his companion. Bahia asked him how he had fared, and he said to her, "Ask your sister. By my faith! she knows it all! Only know, that we have passed the night in mutual pleasures, kissing and enjoying ourselves until now."

Then they changed clothes again, each one taking his own, and the friend told Bahia all the particulars of what had happened to him.

Appreciate, after this, the deceitfulness of women, and what they are capable of.

The Story of the Man who was an Expert in Tricks, and was Duped by a Woman

A story is told of a man who had studied all the ruses and all the tricks invented by women for the deception of men, and pretended that no woman could dupe him.

A woman of great beauty, and full of charms, got to hear of his conceit. She, therefore, prepared for him in the *medjélés* a meal in which several kinds of wine figured, and nothing was wanting in the way of rare and choice foods. Then she sent for him, and invited him to come and see her. As she was famed for her great beauty and the rare perfection of her person, she had roused his desires, and he made haste to avail himself of her invitation.

She was dressed in her finest garments, and exhaled the choicest perfumes, and assuredly whoever had thus seen her would have been troubled in his mind. And thus, when he was admitted into her presence, he was fascinated by her charms, and plunged into admiration of her marvellous beauty.

This woman, however, appeared to be preoccupied on account of her husband, and allowed it to be seen that she was afraid of his coming back from one minute to another. It must be mentioned that this husband was very proud, very jealous, and very violent, and would not have hesitated to shed the blood of anyone whom he would have found prowling about his house. What would he have done, and, with much more reason, to the man whom he might have found inside!

While the lady and he, who flattered himself that he should possess her, were amusing themselves in the *medjélés*, a knock at the house-door filled the lover

404

with fear and trouble, particularly when the lady cried, "This is my husband, who is returning." All in a tremble, she hid him in a closet which was in the room, shut the door upon him, and left the key in the *medjélés*; then she opened the house-door.

Her husband, for it was he, saw, on entering, the wine and all the preparations that had been made. Surprised, he asked what this meant. "It means what you see", she answered. "But for whom is all this?" he asked.

"It is for my lover whom I have here."

"And where is he?"

"In this closet", she said, pointing with her finger to the place where the sufferer was locked in.

At these words the husband started. He rose and went to the closet, but found it locked. "Where is the key?" he said. She answered, "Here!" throwing it to him. But as he was putting it into the lock she burst out laughing uproariously. He turned towards her, and said, "What are you laughing at?" "I laugh", she answered, "at the weakness of your judgment, and your lack of reason and reflection. Oh, you man without sense, do you think that if I had in reality a lover, and had admitted him into his room, I should have told you that he was here and where he was hidden? That is certainly not likely. I had no other thought than to offer you a meal on your return, and wanted only to have a joke with you in doing as I did. If I had had a lover I should certainly not have made you my confidant."

The husband left the key in the lock of the closet without having turned it, returned to the table, and said, "True! I rose; but I have not the slightest doubt about the sincerity of your words." Then they ate and drank together, and made love.

The man in the closet had to stop there until the husband went out. Then the lady went to set him free, and found him quite undone and in a bad state. When he came out, after having escaped an eminent peril, she said to him, "Well, you know-all, who know so well the tricks of women, of all those you know, is there one to equal this?" He made answer, "I am now convinced that your tricks are countless."

Appreciate after this the deceits of women, and what they are capable of.

Story of the Lover who was surprise by the unexpected Arrival of the Husband

It is related that a woman who was married to a violent and brutal man, having her lover with her on the unexpected arrival of her husband, who was returning from a journey, had only just time to hide him under the bed. She was compelled to let him remain in this dangerous and unpleasant position, knowing of no expedient which might enable him to leave the house. In her restlessness she went to and fro, and having gone to the street-door, one of her neighbours, a woman, saw that she was in trouble, and asked her she reason of it. She told her what had happened. The other then said, "Return into the house. I will charge myself with the safety of your lover, and I promise you that he shall come out unharmed." Then the woman re-entered her house.

Her neighbour was not long in joining her, and together they prepared the meal, and then they all sat down to eat and drink. The woman sat facing her husband, and the neighbour opposite the bed. The latter began to tell stories and anecdotes about the tricks of women; and the lover under the bed heard all that was going on.

Continuing her tales, the neighbour told the following one: "A married woman had a lover, whom she loved tenderly, and by whom she was equally loved. One day the lover came to see her in the absence of her husband. But the latter happened to return home unexpectedly just as they were together. The woman, knowing of no better place, hid her lover under the bed, then sat down by her husband, who was taking some refreshment, and joked and played with him. Amongst other playful games, she covered her husband's eyes with a napkin, and her lover took this opportunity to come out from under the bed and escape unobserved."

The wife understood at once how to profit by this tale; taking a napkin and covering the eyes of her husband with it, she said, "Then it was by means of this ruse that the lover was helped out of his dilemma." And the lover, taking the opportunity, succeeded in making good his escape unobserved by the husband. Unaware of what had happened this latter laughed at the story, and his merriment was still increased by the last words of his wife and by her action. Appreciate after this the deceitfulness of women, and what they are capable of.

XII

Concerning Various Observations useful to know for Men and Women

Know, o Vizir (to whom God be good!), that the information contained in this chapter is of the greatest usefulness, and it is only in this book that such can be found. Assuredly to know things is better than to be ignorant of them. Knowledge may be bad, but ignorance is still more so.

The knowledge in question concerns matters unknown to you, and relating to women.

There was once a woman, named Moârbeda, who was considered to be the most knowing and wisest person of her time. She was a philosopher. One day various queries were put to her, and among them the following, which I shall give here, with her answers.

"In what part of a woman's body does her mind reside?"

"Between her thighs."

"And where her enjoyment?"

"In the same place."

"And where the love of men and the hatred of them?"

"In the vulva", she said; adding, "to the man whom we love we give our vulva, and we refuse it to him we hate. We share our property with the man we love, and are content with whatever little he may be able to bring to us; if he has no fortune, we take him as he is. But, on the other hand, we keep at a distance him whom we hate, were he to offer us wealth and riches."

"Where, in a woman, are located knowledge, love and taste?"

"In the eye, the heart, and the vulva."

When asked for explanations on this subject, she replied: "Knowledge dwells in the eye, for it is the woman's eye that appreciates the beauty of form and of appearance. Through this organ love penetrates into the heart and dwells in it, and enslaves it. A woman in love pursues the object of her love, and lays snares for it. If she succeed, there will be an encounter between the beloved one and her vulva. The vulva tastes him and then knows his sweet or bitter flavour. It is, in fact, the vulva which knows how to distinguish by tasting the good from the bad."

"Which virile members are preferred by women? What women are most eager for coitus, and which are those who detest it? Which are the men preferred by women, and which are those whom they abdominate?"

She answered, "Not all women have the same form of vulva, and they also differ in their manner of making love, and in their love for and their aversion to things. The same differences exist in men, both with regard to their organs and their tastes. A woman of plump form and with a shallow uterus will look out for a member which is both short and thick, which will completely fill her vagina, without touching the bottom of it; a long and large member would not suit her. A woman with a deep lying uterus, and consequently a long vagina, only yearns for a member which is long and thick and of ample proportions, and thus fills her vagina in its whole extension; she will despise the man with a small and slender member for he could never satisfy her in coition.

The following distinctions exist in the temperaments of women: the cholic, the melancholy, the sanguine, the phlegmatic, and the mixed. Those with a cholic or melancholy temperament are not much given to coitus, and like it only with men of the same disposition. Those who are sanguine or phlegmatic love coition to excess, and if they encounter a member, they would never let it leave their vul-

va if they could help it. With these also it is only men of their own temperament who can satisfy them, and if such a woman were married to a cholic or melancholy man, they would lead a sorry life together. As regards mixed temperaments, they exhibit neither a marked predilection for, nor aversion against coitus.

"It has been observed that under all circumstances little women love coitus more and show a stronger affection for the virile member than women of a large size. Only long and vigorous members suit them; in them they find the delight of their existence and of their couch."

"There are also women who love the coitus only on the edge of their vulva, and when a man lying upon them wants to get his member into the vagina, they take it out with the hand and place its gland between the lips of the vulva."

I have every reason to believe that this is only the case with young girls or with women not used to men. I pray God to preserve us from such, or from women for whom it is a matter of impossibility to give themselves up to men.

"There are women who will do their husband's commands and will satisfy them and give them voluptuous pleasure by coition, only if compelled by blows and ill-treatment. Some people ascribe this conduct to the aversion they feel either against coition or against the husband; but this is not so; it is simply a question of temperament and character.

There are also women who do not care for coition because all their ideas turn upon the grandeurs, personal honours, ambitious hopes, or business-cares of the world. With others this indifference springs, as it may be, from purity of the heart, or from jealousy, or from a pronounced tendency of their souls towards another world, or lastly from past violent sorrows. Furthermore, the pleasures which they feel in coition depend not alone upon the size of the member, but also upon the particular configuration of their own natural parts. Amongst those the vulva called from its form *el mortebâ*, the square one, and *el mortafâ*, the projecting is remarkable. This vulva has the peculiarity of projecting all round when the woman is standing up and closes her thighs. It burns for the coitus, its slit is narrow, and it is also called *el keulihimi*, the pressed one. The

413

woman who has such a one likes only large members, and they must not let her wait long for the climax. But this is a general characteristic of women. "As to the desire of men for coition, I must say that they also are addicted to it more or less according to their different temperaments, five in number, like the women's, with the difference that the hankering of the woman after the member is stronger than that of the man after the vulva."

"What are the faults of women?" Moârbeda replied to this question, "The worst of women is she who immediately cries out aloud as soon as her husband wants to touch the smallest amount of her property for his needs. In the same line stands she who divulges matters which her husband wants to be kept secret."

"Are there any more?" she is asked. She adds, "The woman of jealous disposition and the woman who raises her voice so as to drown that of her husband; she who spreads scandal; the woman that scowls; the one who is always burning to let men see her beauty, and cannot stay at home; and with respect to this last let me add that a woman who laughs much, and is constantly seen at the street door, may be taken to be a complete prostitute".

"Bad also are those women who mind people's affairs; those who are always complaining; those who steal things belonging to their husbands; those of a disagreeable and imperious temper; those who are not grateful for kindnesses received; those that will not share the conjugal couch, or who inconvenience their husbands by the uncomfortable positions they take in it; those who are inclined to deceit, treachery, slander and ruse.

"Then there are still women who are unlucky in whatever they undertake; those who are always inclined to blame and censure; those who invite their husbands to fulfil their conjugal duty only when it is convenient for them; those that make noises in bed; and lastly those who are shameless, without intelligence, gossips and curious."

"Here you have the worst specimens amongst women."

XIII

Concerning the Causes of Enjoyment in the Act of Coition

Know, o Vizir (to whom God be good!), that the causes which tend to develop the passion for coition are six in number: the fire of an ardent love, the superabundance of sperm, the proximity of the loved person whose possession is eagerly desired, the beauty of the face, aphrodisiac foods, and contact.

Know also, that the causes of the pleasure in coition and the conditions of enjoyment are numerous, but that the principal and best ones are: the heat of the vulva; the narrowness, dryness, and sweet odour of the same. If any one of these conditions is absent, there is at the same time something wanting in the voluptuous enjoyment. But if the vagina unites the required qualifications, the enjoyment is complete. In fact, a moist vulva relaxes the nerves, a cold one robs the member of all its vigour, and bad odours from the vagina detract greatly from the pleasure, as is also the case if the latter is very wide.

The peak of enjoyment, which is produced by the abundance and impetuous ejaculation of the sperm, depends upon one circumstance, and this is, that the vulva is furnished with a suction-pump (orifice of the uterus), which will clasp the virile member, and suck up the sperm with an irresistible force. The member, once seized by the orifice, the lover is powerless to retain the sperm, for the orifice will not relax its hold until it has extracted every drop of the sperm, and certainly if the climax arrives before this gripping of the gland takes place, the pleasure of the ejaculation will not be complete.

Know that there are eight things which give strength to and favour the ejaculation. These are: bodily health, the absence of all care and worry, an unembarrassed mind, natural gaiety of spirit, good nourishment, wealth, the variety of the faces of women, and the variety of their complexions.

If you wish to acquire strength for coitus, take fruit of the mastic-tree (*derou*), pound them and steep them with oil and honey; then drink of the liquid first thing in the morning: you will thus become vigorous for the coitus, and there will be abundance of sperm produced. The same result will be obtained by rubbing the virile member and the vulva with gall from the jackal. This rubbing stimulates those parts and increases their vigour.

A scholar of the name of Djelinouss has said: "He who feels that he is weak for coition should drink before going to bed a glassful of very thick honey and eat twenty almonds and one hundred grains of the pine tree. He must follow this diet for three days. He may also pound onion-seed, sift it and mix it afterwards with honey, stirring the mixture well, and consume this mixture while still fasting."

A man who would wish to acquire vigour for coition may likewise melt down fat from the hump of a camel, and rub his member with it just before the act; it will then perform wonders, and the woman will praise it for its work.

If you would make the enjoyment still more voluptuous, chew a little cubeb-pepper or cardamom-grains of the large species; put a certain quantity of it upon the head of your member, and then go to work. This will procure for you, as well as for the woman, a matchless enjoyment. The ointment from the balm of Judea or of Mecca produces a similar effect.

If you would make yourself very strong for the coitus, pound very carefully pyrether together with ginger, mix them while pounding with ointment of lilac, then rub with this compound your abdomen, the testicles, and the member. This will make you ardent for coitus.

You will likewise predispose yourself for coition, sensibly increase the volume of your sperm, gain increased vigour for the action, and procure for yourself extraordinary erections, by eating of chrysocolla the size of a mustard grain. The excitement resulting from the use of this remedy is unparalleled, and all your qualifications for coitus will be increased.

If you wish the woman to be inspired with a great desire to have intercourse with you, take a little of cubebs, pyrether, ginger and cinnamon, which you will have to eat just before joining her; then moisten your member with your saliva and make love to her. From that moment she will have such an affection for you that she can scarcely be a moment without you.

The virile member, rubbed with ass's milk, will become uncommonly strong and vigorous.

Green peas, boiled carefully with onions, and powdered with cinnamon, ginger and cardamoms, well pounded, create for the consumer considerable amorous passion and strength in coitus.

XIV

Description of the Uterus of Sterile Women, and Treatment
of the Same

Know, o Vizir (God be good to you!), that wise physicians have plunged into this sea of difficulties to very little purpose. Each one has looked at the matter from his own point of view, and in the end the question has been left in the dark. Amongst the causes which determine the sterility of women may be taken the obstruction in the uterus by clots of blood, the accumulation of water, the lack of or defective sperm of the man, organic malformation of the parts of the latter, internal defects in the uterus, stagnation of the periods and the impurity of the menstrual fluid, and the habitual presence of wind in the uterus. Other scholars attribute the sterility of women to the action of spirits and spells. Sterility is common in women who are very corpulent, so that their uterus gets compressed and cannot conceive, not being able to take up the sperm, especially if the husband's member is short and his testicles are very fat; in such a case the act of copulation can only be imperfectly completed.

One of the remedies against sterility consists of the marrow from the hump of a camel, which the woman spreads on a piece of linen, and rubs her sexual parts with it, after having been purified subsequently to her periods. To complete the cure, she takes some fruits of the plant called *jackal's grapes*, squeezes the juice out of them into a vase, and then adds a little vinegar; of this medicine she drinks, fasting for seven days, during which time her husband will take care to have copulation with her.

The woman may besides pound a small quantity of sésame grain and mix its juice with a bean's weight of sandarach powder; of this mixture she drinks during three days after her periods; she is then fit to receive her husband's embraces. The first of these beverages is to be taken separately at the beginning; after this the second, which will have a beneficial effect, if so it please the Almighty God! There is still another remedy. A mixture is made of nitre, gall from a sheep or a crow, a small quantity of the plant named *el meusk*, and of the grains of that plant. The woman saturates a plug of soft wool with this mixture, and rubs her vulva with it after menstruation; she then receives the caresses of her husband, and, with the will of God the Highest, will become pregnant.

XV

Concerning the Causes of Impotence in Men

Know, o Vizir (God be good to you!) that there are men whose sperm is spilt by the inborn coldness of their nature, by diseases of their organs, by purulent discharges, and by fevers. There are also men with the urinary canal in their member deviating owing to a downward curve; the result of such arrangement is that the seminal liquid cannot be ejected in a straight direction, but falls downwards.

Other men have the member too short and too small to reach the neck of the womb, or their bladder is ulcerated, or they are affected by other infirmities, which prevent them from coition.

Finally, there are men who arrive quicker at the climax than women, in consequence of which the two emissions are not simultaneous; there is in such cases no conception.

All these circumstances serve to explain the absence of conception in women; but the principal cause of all is the shortness of the virile member.

As another cause of impotence may be regarded the sudden transmission from hot to cold, and vice versa, and a great number of analogous reasons.

Men whose impotence is due either to the impurty of their sperm owing to their cold nature, or to diseases of the organs, or to discharges or fevers and similar ills, or to their excessive quickness in ejaculation, can be cured. They should eat stimulant pastry containing honey, ginger, pyrether, syrup of vinegar, hellebore, garlic, cinnamon, nutmeg, cardamoms, sparrows' tongues, Chinese cinnamon, long pepper, and other spices. They will be cured by using them.

As to the other afflictions which we have indicated – the curvature of the urethra, the small dimensions of the virile members, ulcers on the bladder, and the other infirmities which are adverse to coition – God only can cure them.

XVI

Temporary Impotence

Know, o Vizir (God be good to you!), that impotence arises from three causes:
Firstly, from temporary impotence.
Secondly, from a feeble and relaxed constitution.
And thirdly, from too premature ejaculation.
To cure temporary impotence you must take *galanga*, cinnamon from Mecca, cloves, Indian cachou, nutmeg, Indian cubebs, sparrow-wort, cinnamon, Persian pepper, Indian thistle, cardamoms, pyrether, laurel-seed, and gilly-flowers. All these ingredients must be pounded together carefully, and one drinks of it as much as one can, morning and night, in broth, particularly in pigeon broth; fowl broth may, however, be substituted just as well. Water is to be drunk before and after taking it. The compound may likewise be taken with honey, which is the best method, and gives the best results.

The man whose ejaculation is too quick must take nutmeg and incense (*oliban*) mixed together with honey.

If the impotence arises from weakness, the following ingredients are to be taken in honey: viz., pyrether, nettleseed, a little spurge (or cevadille), ginger, cinnamon of Mecca, and cardamom. This preparation will cause the weakness to disappear and effect the cure, with the permission of God the Highest!

I can warrant the effectiveness of all these preparations, the virtue of which has been tested.

The impossibility of performing the coitus, owing to the absence of stiffness in the member, is also due to other causes. It will happen, for instance, that a man with his member in erection will find it getting flaccid just when he is on the point of introducing it between the thighs of the woman. He thinks this is impotence, while it is simply the result, may be, of an exaggerated respect for the woman, may be of a misplaced bashfulness, may be because one has observed something disagreeable, or on account of an unpleasant odour; finally, owing to a feeling of jealousy, inspired by the reflection that the woman is no longer a virgin, and has served the pleasures of other men.

XVII

Prescriptions for Increasing the Dimensions of Small members and for making them Splendid

Know, o Vizir (God be good to you!), that this chapter, which treats of the size of the virile member, is of the first importance both for men and women. For the men, because from a good-sized and vigorous member there springs the affection and love of women; for the women, because it is by such members that their amorous passions are appeased, and the greatest pleasure is achieved for them. This is evident from the fact that many men, solely by reason of their insignificant members, are, as far as coition is concerned, objects of aversion to women, who likewise entertain the same sentiment with regard to those whose members are soft, numb and relaxed. Their whole happiness consists in the use of robust and strong members.

A man, therefore, with a small member, who wants to make it grand or fortify it for the coitus, must rub it before copulation with tepid water, until it gets red and extended by the blood flowing into it, in consequence of the heat; he must then apply a mixture of honey and ginger, rubbing it in carefully. Then let him join the woman; he will give for her such pleasure that she objects to him getting off her again.

425

Another remedy consists in a compound made of a moderate quantity of pepper, lavender, galanga, and musk, reduced to powder, sifted, and mixed up with honey and preserved ginger. The member, after having been first washed in warm water, is then vigorously rubbed with the mixture; it will then grow large and vigorous, and afford to the woman a marvellous feeling of voluptuousness.

A third remedy is the following: wash the member in water until it becomes red, and becomes erect. Then take a piece of soft leather, upon which spread hot pitch, and envelope the member with it. It will not be long before the member raises its head, trembling with passion. The leather is to be left on until the pitch grows cold, and the member is again in a state of rest. This operation, several times repeated, will have the effect of making the member strong and thick.

A fourth remedy is based upon the use made of leeches, but only of such as live in water (*sic*). You put as many of them into a bottle as can be got in, and fill it up with oil. Then expose the bottle to the sun, until the heat of the same has effected a complete mixture. With the fluid thus obtained the member is to be rubbed several consecutive days, and it will, by being thus treated, become of a good size and of full dimensions.

For another procedure I will here note the use of an ass's member. Procure one and boil it, together with onions and a large quantity of corn. With this dish feed fowls, which you eat afterwards. One can also steep the ass's member with oil, and use the fluid thus obtained for applying to one's member, and drinking of it. Another way is to crush leeches with oil, and rub the member with this ointment; or, if it is preferred, the leeches may be put into a bottle, and, thus enclosed, buried in a warm dunghill until they are dissolved into a coherent mass and form a sort of liniment, which is used for repeatedly applying to the member. The member is certain to greatly benefit by this.

One may likewise take rosin and wax, mixed with tubipore, asphodel, and cobbler's glue, with which mixture rub the member, and the result will be that its dimensions will be enlarged.

The effectiveness of all these remedies is well known, and I have tested them.

XVIII

Of things that take away the Bad Smell from the Armpits and Sexual Parts of Women and Contract the Latter

Know, o Vizir (God be good to you!), that bad odours from the vulva and of the armpits are, as also a wide vagina, the greatest of evils.

If a woman wants this bad odour to disappear she must pound red myrrh, then sift it, and knead this powder with myrtle-water, and rub her sexual parts with this wash. All disagreeable odours will disappear from her vulva.

Another remedy is obtained by pounding lavender, and kneading it afterwards with musk-rose-water. Saturate a piece of woollen-stuff with it, and rub the vulva with the same until it is hot. The bad smell will be removed by this.

If a woman intends to contract her vagina, she has only to dissolve alum in water, and wash her sexual parts with the solution, which may be made still more effective by the addition of a little bark of the walnut-tree, the latter substance being very astringent.

Another remedy to be mentioned is the following, which is well known for its effectiveness: Boil well in water carobs (locusts), freed from their kernels, and bark of the pomegranate tree. The woman takes a sitz bath in the extract thus obtained, and which must be as hot as she can bear it; when the bath gets cold, it must be warmed and used again, and this immersion is to be repeated several times. The same result may be obtained by fumigating the vulva with cow-dung. To do away with the bad smell of the armpits, one takes antimony and mastic, which are to be pounded together, and put with water into an earthen vase. The mixture is then rubbed against the sides of the vase until it turns red; when it is ready for use, rub it into the armpits, and the bad smell will be removed. It must be used repeatedly, until a radical cure is effected.

The same result may be arrived at by pounding together antimony (*hadida*) and mastic, setting the mixture afterwards onto a stove over a low fire, until it is of the consistency of bread, and rubbing the residue with a stone until the skin, which will have formed, is removed. Then rub it into the armpits, and you may be sure that the bad smell will soon be gone.

XIX

Instructions with regard to Pregnancy and how the Gender of the Child that is to be Born may be known – that is to say, Knowledge of the Sex of the Foetus

Know, o Vizir (God be good to you!), that the certain indications of pregnancy are the following: the dryness of the vulva immediately after coitus, the inclination to stretch herself, attacks of drowsiness, heavy and profound sleep, the frequent contraction of the opening of the vulva to such an extent that not even a *meroud* could penetrate, the nipples of the breast become darker, and lastly, the most certain of all marks is the stopping of menstruation.

If the woman remains always in good health from the time that her pregnancy is certain, if she preserves the good looks of her face and a clear complexion, if she does not become freckled, then it may be taken as a sign that the child will be a boy.

The red colour of the nipples also points to a child of the male sex. The strong development of the breasts, and bleeding from the nose, if it comes from the right nostril, are signs of the same significance.

The signs pointing to the conception of a child of the female sex are numerous.

I will name them here: frequent illness during pregnancy, pale complexion, spots and freckles, pains in the womb, frequent nightmares, blackness of the nipples, a heavy feeling on the left side, nasal hemorrhage on the same side.

If there is any doubt about the pregnancy, let the woman drink, on going to bed, honey-water, and if then she has a feeling of heaviness in the abdomen, it is a proof that she is with child. If the right side feels heavier than the left one, it will be a boy. If the breasts are swelling with milk, this is similarly a sign that the child she is bearing will be of the male sex.

I have received this information from scholars, and all the indications are positive and tested.

XX

Forming the Conclusion of this Work, and Treating of the Good Effects of the Swallowing of Eggs as Favourable to the Coitus

Know, o Vizir (God be good to you!), that this chapter contains the most useful instructions – how to increase the intensity of the coitus – and that the latter part is profitable to read for an old man as well as for the man in his best years and for the young man.

The *Cheikh*, who gives good advice to the creatures of God the Great! he the sage, the savant, the first of the men of his time, speaks as follows on this subject; listen then to his words:

He who makes it a practice to eat every day fasting the yolks of eggs, without the white part, will find in this food an energetic stimulant towards coitus. The same is the case with the man who during three days eats of the same mixture with onions.

He who boils asparagus, and then fries them in fat, and then pours upon them the yolks of eggs with pounded seasoning and eats every day of this dish, will grow very strong for the coitus, and find in it a stimulant for his amorous desires.

He who peels onions, puts them into a saucepan, with seasoning and aromatic substances, and fries the mixture with oil and yolks of eggs, will acquire a surpassing and invaluable vigour for the coitus, if he will partake of this dish for several days.

Camel's milk mixed with honey and taken regularly develops a vigour for copulation which is unaccountable and causes the virile member to be on the alert night and day.

He who for several days makes his meals upon eggs boiled with myrrh, coarse cinnamon, and pepper, will find his vigour with respect to coition and erections greatly increased. He will have a feeling as though his member would never return to a state of rest.

A man who wishes to copulate during a whole night, and whose desire, having come on suddenly, will not allow him to prepare himself and follow the diet just mentioned, may have recourse to the following recipe. He must get a great number of eggs, so that he may eat to excess, and fry them with fresh fat and butter; when done he immerses them in honey, working the whole mass well together. He must then eat of them as much as possible with a little bread, and he may be certain that for the whole night his member will not give him any rest.

On this subject the following verses have been composed:

The member of Abou el Heïloukh has remained erect
For thirty days without a break, because he did eat onions.
Abou el Heïdja has deflowered in one night
Once eighty virgins, and he did not eat or drink between,
Because he'd filled himself first with chick-peas,
And had drunk camel's milk with honey mixed.
Mimoun, the negro, never ceased to spend his sperm, while he
For fifty days without a truce the game was working.
How proud he was to finish such a task!

For ten days more he worked it, not was he yet satisfied.
But all this time he ate but yolk of eggs and bread.

The deeds of Abou el Heïloukh, Abou el Heïdja and Mimoun, just cited, have been justly praised, and their history is truly marvellous. So I will make you acquainted with it, please God, and thus complete the remarkable services which this work is designed to render to humanity.

The History of Zohra

The *Cheikh*, the protector of religion (God, the Highest, be good to him!) records, that there lived once in ancient antiquity an illustrious King, who had numerous armies and immense riches.

This King had seven daughters remarkable for their beauty and perfections. These seven had been born one after another, without any male infant between them.

The Kings of the time wanted them in marriage, but they refused to be married. They wore men's clothing, rode on magnificent horses covered with gold-embroidered trappings, knew how to handle the sword and the spear, and overcome men in single combat. Each of them possessed a splendid palace with the servants and slaves necessary for such service, for the preparation of meat and drink, and other necessities of that kind.

Whenever a marriage-offer for one of them was presented to the King, he never failed to consult with her about it; but they always answered, "That shall never be."

Different conclusions were drawn from these refusals; some in a good sense, some in a bad one.

For a long time no positive information could be gathered of the reasons for this conduct, and the daughters persevered in acting in the same manner until the death of their father. Then the oldest of them was called upon to succeed him, and received the oath of fidelity from all his subjects. This accession to the throne resounded through all the countries.

The name of the eldest sister was Fouzel Djemal (the flower of beauty); the second was calles Soltana el Agmar (the queen of moons); the third, Bediâat el

Djemal (the incomparable in beauty); the fourth, Ouarda (the rose); the fifth, Mahmouda (the praiseworthy); the sixth, Kamela (the perfect); and, finally, the seventh, Zohra (the beauty).

Zohra, the youngest, was at the same time the most intelligent and judicious. She was passionately fond of hunting and one day as she was riding through the fields she met on her way a cavalier, who saluted her, and she returned his salute; she had some twenty men in her service with her. The cavalier thought it was the voice of a woman he had heard, but as Zohra's face was covered by a flap of her *haïk*, he was not certain, and said to himself, "I would like to know whether this is a woman or a man." He asked one of the princess's servants, who dispelled his doubts. Approaching Zohra, he then conversed pleasantly with her till they made a halt for breakfast. He sat down near her to share the meal.

Disappointing the hopes of the cavalier, the princess did not uncover her face, and, pleading that she was fasting, are nothing. He could not help admiring secretly her hand, the gracefulness of her waist, and the amorous expression of her eyes. His heart was seized with an ardent love.

The following conversation took place between them:

The Cavalier: "Is your heart insensible for friendship?"

Zohra: "It is not proper for a man to feel friendship for a woman; for if their hearts once incline towards each other, lustful desires will soon invade them, and with Satan enticing them to do wrong, their fall is soon known by everyone."

The Cavalier: "It is not so, when the affection is true and their intercourse pure without infidelity or treachery."

Zohra: "If a woman gives way to the affection she feels for a man, she becomes an object of slander for the whole world, and of general contempt, whence nothing arises but trouble and regrets."

The Cavalier: "But our love will remain secret, and in this remote spot, which may serve us as our place of meeting, we shall have intercourse together unknown to all."

Zohra: "That may not be. Besides, it could not so easily be done, we should soon be suspected, and the eyes of the whole world would be turned upon us."

The Cavalier: "But love, love is the source of life. The happiness, that is, the meeting, the embraces, the caresses of lovers. The sacrifice of the fortune, and even of the life for your love."

Zohra: "These words are inspired with love, and your smile is seductive; but you would do better to refrain from similar conversation."

The Cavalier: "Your word is emerald and your advice is sincere. But love has now taken root in my heart, and no one is able to tear it out. If you drive me from you I shall assuredly die."

Zohra: "For all that you must return to your place and I to mine. If it pleases God we shall meet again."

They then separated, bidding each other adieu, and returned each of them to their dwelling.

The cavalier's name was Abou el Heïdja. His father, Kheiroun, was a great merchant and immensely rich, whose home stood isolated beyond the estate of the princess, a day's journey distant from her castle. Abou el Heïdja returned home, could not rest, and put on again his *temeur* when the night fell, took a black turban, and buckled his sword on under his *temeur*. Then he mounted his horse, and, accompanied by his favourite negro, Mimoun, he rode away secretly under the cover of night.

They travelled all night without stopping until, on the approach of daylight, the dawn came upon them in sight of Zohra's castle. They then made a halt among the hills, and entered with their horses into a cavern which they found there. Abou el Heïdja left the negro in charge of the horses, and went in the direction of the castle, in order to examine its approaches; he found it surrounded by a very high wall. Not being able to get into it, he retired to some distance to watch those who came out. But the whole day passed away and he saw no one come out. After sunset he sat himself down at the entrance of the cavern and kept on the watch until midnight; then sleep overcame him.

He was lying asleep with his head on Mimoun's knee, when the latter suddenly awakened him. "What is it?" he asked. "O my master", said Mimoun, "I have heard some noise in the cavern, and I saw the glimmer of a light." He rose at once, and looking attentively, he perceived indeed a light, towards which he went, and which guided him to a recess in the cavern. Having ordered the negro to wait for him while he was going to find out where it proceeded from, he took his sabre and entered deeper into the cavern. He discovered an underground vault, into which he descended.

The road to it was nearly impassable, on account of the stones which obstructed it. He contrived, however, after much trouble to reach a kind of crevice, through which the light shone which he had perceived. Looking through it, he saw the princess Zohra, surrounded by about a hundred virgins. They were in a magnificent palace dug out in the heart of the mountain, splendidly furnished and resplendent with gold everywhere. The maidens were eating and drinking and enjoying the pleasures of the table.

Abou el Heïdja said to himself, "Alas! I have no companion to assist me at this difficult moment." Under the influence of this reflection, he returned to his servant, Mimoun, and said to him, "Go to my brother before God, Abou el Heïloukh, and tell him to come here to me as quickly as he can." The servant forthwith mounted upon his horse, and rode through the remainder of the night.

Of all his friends, Abou el Heïloukh was the one whom Abou el Heïdja liked best; he was the son of the Vizir. This young man and Abou el Heïdja and the negro, Mimoun, passed as the three strongest and most fearless men of their time, and no one ever succeeded in overcoming them in combat.

When the negro Mimoun came to his master's friend, and had told him what had happened, the latter said, "Certainly, we belong to God and shall return to him." Then he took his sabre, mounted his horse, and taking his favourite negro with him, he made his way, with Mimoun, to the cavern.

Abou el Heïdja came out to meet him and bid him welcome, and having informed him of the love he felt for Zohra, he told him of his resolution to enter forcibly into the palace, of the circumstances under which he had taken refuge in the cavern, and the marvellous scene he had witnessed while there. Abou el Heïloukh was dumb with surprise.

At nightfall they heard singing, boisterous laughter, and animated talking. Abou el Heïdja said to his friend, "Go to the end of the subterranean passage and look. You will then make excuse for the love of your brother." Abou el Heïloukh stealing softly down to the lower end of the grotto, looked into the interior of the palace, and was enchanted with the sight of these virgins and their charms. "O brother", he asked, "which among these women is Zohra?"

Abou el Heïdja answered, "The one with the irreproachable shape, whose smile is irresistible, whose cheeks are roses, and whose forehead is resplendently white, whose head is encircled by a crown of pearls, and whose garments sparkle with gold. She is seated on a throne incrusted with rare stones and nails of silver, and she is leaning her head upon her hand."

"I have observed her of all the others", said Abou el Heïloukh, "as though she were a standard or a blazing torch. But, O my brother, let me draw your attention to a matter which appears not to have struck you." "What is it?" asked Abou el Heïdja. His friend replied, "It is very certain, O my brother, that licentiousness reigns in this palace. Observe that these people come here only at night time, and that this is a remote place. There is every reason to believe that it is exclusively devoted to feasting, drinking, and debauchery, and if it was your idea that you could have come to her you love by any other way than the one on which we are now, you would have found that you had deceived yourself, even if you had found means to communicate with her by the help of other people." "And why so?" asked Abou el Heïdja. "Because", said his friend, "as far as I can see, Zohra solicits the affection of young girls, which is a proof that she can have no inclination for men, nor be responsive to their love."

"O Abou el Heïloukh", said Abou el Heïdja, "I know the value of your judgment, and it is for that I have sent for you. You know that I have never hesitated to follow your advice and counsel!" "O my brother", said the son of the Vizir, "if God had not guided you to this entrance of the palace, you would never have been able to approach Zohra. But from here, please God! we can find our way."

Next morning, at sunrise, they ordered their servants to make a gap in that place, and managed to get everything out of the way that could obstruct the passage. This done they hid their horses in another cavern, safe from wild beasts and thieves; then all the four, the two masters and the two servants, entered the

439

cavern and entered into the palace, each of them armed with sabre and buckler. They then closed up again the gap, and restored its former appearance.

Now they found themselves in darkness, but Abou el Heïloukh, having struck a match, lighted one of the candles, and they began to explore the palace in every sense. It seemed to them the marvel of marvels. The furniture was magnificent. Everywhere there were beds and couches of all kinds, rich candelabras, splendid lights, sumptuous carpets, and tables covered with dishes, fruits and beverages. When they had admired all these treasures, they went on examining the chambers, counting them. There was a great number of them, and in the last one they found a secret door, very small, and of appearance which attracted their attention. Abou el Heïloukh said, "This is very probably the door which is connected with the palace. Come, O my brother, we will await the things that are to come in one of these chambers." They took their position in a room difficult to reach, high up, and from which one could see without being seen.

So they waited till night came on. At that moment the secret door opened, giving admission to a negress carrying a torch, who set alight all the lights and candelabra, arranged the beds, set the plates, placed all sorts of meats upon the tables, with cups and bottles, and perfumed the air with the sweetest scents. Soon afterwards the maidens made their appearance. Their gait denoted at the same time indifference and languor. They seated themselves upon the divans, and the negress offered them meat and drink. They ate, drank, and sang melodiously.

Then the four men, seeing them giddy with wine, came down from their hiding place with their sabres in their hands, brandishing them over the heads of the maidens. They had first taken care to veil their faces with the upper part of their *haik*.

"Who are these men", cried Zohra, "who are invading our dwelling under cover of the shades of the night? Have you risen out of the ground, or did you descend from the sky? What do you want?"

"Coition!" they answered.

"With whom?" asked Zohra.

"With you, O apple of my eye!" said Abou el Heïdja, advancing.

Zohra: "Who are you?"

"I am Abou el Heïdja."

Zohra: "But how is it you know me?"

"It is I who met you while out hunting at such and such a place."

Zohra: "But what brought you hither?"

"The will of God the Highest!"

At this answer Zohra was silent, and set herself to think of a means by which she could rid herself of these intruders.

Now among the virgins that were present there were several whose vulvas were like iron barred, and whom no one had been able to deflower; there was also present a woman called Mouna (she who appeases the passion), who was insatiable as regards coition. Zohra thought to herself, "It is only by a trick I can get rid of these men. By means of these women I will set them tasks which they will be unable to accomplish as conditions for my consent." Then turning to Abou el Heïdja, she said to him, "You will not get possession of me unless you fulfil the conditions which I shall impose upon you." The four cavaliers at once consented to this without knowing them, and she continued, "But, if you do not fulfil them, will you pledge your word that you will be my prisoners, and place yourselves entirely at my disposal." "We pledge our words!" they answered.

She made them take their oath that they would be faithful to their word, and then, placing her hand in that of Abou el Heïdja, she said to him, "As regards you, I impose upon you the task of deflowering eighty virgins without ejaculating. Such is my will!" He answered, "I accept."

She let him then enter a chamber where there were several kinds of beds, and sent to him the eighty virgins in succession. Abou el Heïdja deflowered them all, and so ravished in a single night the virginity of eighty young girls without ejaculating the smallest drop of sperm. This extraordinary vigour filled Zohra with astonishment, and likewise all those who were present.

The princess, turning then to the negro Mimoun, asked, "And this one, what is his name?" They said, "Mimoun." "Your task shall be", said the princess, pointing to Mouna, "to make love to this woman without resisting for fifty consecutive days; you need not ejaculate unless you like; but if the excess of fatigue forces you to stop, you will not have fulfilled your obligations." They all cried out at the hardness of such a task; but Mimoun protested, and said, "I accept the condition, and shall come out of it with honour!" The fact was that this negro had an insatiable appetite for the coitus. Zohra told him to go with Mouna to her chamber, impressing upon the latter to let her know if the negro should exhibit the slightest trace of fatigue.

"And you, what is your name?" she asked the friend of Abou el Heïdja. "Abou el Heïloukh," he replied. "Well, then, Abou el Heïloukh, what I require of you is to remain here, in the presence of these women and virgins, for thirty consecutive days with your member during this period always in erection during day and night." Then she said to the fourth, "What is your name?"

"Felah" (good futune), was his answer. "Very well, Felah", she said, "you will remain at our disposal for any services which we may have to demand of you." However, Zohra, in order to leave no motive for any excuse, and so that she might not be accused of bad faith, had asked them, first of all, what diet they wished to follow during the period of their trial. Abou el Heïdja had aksed for the only drink — excepting water — camel's milk with honey, and, for nourishment, chick-peas cooked with meat and abundance of onions; and, by means of these foods he did, by the permission of God, accomplish his remarkable exploit. Abou el Heïloukh demanded, for his nourishment, onions cooked with meat, and, for the drink, the juice pressed out of pounded onions mixed with honey. Mimoun, on his part, asked for yolks of eggs and bread.

However, Abou el Heïdja claimed of Zohra the favour of copulating with her on the strength of the fact that he had fulfilled his promise. She answered him, "Oh, impossible! the condition which you have fulfilled is inseparable from those which your companions have to comply with. The agreement must be carried out in its entirety, and you will find me true to my promise. But if one amongst you should fail in his task, you will all be my prisoners by the will of God!" Abou el Heïdja gave way in the face of this firm resolve, and sat down amongst the girls and women, and ate and drank with them, whilst waiting for the conclusion of the tasks of his companions.

At first Zohra, feeling convinced that they would soon all be at her mercy, was all amiability and smiles. But when the twentieth day had come she began to show signs of distress; and on the thirtieth she could no longer restrain her tears. For on that day Abou el Heïloukh had finished his task, and, having come out of it honourably, he took his seat by the side of his friend amongst the company, who continued to eat tranquilly and to drink abundantly.

From that time the princess, who had now no other hope than in the failure of the negro Mimoun, relied upon his becoming fatigued before he finished his work. She sent every day to Mouna for information, who sent word that the negro's vigour was constantly increasing, and she began to despair, seeing already Abou el Heïdja and Abou el Heïloukh coming off as victors in their enterprises. One day she said to the two friends, "I have made inquiries about the negro, and Mouna has let me know that he was exhausted with fatigue." At this words Abou el Heïdja cried, "In the name of God! if he does not carry out his task, aye, and if he does not go beyond it for ten days longer, he shall die the vilest of deaths!"

But his zealous servant never during the period of fifty days took any rest in his work of copulation, and kept going on besides, for ten days longer, as ordered by his master. Mouna, on her part, had the greatest satisfaction, as this feat had at last appeased her ardour for coition. Mimoun, having remained victor, could then take his seat with his companions.

Then said Abou el Heïdja to Zohra. "See, we have fulfilled all the conditions you have imposed upon us. It is now for you to accord me the favours which, according to our agreement, was to be the price if we succeeded." "It is but too true!" answered the princess, and she gave herself up to him, and he found her excelling the most excellent.

As to the negro, Mimoun, he married Mouna. Abou el Heïloukh chose, amongst all the virgins, the one whom he had found most attractive.

They all remained in the palace, giving themselves up to good cheer and all possible pleasures, until death put an end to their happy existence and dissolved their union. God be merciful to them as well as to all Mussulmans! Amen! It is to this story that the verses cited previously refer. I have given it here, because it testifies to the effectiveness of the dishes and remedies, the use of which I have recommended, for giving vigour for coition, and all learned men agree in acknowledging their beneficial effects.

There are still other beverages of excellent virtue. I will describe the following: Take one part of the juice pressed out of pounded onions, and mix it with two parts of purified honey. Heat the mixture over a fire until the onion-juice has disappeared and the honey only remains. Then take the residue from the fire, let it get cool, and preserve it for use when wanted. Then mix of the same one *aoukia* with three *aouak* of water, and let chickpeas be steeped in this fluid for one day and one night.

This beverage is to be drunk during winter and on going to bed. Only a small quantity is to be taken, and only for one day. The member of him who has drunk of it will not give him much rest during the night that follows. As to the man who drinks it for several consecutive days, he will constantly have his member rigid and upright without a pause. A man with an ardent temperament ought not to make use of it, as it may give him a fever. Nor should the medicine be used three days in succession except by old or cold-tempered men. And lastly, it should not be resorted to in summer.

I certainly did wrong to put this book together;
But you will pardon me, nor let me pray in vain,
O God! award no punishment for this on judgment day!
And thou, oh reader, hear me conjure thee to say:
So be it!

Appendix to the Autograph Edition

In the year of grace 1876 some amateurs who were passionately fond of Arabian literature combined for the purpose of reproducing, by autographic process, a number of copies of a French translation of a work written by the Cheikh Nefzaoui, which book had, by a lucky chance, fallen into their hands. Each brought to the undertaking such assistance as his special knowledge allowed, and it was thus that a tedious work was achieved by amateurs, amidst obstacles which were calculated to abate the ardour of their enthusiasm.

Thus, as the reader has doubtless already divined, it was not an individual, but a concourse of individuals, who, taking advantage of a union of favourable circumstances and facilities, not of common occurrence, offered to their friends the first fruit of a work, interesting, and of such rarity that to the present time very few have had the opportunity of reading it, while they could only gather their knowledge from incorrect manuscripts, sophisticated copies, and in-complete translations! It is to this association of efforts, guided by the principle of the division of labour for the carrying out of a great undertaking, that the appearance of this book is due.

The Editor (it is under this name that the Society J.M.P.Q. has been, is, and will be designated) is assured beforehand, notwithstanding the imperfection of his production, of the sympathies of his readers, who are all friends of his, or friends of his friends, and for whose benefit he has worked. For this reason he is not

445

going to claim an indulgence which has been already extended to him; his wish is only to make clear to everybody the exact value and nature of the book which he is offering, and to make known on what foundations the work has been done, in how far the remarkable translation of M … has been respected, and, in short, what reliance may be placed in the title, "Tanslated from the Arabic by M …, Staff Officer."

It is, in fact, important that there should be no misunderstanding on this point, and that the reader should not imagine that he holds an exact copy of that translation in his hands; for we confess that we have modified it, and we give these explanations in order to justify the alterations which were imposed by the attending circumstances.

As far as we are aware, there have been made until now only two proper translations of the work of the Cheikh Nefzaoui. One, of which we have availed ourselves, is due, as is well known, to M …, a fanatical and distinguished Arabophile; the other is the work of Doctor L …; the latter we have never seen.

A learned expounder commenced a translation which promised to leave the others far behind. Unfortunately, death interrupted the accomplishment of this work, and there was no one to continue it.

Our intention, at the outset, was ro reproduce simply the first of the aforenamed translations, making, however, such rectifications as were necessitated by gross mistakes in the orthography, and in the French idiom, by which the manuscript in our possession was disfigured. Our views did not go beyond that; but we had scarcely made any progress with the book when we found that it was impossible to keep to the translation as it stood. Obvious omissions, mistaken renderings of the sense, originating, no doubt, with the faulty Arab text which the translator had at his disposal, and which were patent at first sight, imposed upon us the necessity of consulting other resources. We were thus induced to examine all the Arab manuscripts of the work which we could by any possibility obtain.

Three texts were to this end put under contribution. These treated of the same subjects in the same order, and presented the same succession of chapters, corresponding, however, in this respect, point by point, with the manuscript upon which our translator had to work; but while two of them gave a kind of ab-

stract of the questions treated, the third, on the contrary, seemed to enlarge at pleasure upon every subject.

We shall expatiate to some slight extent upon this last named text, since the study of it has enabled us to clear up a certain number of points upon which M ..., not withstanding his conscientious researches, has been unable to throw sufficient light.

The principal characteristic of this text, which is not exempt from gross mistakes, is the affectation of more care as to style and choice of expressions; it enters more into fastidious, and frequently technical particulars, contains more quotations of verses – often, be it remarked, inapplicable ones – and uses, in certain circumstances, filthy images, which seem to have had a particular attraction for the author; but as a compensation for these faults, it gives, instead of cold, dry explications, pictures which are often charming, wanting neither in poetry nor originality, nor in descriptive talent, nor even in a certain elevation of thought, and bearing an undeniable stamp of originality. We may cite as an example the 'Chapter on Kisses', which is found neither in our translation nor in the other two texts which we have examined, and which we have borrowed.

In our character as Gauls, we must not complain about the obscenities which are scattered about, as if on purpose to excite the grosser passions; but what we must deprecate are the tedious expansions, whole pages full of verbiage, which disfigure the work, and are like the reverse of the medal. The author has felt this himself, as at the conslusion of his work he requests the reader to pardon him in consideration of the good intention which has guided his pen. In presence of the qualities of first rank which must be acknowledged to exist in the book, we should have preferred that it had not contained these defects; we should have liked, in one word, to see it more homogeneous and more earnest; and more particularly so if one considers that the circumstances which we are pointing out raise doubts as to the veritable origin of the new matters which have been discovered, and which might easily be taken for interpolations due to the fancy of one or more of the copyists through whose hands the work passed before we received it.

Everyone knows, in fact, the grave inconveniences attaching to manuscripts, and the services rendered by the art of printing to science and literature by disposing of them. No copy leaves the hands of the copyist complete and perfect, particularly if the writer is an Arab, the least scrupulous of all. The Arab copyist not only involuntarily scatters about mistakes which are due to his ignorance and carelessness, but will not shrink from making corrections, modifications, and even additions, according to his fancy. The literary reader himself, carried away by the charm of the subject, often annotates the text in the margin, inserts an anecdote or idea which is just current, or some puffed-up medical recipe; and all this, to the great detriment of its purity, finds its way into the body of the work through the hands of the next copyist.

There can be no doubt that the work of the Cheikh Nefzaoui has suffered in this way. Our three texts and the one upon which the translator worked, offer striking dissimilarities, and of all kinds; although, by the way, one of the translations seems to approach more nearly in style to the extended text of which we have spoken. But a question of another sort comes before us with respect to this last, which contains more than four times as much matter as the others. Is this the entire work of the Cheikh Nefzaoui, always bearing in mind the modification to which manuscripts are exposed, and does it so stand by itself as a work for the perusal of voluptuaries, while the others are only abridged copies for the use of the vulgar, serving them as an elementary treatise? Or might it not be the product of numerous successive additions to the original work, by which, as we have already suggested, its bulk has been considerably increased.

We have no hesitation in pronouncing in favour of the first of these hypotheses. In the record which the Cheikh gives of it, he says that this is the second work of the kind which he has composed, and that it is in fact only the first one, entitled the *Torch of the Universe,* considerably increased in pursuance of the advice given him by the Vizir Mohammed ben Ouana ez Zouaoui. Might it not be possible that a third word, still more complete than the second, had been the outcome of new studies of the author? Subjects of a particular speciality have certainly been treated in the work of which we speak. In looking at the Notes which serve as a preface to this translation, we find reproaches addressed by the translator to the author, because he has merely hinted at two questions of more than ordinary interest, viz., tribady and paederasty. Well, then, the Cheikh would meet his critic triumphantly by appearing before him with the work in question, for the chapter which constitutes by itself more than half of its whole volume is the twenty-first, and bears the superscription: "The twenty-first and last chapter of the book, treating of the utility of eggs and some other substances which favour coitus; of tribady and the woman who first conceived this description of voluptuousness; of peaderasty and matters concerned with it; of procuresses and the sundry ruses by which one may get possession of a woman; of facetiae, jokes, anecdotes, and serval questions concerning coitus in general."

What would be the surprise of the translator to find a community of views and sentiments existing between himself, a representative of modern civilization, and this Arab, who lived more than three hundred years ago. He could only express his regret for having entertained so bad an opinion of his master, for having believed for one moment in an omission on his part, and for having doubted his competency to deal with the various questions spoken of.

Does not the discovery of a text so complete authorise us to admit the existence of two works, one elementary, the other learned? And might it not be by reason of a little remnant of bashfulness, that the author has reserved for the twenty-first chapter without any previous allusion, the remarkable subjects which we do not find hinted at in any other place?

To put the question in this fashion is at the same time to solve it, and to solve it in the affirmative. That interminable chapter would not be a product of interpolations. It is too long and too serious a work to admit of such a supposition. The little that we have seen of it seems to bear the stamp of a well-pronounced originality, and to be composed with too much method, no to be the work – and entirely the work – of the master.

One may be surprised that this text is so rare, but the answer is very simple. As the translator judiciously observes in his notice, the matters treated in the twenty-first chapter are of a nature to startle many people. See! an Arab, who practises in secret paederasty, affects in public rigid and austere manners, while he discusses without constraint in his conversation everything that concerns the natural coitus. Thus you will easily understand that he would not wish to be suspected of reading such a book, by which his reputation would be compromised in the eyes of his co-religionists while he would, without hesitation, exhibit a book which treated of the coitus only. Another consideration, moreover, suffices to completely explain the rarity of the work; its compass makes it very expensive, and the manuscript is not attainable by everybody on account of the high price it reaches.

However it may be as regards the origin of the text, having the three documents in our possession we have given careful revision to the translation of M.... Each doubtful point has been the object of minute research, and has been generally cleared up by one or the other. When there were several acceptable versions, we chose that which was the most fit for the context, and many mutilated passages were restored. Nor were we afraid to make additions in borrowing from the extended text what appeared to us worthy of reproduction, and for the omission of which we should have been blamed by the reader. We were careful, however, not to overload the work, and to introduce no new matter which would militate against the peculiar character of the original translation. It is partly for this last reason, and still more so because the work required for this undertaking surpassed our strength, that we could not bring to light, to our great regret, the treasures concealed in the twenty-first chapter, as well as a certain number of new tales not less acceptable than those which we have given, and with which we have enriched the text.

We must not conceal that, leaving out of sight these alterations, we have not scrupled to refine the phrases, round off the periods, correct the phraseology, and, in short, to amend even the form of the translation which, in many instances, left much to be desired. It was a matter of necessity that the perusal of the contents of the book should be made agreeable. Now, the translator, with the most praise-worthy intentions, had been too anxious to render the Arabic text, with its short jumbled sentencs, as clearly as possible, and had thus made the reading painfully laborious. Looking at some passages, it may even be supposed that he had only jotted them down, particularly towards the end, and had not been able, for some reason or other, to revise them until it was too late.

Now that the reader has all the necessary information about the French edition of the Cheikh Nefzaoui's work, he will permit us to make, in conclusion, a few remarks upon the *ensemble* of the book.

There are found in it many passages which are not attractive. The extraordinary ideas displayed – for instance, those about medicines and concerning the meanings of dreams – clash too directly with modern thought not to awaken in the reader a feeling more of boredom than of pleasure.

The work is certainly encumbered with a quantity of matter which cannot but appear ridiculous in the eyes of the civilised modern reader; but we should not have been justified in weeding it out. We were bound to keep it intact as we had received it from our translator. We have held with the Italian proverb, *Traduttore, traditore,* that a work loses sufficient of its originality by beeing conveyed from its own tongue into another, and we hope that the plan we have adopted will meet with general approval. Those oddities are, moreover, instructive, as they make us acquainted with the manner and character of the Arab under a preculiar aspect, and not only of the Arab who was contemporary with our author, but also with the Arab of our own day. The latter is, in fact, not much more advanced than was the former. Although our contact with the race becomes closer every day in Tunis, Morocco, Egypt, and other Mussulman countries, they hold to their old medical prescriptions, have the same belief in divination, and honour the same mass of ridiculous notions, in which sorcery and amulets play a large part, and which appear to us supremely absurd. At the same time, one may observe from the very passages which we here refer to, that this people was not so averse as one might believe to witticisms, for the pun (calembour) occupies an important position in the explanations of dreams with which the author has studded the chapters on the sexual organs, apparently for no particular reason, but no doubt with the idea that no matter of interest should be absent from his work.

The reader will perhaps also find that probability is frequently sacrificed to imagination. This is a distinctive mark in Arabic literature, and our work could not otherwise but exhibit the faults inherent in the genius of this race, which revels in the love for the marvellous, and amongst whose chief literary productions are to be counted the *Thousand and one Nights*. But if these tales show such defaults very glaringly, they exhibit, on the other hand, charming qualities: simplicity, grace, delicacy; a mine of precious things which has been explored and made use of by many modern authors. We have pointed out, in some notes, the relationship which we found between these tales and those of Boccaccio and La Fontaine, but we could not draw attention to all. We had to pass over many with silence, and amongst them some of the most striking, as for instance in the case of "The Man Expert in Stratagems Duped by his Wife", which we find reproduced with all the perfect mastership of Balzac at the end of the *Physilogie du Mariage*.

We will not pursue this sketch any further. If instead of commencing the book with a preface we have preferred to address the reader at the end, this was done in order not to impose our views upon him and thus to stand between him and the work. Whether these additional lines will be read by him or not, we believe that we have done our duty by informing him of the direction we gave to our work. We tried, on the one hand, to prove the merits of the translator who furnished the basis for our labours, that is to say, the part which required the most science and study; while, on the other hand, we desired our readers to know in how far his translation had to be recast.

To the Arabophile who would wish to produce a better translation the way is left open; and in perfecting the work he is free to uncover the unknown beauties of the twenty-first chapter to his admiring contemporaries.

Note Concerning Sir Richard Burton's Translation

Around 1850, a French army officer, apparently stationed in Algeria, got hold of a manuscript in Arabic entitled: *Al Raud al atir wa nuzhat al Khatir*. This was the famous *Perfumed Garden*, at that time unknown to the West. The officer whose name is hidden under the designation, "Monsieur la Baron R..., Capitaine d'Etat major", became fascinated by the book and translated it into French. Publication, however, was delayed for nearly a quarter of a century. Partly, perhaps, owing to the difficulty of finding a suitable printing press in Algeria. Four French officers, who were also students and scholars, finally collaborated in the venture of lithographing the volume on the official machines of the French Government. This was performed in secret, but ended abruptly when their activities were discovered by their commanding officer.

This edition, known as the "autograph edition", and the first translation ever to be made, constied of only 35 copies. The title page, contains the following text: *Le Jardin Parfumé (Al-Raud Al-Atir) Par le Sidi Mohammed el-Nafzaoui; Ouvrage du Cheikh, l'Iman, le Savant, le très-Erudit, le très Intelligent, le très-Véridique Sidi Mohammed el-Nafzaoui que Dieu très-Elevé lui fasse Miséricorde par sa Puissance. Amen. Traduit de l'Arabe par Monsieur le Baron R ..., Capitaine d'Etat major.*

The "autograph edition" consists of 283 pages of text, 15 pages of *avis au lecteur*, 2 portraits, 13 *hors textes* on blue paper, 43 erotic illustrations in the text, and at the end of the book, about 10 pages of errata, with a *Table of Contents*. In 1885, this original lithograph edition was so well reproduced in facsimile in Paris, that it is extremly difficult to distinguish between the original and the fake. The facsimile, however, contains an extra portrait, and its cover bears a phallic watermark.

In the year before the counterfeit edition something mysterious happened: the distinguished novelist, Guy de Maupassant wrote personally to a Paris publisher the following letter, suggesting a reprint of the text of the lithograph edition which he had just discovered.

'Oasis de Bou Sàada,
25 aout, 1884.

Monsieur et chèr Editeur,

Je reçois aujourd'hui en plein Sahara votre carte postale.

Envoyez-moi, je vous prie, *le recueil chez moi,* à Paris, 83, rue Dulong (Batignolles), c'est encore le plus sûr. Je le trouverai dans un mois à mon retour.

Maintenant autre chose. Je viens de découvrir ici un livre arabe, lubrique, remarquablement traduit par un officier supérieur français.

L'historie de ce livre est curieuse. Un écrivain arabe allait être mis à mort par ordre d'un bey (celui de Tunis, je crois) quand il obtint sa grâce à la condition qu'il écrirait un livre capable de réveiller les passions mourantes de son souverain.

Il a écrit ce livre et fut gracié. Les dessins de cette traduction sont faits par un officier d'Etat major. Tous sont remarquables. Un d'eux me paraît être un vrai chef-d'œuvre. Il représente deux êtres épuisés après l'étreinte.

Ce livre absolument inconnu de tout le monde me paraît singulèrement intéressant *pour les amateurs de raretés.* Vous irait-il de le publier?

L'officier traducteur hésite beaucoup, ayant grand peur que son nom soit prononcé. Je lui ai affirmé que dans le cas ou cet ouvrage vous agréerait, il pourrait être assuré de la plus absolue discrétion.

Malheureusement il n'a pas osé traduire un des chapitres concernant un vice fort commun en ce pays – «la Pédé-rastie»; mais, en somme, le livre est, en son genre un des plus curieux qu'on puisse trouver.

Si cette trouvaille vous tentait, vous pourriez écrire directment de ma part à M. le Commandant Maréchal, Commandant Supérieur du Cercle Militaire de Bou-Sàada (Algérie).

M. le Commandant Maréchal ne voudrait point entendre parler de question d'argent. Vous lui donneriez tout simplement quelques exemplaires.

Une autre question serait embarrassante. Il a fait autographier ce livre, en secret, par de subordonnés et il hésiterait beaucoup à se separer de ce volume original-relié magnifiquement. Pour les dessins cela pourrait créer un embarras.

457

Veuillez toujours me répondre un mot, *car si la chose ne vous convenait pas, je connais quelqu'un qui la prendrait, immèdiatement.*

Recevez, cher Monsieur, l'expression de mes sentiments empressés et tout dévoués.

Guy de Maupassant

Du 5 septembre au Ier octobre on peut m'écrire à Erbalunga, commune de Brando, près Bastia, *Corse.*

It remains uncertain whether Maupassant was writing to the publisher who issued the counterfeit edition of 1885, to Isidore Liseux (aimed at scholars and collectors), or to his own publisher. Isidore Liseux was a publisher, scholar and bibliophile specialized in the issue of rare, forgotten, or curious works of literary interest. These were always superbly printed and generally decorated with ornamental inital letters. The editing and annotation was always scholarly. Whatever the effect of Maupassant's letter, Liseux was the publisher who first set *The Perfumed Garden* in type, correcting and revising the text, and issuing it in a superb edition limited to 220 copies with the following text on the title-page:

LE JARDIN PARFUME DU CHEIKH NEFZAOUI: *Manuel d'Erotologie Arabe: XVI Siècle. Traduction revue et corrigé. Paris, Isidore Liseux, 1886.*
The Book was reprinted at Paris during 1904 in a 'Réimpression conforme à l'édition publiée en 1886'. No publisher's name was given, bat Liseux was certainly not responsible for the reprint, as he had died about ten years before.
Between 1911 and 1922 further excellent and unlimited reprints of this edition were published at Paris by the Bibliothèque de Curieux in their "Maîtres de l'Amour" series.
The Liseux revised version of the original 1850 translation immediately caught Burton's attention. He mentions it in volume X of his *Arabian Nights*. In the same place he draws attention to the Kama Shastra Society edition of the English translation of *The Perfumed Garden*. This was of course, made direct from the Liseux volume published during 1886, being anonymously translated by Burton, and privately issued from London during the same year.
Altogether five titles were privately issued by the Kama Shastra Society to its subscribers. These, with their dates, were:

1. *The Kama Sutra*, 1883.
2. *The Anaga Ranga*, 1885.
3. *The Perfumed Garden*, 1886.
4. *The Beharistan*, 1887.
5. *The Gulistan*, 1888.

The title-page of Burton's translation of the *Arabian Nights* also bore the name of the Society. This, however, as Penzer has pointed out, was simply because Burton did not wish to employ the name of a publisher or printer – he, himself, in this instance being the publisher. Thus the work cannot rightly be considered as an issue of the Society.

After the appearance of the Liseux version of *The Perfumed Garden*, Burton decided to translate direct from the French. There can be no doubt that this edition ranked as high in his estimation as had the "autograph edition" in the opinion of Guy de Maupassant. The first Kama Shastra Society edition was issued in parts (seven or ten), with paper covers in different tints of grey and fawn. The title-page of each part was printed in black ink, and this page was reproduced, within a fancy border, on the outer wrapper.

The second edition appeared later in the same year, this time as a volume bound in full white vellum with bevelled edges. The title-page reads:

The Perfumed Garden of the Cheikh Nefzaoui: *A Manual of Arabian Erotology (XVI Century): Revised and Corrected Translation. Cosmopoli: MDCCCLXXXVI: for the Kama Shastra Society of London and Benares, and for Private circulation only.* (Pagination: XVI + 256).

Burton's translation, which follows the French of the Liseux text very closely, is yet one more example of the success which can be achieved by the translation of a work from one language into another, and then into a third.

The example had been set during the eighteenth century in the English translation made form Galland's French version of the *Arabian Nights* (orginally published in the French language between 1704 and 1717).

By 1888 a thousand sets of the sixteen volumes of Burton's literal, unabridged, and unexpurgated translation of the *Arabian Nights* had been issued. He had attained the highest degree of acceptance, distinction, and celebrity. In this same year, he began a new translation of *The Perfumed Garden;* this time, apparently, direct from an Arabic manuscript, and with much less concern for secrecy. Why, it may be asked, was this new version necessary? The answer, I think, lies in that sentence in the letter of Guy de Maupassant which stated that the original

French translator had "not dared to translate a chapter concerning a vice very common in this country – that of 'Pederasty'".

Almost throughout his life Burton had been extremely interested in the subject of homosexuality. He may be considered, in fact, the pioneer in the serious study of this subject in England; for, without doubt, he paved the way for that classic volume which forms the second part of Havelock Ellis's monumental *Studies in the Psychology of Sex.*

The new *Garden,* then, was to contain the whole of the very considerable portion of the twenty-first chapter concerning homosexuality, which had been eliminated by the modest and anonymous French translator. Burton died in 1890, leaving the new manuscript of Nefzawi not quite complete. As is now well known, his wife immediatly burnt the book, thus incurring the wrath and exasperation of innumerable eminent scholars throughout the world. In the long run, however, not much appears to have been lost; for according to Dr. Grenfell Baker, who throughout the period that Sir Richard was engaged on this new version daily had intimate converse with him concerning its contents, "it was merely a greatly annotated edition of that issued in 1886" – plus, of course, the controversial section on pederasty.

The general reader therefore has probably lost little by Lady Burton's hasty action. The loss, of course, for scholars, cannot precisely be estimated. All we can be certain of is that Burton reiterated to Dr. Baker the fact that this extra-annotated version of the book was his *magnum opus:* "I have put my whole life and all my lifeblood into that *Scented Garden;* it is my great hope that I shall live by it. It is the crown of my life."

And despite his wife's efforts to consign the *Garden* to oblivion, he *has* lived by it; for, equally with the *Arabian Nights,* the Kame Shastra edition of Nefzawi – however much it may lack the controversial pederastic section – remains his most celebrated work.

Contents